The Modernist Masquerade

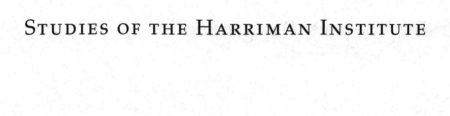

STUDIES OF THE HARRIMAN INSTITUTE

The Modernist Masquerade

Stylizing Life, Literature,
and Costumes in Russia

COLLEEN MCQUILLEN

THE UNIVERSITY OF WISCONSIN PRESS

Publication of this volume has been made possible, in part, through support from the **Andrew W. Mellon Foundation.**

The University of Wisconsin Press
1930 Monroe Street, 3rd Floor
Madison, Wisconsin 53711-2059
uwpress.wisc.edu

3 Henrietta Street
London WC2E 8LU, England
eurospanbookstore.com

Library of Congress Cataloging-in-Publication Data
McQuillen, Colleen, 1972–
The modernist masquerade: stylizing life, literature, and costumes in Russia / Colleen McQuillen.
  pages   cm
  Includes bibliographical references and index.
  ISBN 978-0-299-29614-8 (pbk.: alk. paper)
  ISBN 978-0-299-29613-1 (e-book)
1. Russian literature—19th century—History and criticism.
2. Russian literature—20th century—History and criticism.
3. Modernism (Literature)—Russia.   4. Masquerades—Russia.
5. Masquerades in literature.   I. Title.
PG3020.5.M6M37   2013
791.6—dc23
2013015052

With love,

for **MY FAMILY** and **FRIENDS**

Contents

Illustrations

Acknowledgments

Governing the publication of this book is my belief that knowledge is meaningful only if shared. My mentors instilled in me this belief by modeling scholarly generosity. My first debt of gratitude goes to Irina Reyfman at Columbia University, under whose guidance and steadfast support my ideas on the cultural semiotics of masquerade first took shape as a doctoral dissertation. I am grateful for the support I received from Columbia, including generous fellowship funding from the Harriman Institute that enabled my research and writing. Ron Meyer, Communications Manager of the Harriman, supplied critiques, advice, and encouragement, which were instrumental in propelling forward my work and sustaining my belief in this project.

The University of Illinois at Chicago (UIC) has provided me with a vital community of scholars among whom I have been able to cultivate my interdisciplinary research. A Faculty Fellowship from UIC's Institute for the Humanities allowed me to expand the cultural history component of this project, as did a UIC Faculty Research Support Grant. My participation in The Summer Research Laboratory on Russia, Eastern Europe, and Eurasia at the University of Illinois at Urbana-Champaign (UIUC) was indispensable for executing my second stage of research. Helen Sullivan and other Slavic Reference Service librarians at UIUC guided me toward rich resources through the Individualized Research Practicum and knowledgably replied to my many online queries.

In addition to this institutional support, many individuals have contributed to the success of this project. My colleagues Michal Pawel Markowski, Norma Moruzzi, Susanne Rott, Astrida Orle Tantillo, Alfred Thomas, and Julia Vaingurt at UIC have inspired and aided me with their good counsel and camaraderie. A model of intellectual generosity, Julia has been a consistently insightful reader of my work and a true friend. Elizabeth Kendall, Margo Rosen, Vadim Shkolnikov, Jane Taubman, and Alina Wyman have offered keen suggestions for how to improve portions of this manuscript, as did the fellows at UIC's Institute for the Humanities. I am thankful to the anonymous readers of this manuscript for their constructive critiques. A very special, heartfelt thank-you goes to Olga Peters Hasty, who scrupulously read multiple versions of this manuscript. Her astute observations and unwavering faith in this project have buoyed me over the course of its realization. In the end, however, I alone bear full responsibility for any errors or oversights in the pages of this book.

Several research assistants made significant contributions, especially in securing the photographs and illustrations in this book. Makbal Musina assisted me in locating materials at the Russian State Historical Archive and worked tirelessly to obtain photographs from the Central State Archive of Cinema, Photographic, and Phonographic Documents in Saint Petersburg (TsGAKFFD). Tatyana Gershkovich supplied invaluable help getting high-quality scans of illustrations from newspapers and journals held at the Russian National Library. Stateside, Kate Howe lent her skills in photography and consulted on the book's cover image. In the hectic final stages of manuscript preparation Anton Svynarenko assisted with image scanning and citation checking. I thank these individuals as well as the institutions that rendered their service. I also wish to express my appreciation to the organizations that granted me permission to reproduce images. While I have made every effort to secure all necessary permissions, I invite copyright holders who may not have received a request to contact me, the author.

I extend my deep gratitude to Gwen Walker, acquisitions editor at the University of Wisconsin Press, for her consistent support and firm commitment to publishing my project. The Press's entire editorial staff and production crew impressed me at every stage with their professionalism and made me feel fortunate to have such a talented team tending to my book. The author expresses appreciation to the Schoff Fund at the

University Seminars at Columbia University for their help in publication. The ideas presented have benefited from discussions in the University Seminars on Slavic History and Culture. A subvention from UIC's School of Literature, Cultural Studies, and Linguistics covered the cost of photographs and illustrations.

Material from two chapters appeared in earlier publications. Part of chapter 4 appeared as "Artists' Balls and Conceptual Costumes at the Saint Petersburg Academy of Arts, 1885–1909" (*Fashion Theory* 16.1 [March 2012], 29–48) and under the title "Germenevtika maskaradnogo kostiuma. Dizainerskie novatsii na 'Balakh khudozhnikov' v Sankt-Peterburgskoi Akademii khudozhestv" (*Teoriia mody: odezhda, telo, kul'tura* 21 [fall 2011], 30–51); chapter 6 as "From *The Fairground Booth* to Futurism: The Sartorial and Material Estrangement of Masquerade" (*The Russian Review* 71.3 [July 2012], 413–435). I thank the editors of *Fashion Theory*, published by Berg, of *Teoriia mody*, published by Novoe Literaturnoe Obozrenie, and of *Russian Review*, published by Wiley Periodicals, for all allowing me to reprint this material.

Family and friends have nurtured me with boundless love and encouragement. I thank my mother Elizabeth Mokrzecki and my father Kevin McQuillen for instilling in me the curiosity, vision, and determination to realize a project of this magnitude, and for believing in my choices and my abilities. Sean Conway, Brad Courtney, Laura DeMarco, Irina Nenciu, Mihnea Popa, and Christof Sparber are among my other loved ones whose warmth and good cheer have brightened my days of work. The greatest things in life are never done alone and this book is no exception.

A Note on Transliteration and Abbreviations

I have used the Library of Congress system of transliteration for quotations, bibliographic information, terms that would be of importance to scholars, and most names. However, I have preserved conventional spellings of well-known authors' names. All translations are mine unless noted otherwise. In citations and photo captions I use the following acronyms for the sake of brevity: RGIA (Russkii gosudarstvennyi istoricheskii arkhiv) and TsGAKFFD (Tsentral'nyi gosudarstvennyi arkhiv kinofonofotodokumentov).

The Modernist Masquerade

Introduction

Masquerades in Russian History and Culture

Masked and costume balls thrived in Russia at the turn of the last century, most notably in Saint Petersburg, the geographic center of the Silver Age's cultural florescence. Held in private and state-operated theaters; in cabarets, outdoor gardens, and skating rinks; in the palatial homes of the city's well-heeled denizens and in the bohemian quarters of the literary vanguard—masquerades (a term I use for the category of entertainment that comprises masked and costume balls) constituted a vital component of Russian social life and cultural fabric in the late nineteenth and early twentieth centuries. Socialites, philanthropists, entrepreneurs, actors, writers, and students organized costume balls and parties for amusement as well as civic benefaction. Whereas masked balls in the eighteenth and early nineteenth centuries were occasions for anonymity and disguised identity, costume balls in the modernist era (defined in this study as 1872–1914) gave full rein to creative personal expression. In addition to the highly inventive and elaborate costuming that characterized the events, lavish décor, tableaux vivants and theatrical sketches, musical concerts and dancing were integrated in various combinations into the programs, creating

comprehensive artistic experiences that preceded the sumptuous productions of the Ballets Russes.

Take, for example, the Monster Masquerade, held at the Saint Petersburg Noblemen's Assembly on January 24, 1901. Billed as "a new and
original, international-artistic masquerade ball" and parenthetically
described as "a decadent ball," this event promised a dizzying array of
entertainments and attractions.[1] According to the advertising poster
drawn by Paul Assaturov, guests would enjoy a host of kiosks and
pavilions, including an igloo, a Turkish coffeehouse, a Caucasian tavern,
a house of geishas, a tea tavern, and an elaborate Persian dessert table
(figure 1). The poster heralded such wonders as "flowers that do not
wilt" and a new, mysterious amusement called "Masquerade Mail." In
addition to the exotic floral phenomena and the novel epistolary game,
guests could also look forward to entertainment by a gypsy choir (directed by I. F. Shishkov), a Romanian orchestra, a culinary exhibition
and cooking contest, and contests for best male and female costumes, as
well as nonstop dancing and unspecified "international diversions."[2]

The ornate, brightly colored illustration on the announcement
mirrors in its graphic dynamism the poster's breathless cataloging of
attractions. Assaturov's poster depicts a svelte woman wearing a form-
fitting, strapless bodysuit, mottled with robust red and black flowers.
She sports a seductive long black glove on her right arm and a decorative heart-shaped bracelet on her left. Radiating up from behind her
head is a red and black half-mask, the outline of which is scalloped, a
design feature that organically unites the mask with the garland of lime-
green flowers entwined with the woman's body. Her eyes closed, lips
parted in a coy smile, and golden tresses cascading to her knees, this
racy femme fatale is a fitting envoy to the "decadent ball." The poster's
visually stimulating imagery anticipates the masquerade's aesthetic
marvels and the sensory excitement that the entertainments promise to
arouse. The Monster Masquerade's aesthetic exuberance and diversionary richness highlight how modernist costume balls were simultaneously a collaborative creative enterprise, a forum for individual self-
expression, and a zone for sanctioned play among adults.

Among urban dwellers who frequented leisure-time masquerades
several times a week during the winter season, donning custom- and
homemade costumes for masquerades reflected a new understanding of
social identity as a creative and oftentimes polemical construct. Although
the public performances of identity explored in part I of this book differed in key ways from the designing of costumes for balls and parties

Figure 1. Advertising poster for "Monster Masquerade" by Pol' Assaturov (1901). (State Russian Museum, Saint Petersburg; reproduced from Eleanora Glinternik, *Reklama v Rossii XVIII–pervoi poloviny XX veka*)

addressed in part II, both types of self-fashioning conferred upon the individual a newfound political and artistic agency that accompanied the social and aesthetic changes sweeping Russia by the end of the nineteenth century. A metaphor for the contingent relationship between appearance and essence, masquerade expressed the relativistic and dynamic worldviews that were replacing absolutist paradigms in the physical and social sciences. The masquerade motif in the literary movement of Symbolism corresponded to the privileging of subjectivity and mystery, while in Decadence and Futurism it stood for radical aestheticism and the theatricalization of life. In tandem with the modernist craze for masquerades as a social diversion, cross-dressing, mystifications, impersonations, and the use of pseudonyms abounded on the stage, in the streets, and in literature.

Masquerade is a master trope of Russian modernist literature on the levels of plot and discourse. As a plot feature, the masquerade brings together disparate characters, exposes the tensions among them, and functions as a barometer of social discord. Such writers as Fyodor Dostoevsky, Fyodor Sologub, and Andrei Bely portrayed the masquerade as a volatile social space in which taboos are violated and conventions overturned. Others invested masquerade costumes with symbolic significance: Leonid Andreev and Alexander Blok employed them allegorically, while Anna Akhmatova used denotative character costumes as intertextual allusions. Masquerade functions as an apt metaphor for experimentations with narrative voice and lyrical persona in the writings of Zinaida Gippius and Elizaveta Dmitrieva, where it also facilitates a discussion of veiled discourse.

The Modernist Masquerade examines how the social practices and artistic representations of costume balls reflected the evolution of identity from an essentialist trait to a fluid construct during the final decades of tsarist Russia. The popularity of wearing imaginative costumes and metaphorical masks signaled a reconceptualization of the individual's relationship to the public sphere, which resulted in a newfound sense of political and artistic agency. The era's emergent spirit of individualism stimulated unbridled artistic experimentation: fashion and costume design gained acceptance as artistic disciplines, which both inspired and drew inspiration from the period's fanciful masquerades.[3] The following section charts the history of masquerade in Russia and provides key insights into the cultural myths and traditions that the modernists reworked.

History of Masquerade in Russia

The Russian cultural imagination associates the masquerade with tsarist splendor in the eighteenth and nineteenth centuries, in particular the opulent balls that accompanied the celebrations of a tsar's coronation and the holiday festivities of the nobility. In 1825 the newspaper *The Northern Bee* offered a fulsome description of an Imperial-court masquerade celebrating *maslenitsa*. For the occasion an artificial cascading waterfall was built onstage, and "the tables were decorated just as magnificently: the silver and bronze pieces of exquisite craftsmanship [were] astonishing and the real fresh flowers bewitch[ed] the gaze." Equally enchanting were the ladies' costumes that were "sprinkled with diamonds and pearls." The splendor of the scene evidently overwhelmed the rapturous reporter, who declared his journalistic skill impotent before such wonders, explaining, "the theater [. . .] was decorated with exceptional taste and a magnificence of which it is impossible to give an accurate account: you must see it for yourself."[4] As a leisure activity initially enjoyed exclusively at the Imperial court and among the aristocracy, the masquerade boasted a reputation for aesthetic refinement and conventions of proper comportment that were correlated to its exclusivity.

However, the elegance of the European-style courtly masquerade belied its anthropological roots in ancient carnival celebrations, which epitomized egalitarianism and a lack of social or aesthetic pretension. In his analysis of literary works by Rabelais and Dostoevsky, Mikhail Bakhtin explored the ritual significance and symbolism of ancient carnival celebrations and highlighted the importance of the natural cycle of death and rebirth. While carnival was not native to Russia, the holiday of maslenitsa, which has pagan roots but was assimilated into the Christian calendar, most closely approximates carnival's symbolic significance.[5] For pagans it was a celebration of the vernal equinox, the calendrical death of winter, which maslenitsa marks through the ritual of burning an effigy. For Eastern Orthodox Russians, maslenitsa is a period of revelry, equivalent to Mardi Gras or Shrovetide, that precedes Lent, a time of repentance and abstemiousness before Easter.

During the Renaissance in Europe, urban carnival celebrations branched in two directions: while some festivities continued in the public square where they were born, others migrated indoors and away from their folk origins and street-style rowdiness. The blossoming of an entertainment culture in eighteenth-century Russia stemmed partly from the transference of ritual satisfaction out of the church and into other forms of collective experience, such as secular holidays and amusements.[6] Indoor urban masquerades proliferated in Imperial Russia during the winter Yuletide (*sviatki*) and spring Shrovetide (*maslenitsa*) holiday seasons. The tradition of mumming, integral to Yuletide and Shrovetide festivities in Russia and England, entailed donning fancy dress as well as performing theatrical skits and singing carols while traveling from house to house in exchange for holiday libations. In Russia, mummers frequently chose their costumes based on the antithesis of native (*svoi*) and alien (*chuzhoi*): the wearer's adopted identity was supposed to oppose his actual social identity in terms of age, sex, species, ethnicity, or profession.[7] The *svoi-chuzhoi* premise of mummers' costume selection is an example of how carnivalesque celebrations favored the simplicity of binary oppositions, a tendency inscribed by the natural death-rebirth cycle that the springtime holiday marked.[8] The practice of dressing in costume was a key legacy bequeathed to the courtly masquerade by such folk celebrations as carnival and maslenitsa. The masks and costumes worn at ancient folk celebrations and modern urban masquerades ostensibly afforded participants temporary freedom from hierarchies and social expectations, and proffered immunity from restrictive taboos. The costumes worn to urban courtly masquerades from the eighteenth century on complicated the carnival binarism with a growing array of options for altering or disguising identity, including the ubiquitous black half-masks and dominos. Toward the beginning of the twentieth century, whimsical, non-representational costumes grew increasingly fashionable (as I discuss in chapter 4); this development further eroded the traditional *svoi-chuzhoi* binary that had characterized folk costuming.

The courtly masquerade shared with carnival and related festivities not only the practice of sporting masks and costumes, but also the suspension of certain social codes of behavior, albeit to differing degrees. Iurii Lotman has called the nineteenth-century cultural institution of the high-society masquerade ball a form of prearranged, organized, and controlled chaos, a culturally sanctioned antidote to the society ball's tyrannical strictures.[9] Whereas Bakhtin's analysis of carnival underscored the disruption of order and transgression of social boundaries typifying the ancient folk celebrations, urban courtly masquerades exhibited substantially more subdued forms of transgression because their sophisticated social settings dictated good manners among aristocratic guests. Into the early twentieth century masquerade participants delighted in festive spontaneity and novelty, which entailed a break from quotidian and prescribed behaviors. The mildly transgressive spirit of the masquerade became a dominant aspect of the literary trope during both eras of its popularity, in the 1830s and 1890s–1910s. In Romantic-era and modernist works of literature, masked and costume balls functioned as sites for scandal that could generate an array of delicious possibilities for plot intrigue, a dynamic that is at the heart of chapter 1.

The courtly masquerade, which flourished during the Renaissance and Enlightenment in England, France, and the Venetian Republic, entered Russia in the era of Peter the Great. Initially introduced as part of Peter's westernization program, the court *assemblei* was a gathering orchestrated for the purpose of entertainment. Although guests did not wear costumes in the currently accepted sense of fanciful dress or disguise, the members of the Russian nobility attending Peter's gatherings were subject to his sartorial decrees mandating western-style clothing. Obligated to dress in accordance with foreign fashion when appearing in public, the nobility was thus continually cloaked in a mode of dress different from its native Russian style. In addition, Peter reportedly organized masked gatherings, among other forms of boisterous revelry, in Saint Petersburg's central Troitskaia Square.[10] His fondness for such masked amusements also manifested itself metaphorically in the "game of tsar," an unstaged performance in which he would temporarily relinquish his identity as monarch in order to reinforce his authority. Such manipulations of public identity constituted a political strategy for acquiring and maintaining power, both rightful and illicit, which I explore in chapter 2.

During Anna Ivanovna's reign (1730–40) the western-style indoor masquerade gained currency, although the empress herself never compromised her dignity by dressing in costume or wearing a mask. Because masks had long-standing folk and religious associations with demonic, impure powers, Anna and her court related to them cautiously: for example, guests were required to shed their disguises when they heard the command "down with the masks" (*maski doloi*) as they sat down to supper.[11] In contrast to Anna's demand that her guests reveal their true identity before breaking bread, Catherine the Great insisted on the sacredness of anonymity at public masquerades. In Alexander Sumarokov's *Sketches of Catherine the Great* (1819) he recalled a particular instance when Catherine was attending a public masquerade incognito and angrily reprimanded a fellow masker who had exposed her.[12] Driven by curiosity, the masker violated etiquette by tearing off the empress's mask. Catherine scolded, "You have ruined the order preserved by all. One must respect every mask."[13] Catherine and her predecessor Elizabeth hosted lavish masquerades and earned renown for their spirited embrace of men's military garb at their "vice versa" (*prevrashchennye*) balls, for which guests were required to dress as the opposite gender. To celebrate Elizabeth's coronation in May 1742, there were no fewer than eight such events, over the course of which she was rumored to have worn every type of Russian military uniform.[14] The political expediency of dressing as men helped the empresses establish legitimacy as leaders of Russia, which was particularly important for the German-born Catherine, who ascended the throne after her husband Peter III's death.[15]

The Imperial court organized masquerades to celebrate major holidays as well as such politically significant occasions as coronations, royal weddings, and declarations of peace. From the late eighteenth century on, certain Imperial-court masquerades were open to all social classes. This surprising level of inclusiveness was a politically shrewd strategy for fostering the monarch's popularity. At one New Year's celebration, the court of Alexander I organized a masquerade that was attended by over 30,000 guests representing a wide range of social classes.[16] A report in *The Northern Bee* about the Imperial-court maslenitsa masquerade of 1825 noted that the attendees' dress reflected their class, pointing out that in contrast to the nobility, who presumably came in costume, the "Russian merchants wore their regular dress."[17] A quarter century later the Belgian newspaper *Le Nord* noted with amazement that "the public of the streets, the rabble of society" were allowed to "enjoy the luxury and magnificence destined for the select of society" at a masquerade celebrating Alexander II's coronation.[18] Although the masquerades were open to members of the lower social strata, the various classes did not necessarily comingle. In fact, members of the nobility and commoners sometimes had physically separate spaces in which to enjoy the festivities. At some court masquerades, members of the Imperial family would appear in a solemn procession to open the event, after which they retreated to a special gallery or balcony from which to watch the spectacle.[19]

Up until the second half of the eighteenth century, masquerades were held mainly at the Imperial court and attended chiefly by an elite circle of noblemen.[20] However, during Catherine the Great's reign and thereafter, entrepreneurial masquerades proliferated at Imperial theaters and noblemen's clubs, often with guidance from western impresarios. In Moscow's Petrovsky Theater the Englishman Michael Maddox built a massive rotunda in 1780 solely for masquerades, which he advertised in newspapers and for which he sold tickets.[21] The emergence of entrepreneurs organizing for-profit masquerades made the amusement accessible to those who had enough money to purchase tickets and acquire costumes, thus attracting a wider spectrum of attendees. As was the case at nineteenth-century Imperial-court masquerades, participants of various classes attended the commercial events but did not necessarily interact. One Moscow memoirist, Pyotr Vistengof, described in *Sketches of Moscow Life* (1842) how participants preferred to socialize with their own, noting that "In the left corner members of higher society usually congregate [. . .] here you will meet the noble, pale, proud and attractive faces of our lady aristocrats; on the right [. . .] almost everyone who runs to Moscow from the provinces in the winter [. . .] doctors' wives, bureaucrats, students, army officers."[22] While entrepreneurial masquerades did not dismantle Russia's social hierarchy, they did expand access to shared leisure-time activities.

In the 1830s a masquerade craze swept Saint Petersburg. Theaters and public entertainment parks regularly hosted and charged admission for masquerades. The Demidov Garden in Saint Petersburg, for example, boasted masquerade balls every Wednesday and Sunday, charging 1 ruble for admission; guests were free to wear a mask or not, according to personal preference.[23] As I discuss in chapter 1, Russian literature from the 1830s reflects the period's enthusiasm for masquerades, most notably in Mikhail Lermontov's classic drama *Masquerade* (1835–36). Many society tales and Yuletide stories, including V. Dmitriev's "Masquerade" (1832), Mikhail Zagoskin's "Concert of Demons" (1834), and V. N. Olin's "Strange Ball" (1838), also feature prominent masked or costume ball scenes. The increasing prevalence of entrepreneurial masquerades during this period attracted a broad social spectrum of attendees, including members of the royal family, who relished breaks from the court's restrictive decorousness. In Saint Petersburg Tsar Nikolai I and Grand Duke Mikhail Pavlovich attended public masquerades (albeit usually without mask or costume) at such venues as the one that V. V. Engel'gardt opened at the Rastrelli Palace in 1828.[24] The tsar reportedly derived pleasure and amusement from listening to the improper conversation and jokes that would ordinarily not be relayed in his presence. Ladies were free to approach the tsar and intertwine their arms with his to lead him off for private socializing. Regarding Nikolai's keenness for female company and the host's need to supply women appropriate to the task, Baron M. A. Korf (who served as a state secretary) recorded, "One of the directors of the Noblemen's Assembly told me that for the masquerades held there they gave out up to 80 complimentary tickets to actresses, socialites and other such Frenchwomen, with the goal of entertaining the Monarch and engaging him in intrigue (*intrigovat' i zanimat' Gosudaria*)."[25]

The tsar's flirtations befitted the loose atmosphere reigning at the public masquerade, which had a reputation for spurring romantic indiscretions. The diversity and sheer number of participants (Saint Petersburg's Bol'shoi Kamennyi Theater could accommodate upward of 12,000 people) assured them of ample opportunities for intrigue under protective disguise: because it was unlikely that participants would encounter and recognize each other at future events, these masquerades offered the possibility of immediate sensual gratification without consequences. Anonymity was key to encoding the nineteenth-century masquerade as a zone of seduction and betrayal, a topos that was widely reflected in Romantic-era literature and epitomized in Lermontov's *Masquerade*. Judging from reminiscences and diaries, anonymity was actual and afforded as much juvenile pleasure as it did opportunity for adult indiscretion. Daryia Fyodorovna Fikel'mon, wife of the Austrian ambassador, recorded in her diary on February 13, 1830, the playful antics in which she participated with the empress the previous evening:

> Ball-Masquerade in the Engel'gardt building. The Empress [Alexandra Fyodorovna, née Charlotte of Prussia] wanted to go, but in the most discreet fashion, and she chose me to accompany her. [. . .] I left the palace together with the Empress in a hired carriage and under the name of Mlle Timasheva. The Tsaritsa laughed like a child, but I was terrified. . . . When we showed up in the crowd it got worse—they were elbowing her and crushing her with little respect, just like any other masker. It was all new to the Empress and it entertained her. We attacked (*atakovali*) many. Meyendorf, a fashionable young man who was always trying to win the Empress's favor, was so inattentive that he absolutely did not recognize her and treated us very poorly. Lobanov immediately recognized us both, but Gorchakov, who spent an entire hour with

us and seated us in the carriage, didn't suspect who we were. [. . .]
Finally, at three in the morning I dropped her off at the palace,
whole and unharmed.[26]

The empress's thrill at remaining unknown stemmed largely from
the freedom her disguise accorded and the novelty of her temporarily
altered social status. As Fikel'mon recollected, the anticipation of engaging in a forbidden activity and capering among her subjects under
protective cover elicited from the empress childlike laughter and glee
at the prospect of duping strangers and acquaintances alike.

Anonymity also encouraged practical jokes at masquerades. The 1859
memoir of Maria Miliutina, wife of a prominent government official,
contains the description of a comical scenario in which a cavalier's
pursuit of a "female" masker proved fruitless because "she" in fact was
a male prankster. "Several young men dressed as ladies in elegant
dominos flirted with their superiors and nearly drove them mad. For
example, Sukhozanet sat with a pink domino for nearly the whole
evening, courted her to the utmost, praising her sweetness and cleverness, kissed her hand and inquired of everyone, 'Who is that charming
woman?' I don't know whether or not he finally got the truth, but many
soon found out that the most charming of women was no one other
than the aide-de-camp Kavelin."[27] A man pursuing a female masker
and imploring her to reveal her identity was a form of masquerade
courtship. A cavalier's persistent attempts to unmask a lady's identity
ostensibly signaled his ardor's sincerity. His entreaties and her rebuffs
constituted a cat-and-mouse game, the challenge stimulating his desire
and heightening the anticipation of conquest. Fifty years after Miliutina's report the newspaper *Sibirskii listok* wrote about a similar incident
of highly effective cross-dressing that duped a cavalier at a masquerade: the masker who won the prize for best costume at a January 1, 1909,
masquerade was not a woman (as had been thought) but rather a man
who "was so well made up with cosmetics that one of the masker's
suitors kissed her hand."[28]

Both the romantic intrigue and comedic aspects of the public masquerade, which could take place thanks to the participants' supposed
anonymity, persisted as part of the cultural myth of masquerade into the
early twentieth century. Two anecdotes from 1909–1910 that appeared in
the satirical journal *Listok kopeiki* wed the trope of the masked amorous
liaison with the situational humor that arises from mistaken identity.[29]

At the Masquerade

First Man: So you're here with your spouse?

Second Man: Please! Really, would a man who loves his wife take her to such a shady place? It's so stuffy here, there's such an intolerable crowd!

First Man: But who is your lady friend?

Second Man: You don't recognize her? You're such a comedian, man. It's none other than your lawful spouse![30]

The Masker

A husband set off for the club and there he met a very interesting and elegant masker. He began to court her persistently and finally took her off to a restaurant.

—You are charming, sweet, lovely! . . . Take off your mask!

The masker passed out and . . . before him awoke his very own wife.

—We've been married for how many years, she said, and you never found me sweet or lovely. Why is that?

—Because I never once saw you in a mask, the husband answered without missing a beat.[31]

In both anecdotes the husband's failure to recognize his spouse in the face of a potential romantic infidelity has the tone of light social satire. However, such extramarital dalliances were potentially perilous in real life. The January 10, 1911, issue of the newspaper *Rul'* reported on the murder of a wife by her jealous husband at a masquerade in the eastern city of Chita. The column "Daily News" explained that the land surveyor Iankovsky killed his wife with two bullets to the head before turning the gun on himself.[32]

While anonymity may have served as an aphrodisiac in certain circumstances by making encounters more piquant, it was also an obstacle for the hopeful yet shy paramour. The newspaper *Novoe vremia* published in 1908 the following "missed-connections" style entreaty under the heading "At the Masquerade": "Mariinskii Theater, Jan 26. You were with Shurochka, when you left I placed a black lace scarf over your shoulders. You were in a light-blue bonnet. I imploringly request your mailing address."[33] This touching plea for the possibility of kindling a romance suggests that not all masquerade attendees had the moxie to pursue amorous pleasures *in situ*.

While anonymity and romantic dalliance characterized the nineteenth-century public masquerade and persisted into the twentieth century as part of the cultural script, the domestic costume ball, at which guests were acquainted with one another, was less likely to promote promiscuous behavior. As N. F. Pavlov explained in *Recollections about Moscow Balls* (1835), "It's enjoyable to see in costumes the same individuals whom we see every day, and to behold how they look dressed up. . . . It's enjoyable to transport familiar faces to distant centuries and distant locales. It somehow pleasantly arouses curiosity."[34] At home masquerades, the warmth of friendship and the pleasure of seeing one's close acquaintances in a new light prevailed over the allure of sexual frisson. Unlike the entrepreneurial masquerades, entrance to which could be purchased, private gatherings organized by members of high society were exclusive events that promised a genteel community of attendees an evening of opulence and refinement. Not surprisingly, women were the driving force behind the sartorial elegance and decorative sophistication that characterized the balls held in private mansions. At the end of the nineteenth century women were praised in newspaper articles for their warm hospitality and skillful interior decorating, and their costumes were attentively, even rapturously, detailed. The domestic costume ball was a feminine space where women were accorded respect for their good taste and generosity.

The illustrated images of women on advertising posters played to their vanity by showcasing beautiful, alluringly dressed figures. Ladies were expected to appear at costume balls and parties elaborately and thoughtfully bedecked. Those who were strapped for time or resources, or who simply lacked ingenuity, could wear a half-mask and domino (as could men) or rent a costume; but the more creative and sophisticated outfits elicited flattering public recognition in the form of prizes and praise in the press. Sartorial requirements for women and men at masquerades differed. An advertising poster for a masquerade ball to be held on January 9, 1899, at the Mariinskii Theater stipulated that women must come in masks (*damam obiazatel'no byt' v maskakh*) and keep them on for the first three hours (11 pm–2 am) of the five-hour event, although there was no such stipulation for the men.[35] Invitations and advertisements for private and public masquerades often specified that men could wear a tuxedo or military uniform in lieu of a costume. The advertisement for the Monster Masquerade described earlier advised male guests who elected not to dress in costume to wear tuxedos (a point that Assaturov drove home with three exclamation points).

In addition to courtly, entrepreneurial, and domestic masked and costume balls, benefit masquerades became fashionable starting in the mid-nineteenth century. Organized by civic, philanthropic, and professional societies and often held in Imperial theaters such as the Mariinskii and Aleksandriiskii, benefit masquerades had the goal of raising money for the aid and protection of indigent children, students, widows, and pensioners. A particular type of winter-holiday costume party for children (*elka*) enjoyed great popularity in the second half of the nineteenth century as a philanthropic event held to assist orphans and other needy youngsters.[36] Benefit masquerades held in public theaters had the advantage of being able to borrow repertory costumes and stage sets, as was the case at the Academy of Arts balls, which I discuss in chapter 4. The Society of Civil Engineers, the Society for the Promotion and Protection of Private Ministerial Work, the Russian Theatrical Society (specifically under the leadership of A. E. Molchanov and the well-known actress M. G. Savina),[37] and the Saint Petersburg Academy of Arts are examples of organizations that regularly sponsored philanthropic evenings.[38] The costumed allegorical quadrille in Dostoevsky's *Demons*, which Iuliia Mikhailovna organized to benefit the local governesses, was a parody of a certain "buffoonish dance" (*shutovskaia pliaska*) in costumes that took place at an event aiding invalids, which was held at the Noblemen's Assembly on February 28, 1869.[39] The philanthropic nature of benefit masquerades bespeaks the privileged social status of their attendees, who included the nobility, aristocracy, military officers, and—toward the end of the nineteenth century— merchants and industry tycoons.

Philanthropic costume balls at the turn of the century catered to an aristocratic clientele accustomed to cosmopolitanism and opulence. A poster by Ivan Porfirov for a benefit masquerade presented practical information about date and venue, as well as enthusiastic descriptions of the artistic pleasures that awaited guests (figure 2). Written in both Russian and French, the poster communicated a Continental patina of elitism along with the necessary facts and fanfare. Set for January 9, 1899, at the Mariinskii, this masquerade ball (*bal masqué et costumé*) was organized for the express purpose of financially supporting the construction of the Nikolaevskii and Okhotenskii Children's Homes.[40] The poster boasted that decoration of the hall was under the artistic direction of painter Valery Ovsiannikov, a fact that aimed to legitimize the ball's

Figure 2. Advertising poster for a masquerade ball at the Mariinskii Theater by Ivan Porfirov (1899). (State Russian Museum, Saint Petersburg; reproduced from Iuliia Demidenko, ed., *Veseliashchiisia Peterburg*)

pretensions to high culture. The event's attractions included an illuminated fountain (*fontaine lumineuse*), two orchestras, tableaux vivants,
and a buffet. As extra enticements, there were two lotteries, one of
which was free to enter and rewarded the winners with original watercolor paintings donated by the Society of Russian Watercolorists. The
poster also trumpeted in large letters a *lotereia-allegri*, a very popular
type of lottery that revealed the results to the participant immediately
upon obtaining a ticket for the price of 25 kopecks. (The prize was
named on the ticket.) In addition to lottery winnings, guests could
aspire to claim a prize for best toilette or best costume. Porfirov's poster
announced that four such prizes would be given out, two of which
would be reserved exclusively for best costume among members of the
general public (i.e., all but actors, actresses, and members of the organizing committee). Finally, the poster listed the names and addresses of
stores and restaurants in Saint Petersburg where one could purchase
entry tickets at the prices of 5 rubles 10 kopecks for men and 3 rubles 10
kopecks for women.

In addition to enumerating entertainments and prizes, the poster
includes imagery that suggests yet one more type of titillation: the
thrill of romantic pursuit. The female figure at the poster's center is in a
décolleté-baring ivory dress that nearly matches her skin tone, which
invites the viewer to imagine her undressed, as does her almost fully
exposed left breast. This coquette is further sexualized by the two vo-
luptuous, art-nouveau-style ivory flowers resting in her hair, their
stamens protruding. Her dynamic posture suggests that she is rushing
forward, seemingly to provoke a male suitor whose hand stretches into
the frame of vision and is poised to clasp her wrist. Her other hand
holds a black half-mask not far from her face, as if she has just removed
it in a gesture of capitulation.

An advertising poster by Fyodor Bukhgol'ts for the same masquerade benefit the following year is less explicit about the masquerade's
potential for romantic escapades, but it too prominently features a
female masker in a flirtatious stance. She wears a sleeveless white ball
gown with a plunging neckline and two pompoms on the front as well
as one adorning each of her shoulders. The dress's puffy bustle accen-
tuates her hips and echoes the spherical shape of her white hat, also
topped with pompoms, and of the tufted white purse that she playfully
swings. Her snowy, pneumatic look conveys an innocence befitting the
children's benefaction, while her bare arms and dramatic décolletage
hint at adult intrigue. Heralding the event set for January 29, 1900, at

the Mariinskii Theater to raise money for enlarging the orphans' wards at children's shelters, the bilingual French-Russian poster announces attractions similar to the last year's: an illuminated fountain, "character dances" (*kharakternye tantsy*) by famous performers, one military and one ballroom orchestra, a buffet, and two lotteries (with the same benefactors and terms as the previous year's free lottery and big *lotereia-allegri*).

In the early twentieth century, masquerades also proliferated in private experimental theaters and cabarets, including the celebrated Stray Dog, as well as in non-performance spaces such as outdoor ice-skating rinks and indoor roller rinks.[41] A photograph from 1900 captured several participants of a daytime masquerade at the Iusupovsky Garden depicting a scene from a Russian folktale (figure 3). Posing outdoors on a frozen pond and clad with ice skates, maskers were dressed as folk characters who included Father Frost and his helper, the Snow Maiden. In 1910 the journal *Ogonek* featured an illustration by N. N. Gerardov that recorded another masquerade on ice, which took place on February 23, also at the Iusupovsky Garden (figure 4). Among the skating costumed figures were the following: a sorcerer in a conical cap and suit with short breeches, both of which were made from dark material and spangled with light-colored stars; a Napoleon lookalike; a Pierrot in a white costume studded with black pompoms down the front and an enormous black ruff; a man in a top hat and tails; and a woman in the foreground wearing stylish winter apparel and a black half-mask. In the center of the picture skates a young boy dressed as a chef with a toque perched atop his head and a ladle in his right hand. This singular child in Gerardov's illustration is a surprising presence inasmuch as adults constituted the primary demographic of public masquerade attendees. Perhaps the wholesomeness of outdoor daytime skating was more appropriate for children than the erotically charged, late-night masquerades held in indoor theaters. The extensive caption beneath the picture reports that the masquerade ball, which was an annual event at the Garden, was illuminated with electric lights and small sparklers known as Bengal lights (*bengal'skie ogni*). Describing the activity, the caption raved, "the festive masquerade crowd in picturesque costumes floated across the glistening ice, executing impressive dance figures." However, the fireworks displays, which evoked the period's engineering wonders with names like "The Eiffel Tower" and "Airplane," consti-tuted the event's chief novelty.[42]

The roller-skating rink at Mars Field was also a popular venue for masquerades. The American-style amusement's kinetic exoticism

Figure 3. Photo of costumed participants at the Iusupovsky Garden ice-skating rink in Saint Petersburg portraying a scene from a Russian folk tale (1900). (from the studio of Carl Bulla; image courtesy of TsGAKFFD, Saint Petersburg)

Figure 4. Illustration of costume party at the Iusupovsky Garden ice-skating rink by Nikolai Gerardov. (from *Ogonek*, no. 10 [March 19, 1910])

enhanced the aesthetic thrill of dressing up. An arranged group photo from 1911 at the rink shows 28 men and women sporting an array of costumes, but with at least four men and three women dressed similarly as Pierrot in white costumes punctuated with trompe l'oeil pompoms (figure 5). Additional photographs taken at the Mars Field skating rink from 1913 and tagged with the moniker "White Ball" show that the customary white costume of the commedia dell'arte figure Pierrot enjoyed popularity as at the 1911 masquerade. One of the photos shows five Pierrots lined up in the rink's buffet area, playing various stringed instruments for an appreciative dining audience (figure 6). Above the heads of the white-clad minstrels stretch garlands of white flowers that complement the strings of electric white light bulbs. Another photograph of the White Ball reveals, however, that Pierrot costumes were not the limit of the public's vestimentary imagination: Greek warriors and figures representing other ethnicities (Spaniards, Chinamen, Arabs) all sported primarily white outfits, accented with dark detailing and accessories (figure 7). The ladies wore white dresses with no particular identifying features. Two notable exceptions were the bare-armed Greek goddess holding a flag and the centrally positioned Snow Maiden, behind whom she stood. The roller rink's walls were exceptionally ornate on this occasion, decorated in friezes featuring, from the top downward, Grecian figures, bas-relief mythical animals, and arches painted with enormous lilies of the valley, white lilies, and five-pedaled flowers to captivate the beholder's eyes. More striking still were the seven boys in blackface sitting in front of the standing adults. Cross-legged, with their roller-skate-shod feet prominently displayed, the boys' identical black faces, black hair, and black limbs were broken up only by their identical white shorts and thin white necklaces. Although it is unclear what role these boys played in the event, their racial exoticism, young age, primitivist costumes, and seated position suggest that they play a subservient role in relation to the white-skinned adults towering over them from behind.

As these examples show, masquerades (comprising both costume and masked balls) were a prominent feature of cultural life in Russia during the years spanning the late nineteenth and early twentieth centuries. Throughout the chapters that follow I bring forth additional examples of historical masquerades drawn from visual and written records, and I analyze them in order to illuminate how they stimulated and reflected the lively artistic experimentation and creative élan that characterized the rich period of cultural production known as the Silver Age.

Mistifer, behind a group she stood. Cascadier Pink's smile was recep-

totally erased in 1919 Carnot. Beyond Cle, these festivities, thanks

Figure 7. Photo of participants of a "White Ball" in masquerade costumes at the Mars Field Skating Rink in Saint Petersburg (1913). (from the studio of Carl Bulla; image courtesy of TsGAKFFD, Saint Petersburg)

Figure 5 (*top left*). Photo of a group of roller skaters in masquerade costumes at the Mars Field Skating Rink in Saint Petersburg (1911). (from the studio of Carl Bulla; image courtesy of TsGAKFFD, Saint Petersburg)

Figure 6 (*bottom left*). Photo of participants of a "White Ball" in masquerade costumes at the buffet at the Mars Field Skating Rink in Saint Petersburg (1913). (from the studio of Carl Bulla; image courtesy of TsGAKFFD, Saint Petersburg)

The Masquerade Motif in Decadence and Symbolism

During the years that bridged the two centuries, Decadence and Symbolism emerged in Russia as the dominant literary movements. While some
literary historians argue that they represent one movement, I distinguish
between the two while also acknowledging their common ground.
Such an approach bears some resemblance to the Soviet-era Russian
paradigm that divided writers into the older, or "first-generation"
Symbolists (Valery Briusov, Sologub, Gippius, and her husband,
Dmitry Merezhkovsky, who are classified by American scholars Joan
Delaney Grossman and Kirsten Lodge as Decadents[43]) and the younger,
"second-generation" Symbolists (Bely, Blok, and Viacheslav Ivanov).
This classificatory scheme unites the literature of these writers roughly
from the years 1890–1910, while allowing for discernible differences in
style and themes. Referring to the "first generation" of Symbolists as
Decadents points to the strong influence of French Decadence (and its
companion movement in Britain, Aestheticism) on the Russian literary
tradition. For the purposes of my study, this terminological distinction
serves as shorthand for evoking distinct artistic and philosophical
priorities. When I speak of Decadence I draw on the French Decadent
tradition of stylizing physical appearance, including the inversion of
traditional gender markers. In chapter 3, on gender masquerades, I
trace the parallels in literary trends and practices of self-fashioning in
fin-de-siècle France and Russia, which are united under the rubric of
Decadence. In chapter 6 I also speak of Decadence when pointing out
the continuities in the exuberant aestheticism between turn-of-the-
century self-stylizing and the outrageous costumes of the Russian
Futurists. In the context of this study, Decadence signals an emphasis
on form and appearance. Accordingly, I align what is commonly termed
"life-creation" (*zhiznetvorchestvo*), the aesthetic organization of behavior
and conscious construction of a social self, with Decadence, whereas
others refer to it as a Symbolist phenomenon.[44]

This Decadent practice does, however, pivot on a fundamentally
Symbolist premise: the contingent relationship between surface and
essence. In this regard Decadence may be considered a subgenre within
Symbolism. Symbolism treated the sign as open-ended, thereby atten-
uating the idea that each signifier ought to have but one signified. This
challenge to the referential stability of the word granted important roles
to subjectivity and personal interpretation. The openness of the Symbol
enabled the reader to enlarge through association the sphere of

meanings present in a work of art.[45] While detractors viewed this
boundlessness as a crisis of signification, the Symbolists believed that
the poet's intuitive imagination and unique ability to think metaphorically transcended the denotative power of literal language and representational art. The Symbolists' permissive attitude toward signifier-
signified relationships allowed them to rupture the semantic link for the
sake of creating an artistic effect. Just as the literary symbol challenged
referential authority, Decadent self-fashioning challenged the idea of a
single, stable identity. Intentional constructions of social identity refute
an essentialist identity in the same way that the subjective interpretation
of a symbol upends the notion of an inseparable link between word or
image and its referent. Contingency and subjectivity reign in these relativistic approaches to art and self, and also characterize literary scholar
Judith Butler's metaphor of social identity as a masquerade. Butler
argues that individuals adopt performative masks to interface with the
changing social spheres they inhabit, and these masquerades of identity
may be playful, parodic, or deceptive.[46]

While there is a formal affinity between Decadent attitudes toward
identity and Symbolist poetics, Symbolism as a literary movement en-
compassed more than the formal method of the symbol. I view the
dominant trait of Russian Symbolism as its mysticism, the gravitas and
solemnity of which oppose the playfulness of Decadent stylizing as
well as the morbid Decadent thematic obsession with death and despair.
Inspired by the religious philosophies of Vladimir Solovyov and Nikolai
Fyodorov, Russian Symbolism probed the mysteries of the spirit and
the universe. Poetry oriented toward this high-minded and abstract
metaphysics fostered an atmosphere of ambiguity: the haziness of the
symbol was appropriate for treating fundamentally enigmatic subjects.
These are the attributes of Symbolism that I highlight in chapter 4,
where I discuss the role of figurative and allegorical costumes at modernist masquerades.

In this book I consciously distance the social and literary practices of
masquerade from the rubric of life-creation principally because of its
imputed metaphysical program. Olga Matich has traced the origins of
life-creation to Solovyov's ideas and explained that certain writers sought
to unite life and art into one erotically charged creative enterprise, thereby
acquiring a god-like power to overcome the inevitability of death that
is associated with procreation and to transform reality according to
their artistic vision.[47] The philosophical seriousness with which most
Symbolists approached their life-styling contradicted the playfulness

of Decadent role-playing. Bely's experience with the circle of Argonauts offers a telling example of how the imputed earnestness of life-creation was at odds with a spirit of play. The Argonauts was an informal, non-literary group of individuals united by a metaphorical quest for the sun, which represented their goal of reconciling the earthly and the heavenly kingdoms.[48] Self-mocking rituals such as the "*kozlovak*" and "harlequinades" intentionally undermined the group's mystical pretensions and aspirations, however. Writes Bely, "We ourselves threw a veil of jokes over our cherished dawn . . . and we began at times to play the fool and joke about how we seemed to the 'uninitiated,' and about what sophisms and paradoxes would result if we exaggerated in overblown forms what was not put into words; i.e., we envisioned a 'harlequinade' of ourselves."[49] By imagining a parody of their own mythmaking practices, the Argonauts could see themselves as role-playing figures at a masquerade. This critical distance between their parodies of mythmaking and the mythmaking itself, which Alexander Lavrov has defined as a manifestation of the Symbolist life-creation ethos,[50] highlights how their mystical agenda contravened the ironic detachment of their harlequinade. My differentiation between Decadence and Symbolism, while running the risk of reductionism, is meant to foreground two distinct trends, each of which variously illuminates how masquerade operated as a trope in Russian modernism.

Symbolism and the Mask

While the masquerade served as an apt metaphor for Decadent self-stylizing and the contingency of identity enacted through costuming echoed the Symbolist attenuation of the link between surface and essence, the mask found widespread use as an emblem of the individual (*lichnost'*) in fin-de-siècle Russian literature. Although the mask motif is not explored systematically in this book because it had cultural significance separate from that of the masquerade, it warrants a brief excursus because certain writers repeatedly returned to it in their fiction and essays. Mask imagery was tied up with philosophical questions about the spiritual and social nature of the individual. Schopenhauer's division of so-called reality into the noumenal (invisible) and the phenomenal (visible) in *The World as Will and Idea* was highly influential, especially in guiding Symbolist ideas about the individual's spiritual relationship to the surrounding world. According to Schopenhauer, the noumenal comprises one universal will of which every individual is a part. Individuals live separate from the one will under their masks (misleading symbols of individuality), which are elements of the phenomenal world that blind us to the noumenal truth. Sologub embraced this conception, which left its imprint on his collection of stories *Mouldering Masks* and in his theoretical essay "Theater of One Will."[51]

Bely also used the mask to elucidate his ideas about phenomenology. His essays from the first decade of the twentieth century revealed the influence of Schopenhauer as well as Nietzsche. "The Mask" (1904) and "Apocalypse of Russian Poetry" (1905) develop the idea of the mask as a visible manifestation of the invisible and menacing forces lurking behind it, drawing on Nietzsche's articulation of the mask in *The Birth of Tragedy* as an emblem of Apollonian order behind which stormed Dionysian chaos. Bely asserted in "Apocalypse," "To know reality is to tear off the mask from the Invisible (*Nevidimaia*), which steals up to us under many guises (*lichinami*)."[52] In "Why I Became a Symbolist" (1928) Bely pointed to his own contingent identity made manifest as pseudonyms to illustrate the divorce between the instantiations of the individual and his true essence. He explained how since his early childhood he practiced adopting masks or guises (*lichiny*) and alternating personas (*lichnosti*), all the while not revealing his true self, his *Individuum*. Born Boris Bugaev, his various monikers (Boren'ka, Andrei Bely and *Unser Freund*, a German nickname his fellow anthroposophists bestowed) reflected different selves, not one of which represented him completely.[53]

Fellow traveler and poet Maksimilian Voloshin expressed a kindred sentiment about the relationship between the formless, noumenal spirit and physical form. He composed a series of essays between 1906 and 1910, which he published under the title *Guises of Art* (*Liki tvorchestva*) about contemporary writers, modeling it on French Symbolist Remy de Gourmont's *Book of Masks* (1896–98).[54] Guiding it was a philosophical idea similar to that which he expressed in his notebook of 1907–9, where he wrote, "In all searches for the formless one must bow before form [. . .]. The faceless makes itself known through the face. [. . .] Each is still searching for a face for himself, and the formless world knocks at the heart of the artist in order to find for itself an incarnation."[55] For Voloshin as for Bely and Sologub, the mask was a symbol for the individual and an instantiation of the primal life force that unites humanity.

Viacheslav Ivanov investigated the relationship between the individual (*lichnost'*) and the countenance, which he characterized as either a divine face (*lik*) or a soulless mask. In his essay "Dostoevsky and the Novel-Tragedy" (1911) he described how the individual is both separate from and merged with others; its borders are "indeterminate and mysterious." The primary subject of his essay is the character Nikolai Stavrogin's (from Dostoevsky's *Demons*) lack of a moral center, a fact betrayed by his mask-like visage. In the novel and in Christian theology, the mask represents the condition of facelessness that corresponds to spiritual bankruptcy or corruption, in contrast to Christ's effulgent face that evinces his divinity.[56]

Methodology and Overview of the Chapters

Bakhtin categorized masquerade as part of the "popular-festive tradition" that owes its existence in part to the carnival tradition.[57] This genetic link would seemingly suggest the profitability of reading modernist masquerades and their literary representations through the lens of Bakhtin's theory of carnival and carnivalized literature. However, Bakhtin also asserted that masquerade has diverged significantly from carnival over the millennia: "Having followed the line of court masquerades combined with other traditions, the style of popular festive forms began, as we have said, to degenerate. It acquired alien elements of ornate and abstract allegory. The ambivalent improprieties related to the bodily lower stratum were turned into erotic frivolity. The popular utopian spirit and the new historic awareness began to fade."[58] In *Problems of Dostoevsky's Poetics* he rearticulated the distance between modern masquerades in particular and carnival celebrations, going so far as to belittle the masquerade for its deviation: "To understand correctly the problem of carnivalization, one must dispense with the oversimplified understanding of carnival found in the *masquerade* [italics in original] line of modern times, and even more with a vulgar bohemian understanding of carnival."[59] Bakhtin believed that the modern-day masquerade lacks the social purpose of ritual—in contrast to ancient carnival, in which there was not "a grain of empty frivolity or vulgar bohemian individualism."[60]

Influential in my decision to sidestep Bakhtin's theorization of carnival is his disparagement of masquerade's "vulgar bohemian individualism," which denigrates what I see as an important defining feature of the modernist masquerade. The central role accorded to the individual, his subjectivity and creativity, deeply influenced the emergence in the late nineteenth and early twentieth centuries of distinctive masquerade-ball practices, such as wearing whimsical, inventive, and polemical costumes. Bakhtin's own statements controvert the suitability of his theoretical approach for the subject of my current study. Although one can dispute his argument that modern-day masquerade is an oversimplified iteration of ancient carnival, doing so would not enrich our understanding of Russian modernism, which is the goal of this book. My theoretical approach to the study of masquerade therefore does not rely on Bakhtin's reading of carnival, which was important for the only other monograph-length scholarly treatment of masquerade (Terry Castle's study of the phenomenon in eighteenth-century England).[61] I do, however, employ his theorization of double-voiced discourses in my discussion of parody in chapters 1 and 3.

This book is divided into two parts, which are united in their intertwining of social history and artistic expression. Each chapter supplies historical accounts of actual and metaphorical masquerades drawn from memoirs, journals, and newspapers, which I use to frame my readings of literary works and modernist aesthetics. While I actively seek correspondences and trends, I am also attentive to the disjunctures between social experience and creative cultural production. The first half of the book concentrates primarily on issues of representation and examines the theoretical problems surrounding parody, imitation, and stylization as discursive strategies in literature and in social performances of personal identity. The second half inquires into issues of reception and interpretation by treating costume design as a type of legible poetics that avails itself to reading.

In chapters 1 and 3, I apply Bakhtin's conception of parody as a double-directed discourse to literary and nonliterary utterances. Distinct from his discussion of parody as a feature of carnivalized literature, which he elaborates in "Characteristics of Genre and Plot Composition in Dostoevsky's Works," is his characterization of parody as a form of double-directed or double-voiced discourse in "Discourse in Dostoevsky."[62] Bakhtin explained that the two "voices" are parallel but that the imitative voice of parody antagonistically appropriates for its own purposes the original discourse. Bakhtin acknowledged the variety of forms that parodistic discourse can take: "One can parody another person's style as a style; one can parody another's socially typical or individually characterological manner of seeing, thinking and speaking."[63] Imitative masquerade costumes and campy impersonations, for example, adopt and intentionally alter (perhaps hostilely) attributes of the originals they imitate. Literary and nonliterary parodies operate similarly by creating a copy that distorts an original and usurps its semantic authority.

The clichés of comportment and sartorial conventions of courtly masquerades are vulnerable targets for parody because they constitute a particular set of attributes that are easily manipulated. In certain works of modernist literature, representations of masquerade read as parodies because they travesty masquerade's longstanding associations with high-society refinement. Chapter 1 offers a brief analysis of four literary works written between 1830 and 1840, which contain the key attributes of the masquerade topos that availed themselves to imitation and deformation in modernist literature. I have selected texts that are highly illustrative of the topos's defining traits: Zagoskin's "Concert of Demons," Lermontov's *Masquerade*, Olin's "Strange Ball," and Vladimir Sollogub's "High Society" (1840). The chapter examines the costume party scenes in Dostoevsky's *Demons* and Sologub's *Petty Demon* as two modernist parodies of the early nineteenth-century topos. Dostoevsky deeply influenced Russia's modernist writers, and many of his works evince a proto-Symbolist sensibility. His novel and that of Sologub feature costume gatherings that devolve into scandal. These scenes travesty the Romantic-era masquerade as a locus of refinement and romance, and forge a link between the moral debasement that spoils the balls and demonism, which is alluded to in the novels' titles. The costume parties are sites of scandalously inappropriate and even criminal behavior. The spoiled balls associate disguise with demonism, a connection that is rooted in Russian folk and Orthodox Church beliefs about the infernal powers invested in disguises and masks. Dostoevsky and Sologub correlate aesthetics and ethics, where all that is beautiful and orderly (contained in the religiously inflected *obraz*, meaning icon) is good, and all that is deformed and defaced (united under the rubric of *bezobrazie*) bespeaks impurity. This direct link between appearance and essence stands out as part of the essentialist paradigm of identity that was being revised at the turn of the last century, a principle illustrated by the numerous examples of modernist masquerades that this book brings forth.

Chapter 2 expands the definition of masquerade to include social performances of identity, in particular politically motivated acts of impersonation and constructions of national identity in the context of the turbulent year 1905. The chapter's discussion of political agency is distantly informed by Hannah Arendt's *On Revolution*, in which she argues that the political actor must unify his disparate private selves under the guise of a constant, stable public mask in order to foster and sustain power. Political scientist Norma Moruzzi has examined Arendt's ideas through the lens of Joan Riviere's 1929 essay "Womanliness as Masquerade" to distill a model of political agency based on a strategic performance of social identity in the public sphere.[64] While Moruzzi's analysis focuses on the benefits of the social mask for wielding rightful power, I interrogate the link between social masking and political agency from the perspective of illegitimate claims to power or destabilizations of rightful power, including those of terrorist organizations. By reading Boris Savinkov's *Pale Horse* and Bely's *Petersburg* against the backdrop of Russia's historical experience with political impostors, affirmations of nationhood, and masked threats to the tsarist regime, the chapter illuminates the relationship between political agency and constructions of national identity (especially as constituted through national costume). As journalistic reports that I examine make clear, the years surrounding the tumult of the Russo-Japanese War (1904–1905) and attempts at domestic political reform in 1905 witnessed a mainstream interest in wearing national and ideologically inflected costumes to masquerade balls. In the first decade of the twentieth century, bold individuals used their masquerade costumes to express individual opinion on political issues at the same time as terrorists used costumed impersonations in the public sphere to blur the line between internal and external threats to Russia's statehood.

Moving from masquerades of national identity to gender masquerades, chapter 3 investigates the various constructions of female identity undertaken by men and women in cabaret performances, in episodes of social self-fashioning, and in literature. As in France and England, experiments with personal appearance and lyrical voice that manipulated traditional gender markers permeated cultural production in fin-de-siècle Russia. This chapter puts the performances of femininity by Russian women writers Zinaida Gippius and Cherubina de Gabriak, the *nom de plume* of Elizaveta Dmitrieva, into the context of Decadence and Aestheticism to foreground their modernist practice of manipulating form. Using Bakhtin's paradigm of veiled discourses, I examine the formal and polemical differences between Gippius's parody of the conspicuous cosmetic artifice attributed to the archetypal Decadent femme fatale, and Dmitrieva's stylization of the enduring Mary and Eve archetypes.[65]

Part II approaches the first part's work on issues of representation from the vantage point of reception, inquiring into hermeneutical problems by treating costume design as a type of legible poetics.

Drawing on the work of cultural semiotician Iurii Lotman, I start with the fundamental premise that analogous interpretive strategies may be applied to text and textile. As Roland Barthes laid out in *Fashion System*, sartorial semiotics has an economy of signification regulated by its own internal laws.[66] Dress and physical appearance express meaning, which may be augmented by behavioral cues and verbal utterances, as in theatrical performance. When the wearer dons and animates his costume, he plays a corresponding role, enacting his newly adopted identity. The connection between costume and performance that characterizes theater also typifies masquerade. However, the fundamental difference between theater and masquerade is one of narrative: whereas the dramatic script provides cohesiveness to the theatrical production, interactions among masquerade participants are spontaneous and unbounded by an overarching narrative.

Chapter 4 compares the signification strategies of figurative and nonrepresentational costumes worn at actual costume balls hosted by the Saint Petersburg Academy of the Arts to those described in Leonid Andreev's play *Black Maskers*. As with metaphors, the intelligibility of nonrepresentational costumes (costumes with names like "Dawn," "Fantasy," or "Duma") depends heavily on their beholder's adeptness at interpretation. Inventive and whimsical costumes, such as those worn at the Artists' Balls and representing polemical positions or intangible concepts, risked communicative failure. The figurative costumes of Andreev's allegorical maskers and of the Artists' Ball participants highlight how the body serves as a legible yet hermeneutically challenging exhibition space. Enrobed in a sartorial code devised through associative, metaphorical thinking, the masker posed as a poetic puzzle.

The following chapter examines the specificity of character costumes, which in contrast to the figurative costumes of chapter 4 are guises that represent fictional, mythological, or historical figures. The character costume replaces a reliance on the wearer's imagination and beholder's subjective interpretation with a dependence on shared cultural literacy for the communication of meaning. The character costumes and identities assumed by poet Viacheslav Ivanov and the guests at his "Evenings of Hafiz" salon, for example, come from eastern and western cultures as well as disparate historical periods ranging from classical antiquity to the nineteenth century. Echoing Ivanov's intertextual approach to costume selection, Anna Akhmatova used character costumes in *Poem without a Hero* as part of her dialog with world culture. Chapter 5 portrays the chronotope of such philological masquerades, as I call them, as one of cultural syncretism: like an art museum, the philological masquerade unites and displays cultural monuments from different nations and epochs.

Whereas chapters 4 and 5 address costumes with underdetermined and overdetermined identities, respectively, chapter 6 looks at the subjective revaluation of sartorial signifiers that members of the Russian avant-garde undertook. The famously brash habits of dress and toilette practiced by such writers as Vladimir Mayakovsky and Aleksei Kruchenykh mirrored their rebellious literary poetics. The practice of material substitution (such as using a utilitarian spoon for a decorative boutonniere in a jacket's lapel) was one particular strategy of semantic rearrangement that played out in the avant-garde's vestimentary escapades and in three performance pieces that boldly broke with Realist costume design practices: Blok's *The Fairground Booth*, Mayakovsky's *Vladimir Mayakovsky: A Tragedy* and Aleksei Kruchenykh's *Victory over the Sun*. This chapter applies the ideas of Formalist Viktor Shklovsky on artistic estrangement or alienation (*ostranenie*) to the costuming practices on stage and in life among avant-garde writers and artists. Outré costumes shocked the public and communicated their wearers' rejection of the bourgeois status quo, and also parodied the Decadent dandies' refinement. The expressive value of avant-garde sartorial deviations resided in the act of rebellion instead of in the costumes' symbolism, which was intentionally scrambled. In the years 1913 and 1914, high-society and student-organized costume balls alike witnessed some of the avant-garde's tactics of vestimentary estrangement, adopted either out of the wearers' wish to be au courant with haute fashions or to mock them through parody.

The book's final chapter continues to treat the body as a legible exhibition space. However, instead of examining costumes, chapter 7 engages with nudity on the performance stage, which was a Russian cultural obsession in the years surrounding 1910. While seemingly the antithesis of sartorial self-fashioning and symbolic ambiguity, absent or minimalist costumes did not remove the need of an audience to make sense of the bodies that it beheld. Critical and essayistic writings about such figures as Isadora Duncan and Olga Desmond by Symbolist MaksimilianVoloshin, theater director Nikolai Evreinov, and actor Fyodor Komissarzhevsky, among others, reveal that the bared bodies of these women served as an occasion for the subjective reveries of their male spectators. While one cannot overlook the skewed power dynamic implicit in men appropriating narrative control over women's bodies, the subjectivity of their readings matched the spirit of individual self-expression celebrated by Duncan and modern dance.

In addition to rearticulating the book's main points about constructions of identity and costume design in prerevolutionary Russia, the conclusion looks at how the contingency, ambiguity, and illegibility of identity also manifested themselves in the early Soviet paranoia about impersonations and the accompanying rhetoric of unmasking enemies of the state.

This book approaches the topic of masquerade from the disciplinary fields of literary and cultural studies, which it unites through its examination of discursive and semiotic strategies of representation. While this study consciously seeks out parallels between the literary and the social, it also acknowledges the limits of applying analogous interpretive strategies to texts, textiles, and performative actions. The most significant point of disjuncture centers on issues of narrative completeness: the literary text presents itself as a stable, bounded entity that avails itself to close reading. The work of literature is whole; it is a system unto itself, and it typically has a cohesive narrative. In contrast, the costumes created by individuals and performative acts of masquerading are evanescent, recorded incompletely in memoirs, diaries, and newspaper articles. The performative act in particular cannot be reconstituted in its entirety as a complete, cohesive entity; this differentiates it from the recuperable literary work. Actual costumes were likewise rarely preserved, a fact that necessitates a near total reliance on illustrations, photographs, and journalistic descriptions to reconstitute their appearance. However, the abundant documentary evidence available in archives and periodicals enables this study to reveal new insights into modernist leisure practices as well as modernism's dominant aesthetic values. As an integral part of urban life at the turn of the last century, masquerades charted the social values and artistic trends that their attendees encountered and reproduced in other creative spheres.

Because this study is organized around a master trope of Russian modernism, it does not aim for an exhaustive account of any single writer, literary text, or movement. Using masquerade as an organizing principle for the study of a specific historical period refracts traditional scholarly disciplines, literary tendencies, and artistic media, thereby showcasing the period's creative output as a diverse yet interconnected whole. This thematic approach illuminates a constellation of political issues and aesthetic debates in the late nineteenth and early twentieth centuries that continued to ramify in the early Soviet era. While

Symbolism's worldview and poetics found apt expression in the metaphor of the mysterious and volatile masquerade, historical examples of actual costume balls and public acts of masquerading also shed light on the flamboyant self-fashioning typical of Decadence and Futurism. At stake is not the overturning of a single accepted interpretive paradigm but rather a loosening of strictures that typically organize scholarly studies and an expanded definition of modernist cultural production, which together afford new insights into fundamental issues of creativity and representation in Russia's Silver Age.

Part I

IMITATION AND STYLIZATION

1

>-⦁-⦁⟩-⦁-⊙-⦁-⟨⦁-⦁-⦁<

The Travestied Masquerade
Aesthetics, Ethics, and Demonism

The contingency of identity was a significant part of the modernist experience of masquerade. The growing awareness of social identity as a construction, as well as the importance of highly inventive masquerade costumes in social life, challenged assumptions about the direct correlation between appearance and an imagined essential self. However, many ordinary Russians outside urban centers harbored beliefs, informed by folk culture and Orthodox Church doctrine, about the interconnectedness of appearance and essence. Folk and Orthodox traditions both supposed that a change to the physical exterior either results from an inner, spiritual corruption or signals to the dark powers that an individual is vulnerable to such corruption. These ideas pivoted on a direct correlation between aesthetics and ethics: unadorned appearance (especially of the face) signaled wholesomeness and purity, whereas disguise (and masks in particular) implied menace and moral peril.

The direct relationship between the authenticity of a human face and that individual's spiritual purity and virtuous behavior manifests itself variously through the masquerade motif in Russian literature from the nineteenth and twentieth centuries. This chapter explores how cultural beliefs about the relationship between appearance and essence ramified in the literary representations of masquerade found in Romantic-era literature, and later in Dostoevsky's *Demons* and Sologub's *Petty Demon*. In these two novels aesthetic form and ethical actions are each presented in the antithetical terms of *obraz* (image, icon, order) and *bezobrazie* (the state of being without an image or shape, i.e., deformation, ugliness, disorder). Whereas characters associated with *obraz* evince beauty, harmony, integrity, and goodness, those associated with *bezobrazie* evince the opposite. This correlation between defiled appearance and essence is evident in the idiom and practice of disguise associated with the novels' anti-heroes (Stavrogin, Verkhovensky and the nihilist pro-vocateurs in *Demons*, and Peredonov in *Petty Demon*,) and in their actions, which range from wayward to injurious. It also governs the novels' costume parties that erupt into scandal when certain maskers violate so-cial taboos and moral strictures. The mask contravenes the sanctity of the face and therefore presents a challenge to order (*obraz*): costume-party maskers ignite outbreaks of chaos and violence (*bezobrazie*).

Dostoevsky and Sologub restyled the literary treatment of the Romantic-era masquerade into a travesty of refinement and urban so-phistication, casting the thematic conflict between *obraz* and *bezobrazie* (both physical and spiritual) in the tension of parodic discourse. Mas-querade imagery in short stories from the 1830s and 1840s reflects the aristocratic origins of the leisure-time activity in Russia. In literature and in the press, costume parties were described in superlative terms and symbolized grandeur and social prominence. Dostoevsky and Sologub inverted the hallmarks of the high-society costume ball, thereby parodying tropes of glamour and decorum as part of their social satires. Their deformation of traditional masquerade imagery through the double-voiced discourse of parody echoes and reinforces the thematic degradation of *obraz* into *bezobrazie*. In other words, the parodies of the high-society masquerade ball, which travesty Romantic-era imagery, expose the intimate relationship between distorted aesthetic form and satirical message content, a variant on the appearance-essence paradigm.

Demonism and the Mask

Russian celebrations of Yuletide in winter and Shrovetide in spring honor Christian and pagan holidays. Pagan festivities marking the winter solstice coincided with the Christian holiday celebrating Christ's birth and the arrival of a new year. Pagan springtime rituals such as carnival, called maslenitsa in Russia, roughly coincided with Christ's resurrection at Easter. Wearing masks and costumes was an important aspect of pagan ritual culture, which endured in the Yuletide and Shrovetide folk practice of mumming. Mumming entailed dressing in costume and parading outdoors in the town square. In the eighteenth century masquerade balls replaced mumming in the Imperial-court Yuletide and Shrovetide celebrations, and thus the tradition of wearing holiday costumes split into two branches: mumming endured among the folk, but in urban aristocratic circles it evolved into the exclusive amusement of costume balls. While the secular courtly entertainment was distant from ritual folk mumming, deep-rooted beliefs about the spiritual dangers of donning costume persisted in literary representations of holiday masquerades.[1]

Folk superstitions, often a legacy of paganism, frequently associated the mummer with infernal powers. One Russian folk belief held that the mummer was vulnerable to possession by demonic spirits because his guardian angel could not recognize him under a disguise. By changing his physical appearance with masks and costumes, the mummer put his soul at risk and could become an agent of the underworld. While the mummer was not necessarily destined to perdition, this folk belief demonstrates the implicit link between disguise and the danger of spiritual corruption. A more definitively damning version of the folk belief regarding mummers maintained that they hailed from the netherworld and wielded black-magical powers.[2] The mummer no longer recognizable as himself was categorized as foreign or other (chuzhoi), which conferred upon him a mysteriousness that portended danger.

These anxieties about disguise heralding peril shaped nineteenth- and twentieth-century literary representations of masquerade, as did Orthodox Church doctrine about the sanctity of the face and the sinfulness of disguise. The seminal tale in the Bible linking sartorial cover with impurity is that of Adam and Eve in the Garden of Eden: the groin-covering fig leaf became emblematic of man's fall from innocence. Medieval Russian Orthodox Church manuscripts and hagiographic literature extended the Old Testament's sartorial metaphor of purity and sinfulness into a distrust of costumes and performance, including mumming, which was called a form of "demonic play and shameful spectacle."[3] A 1636 petition from the priests of Nizhnii Novgorod to the Church sought an injunction against mumming because of its demonic impropriety. They asserted that the costumes were "like demons made visible": "On their faces they place shaggy and beast-like masks and the like in clothing too, and on their behinds they fix tails [. . .], and they wear shameful members on their faces, and bleat like goats all manner of devilish things and display their shameful members, and others beat tabors and clap and dance and perform other improper deeds."[4] The priests' breathless list of the mummers' misdeeds bespeaks their exasperation, especially with the perceived licentiousness of the costumes and their wearers. Their goat-like bleating recalls Satan's own goat-like appearance, as well as the mythical half-goat pagan deity of fertility, Pan, and his prominent genitalia. In addition to the Church's indictment of festival mummers, it opposed *skomorokhi* (jester-like performers) because of their masks, costumes, and bawdy behavior. So deep was the conviction that costumed merriment stemmed from an impure spirit and could inspire the same, the Moscow Stoglav Church Council in 1551 forbade the skomorokhi from public displays.

Certain early nineteenth-century works of literature transferred the negative folk and religious beliefs about mumming onto representations of the secular, high-society seasonal masquerades. The society tale reached the height of its popularity in the 1830s and 1840s during the first wave of masquerade mania. As a prominent feature of the period's social life, masquerades commonly appeared in society tales. A dark supernaturalism characterizes many of the society tales that involve holiday masquerades, such as Mikhail Zagoskin's "Concert of Demons" (1834) and V. N. Olin's "Strange Ball" (1838).[5] The frightful fantastic element of these stories also typifies many Yuletide stories that featured mummers or costume balls, such as A. N. Budishchev's "Mummers" (1886), which connects holiday disguise with the netherworld.[6] While some Romantic-era society tales set during the winter holidays might rightfully be considered Yuletide stories as well, the Yuletide genre became distinctive and swelled in popularity only in the late nineteenth century. First-rate writers including Nikolai Leskov, Anton Chekhov, Valery Briusov, and Anastasia Chebotarevskaia wrote Yuletide stories for prominent newspapers and journals; in contrast, literary epigones penned most Russian society tales. What certain society tales and Yuletide stories share in common is a negative valuation of mummers and masquerades, an attitude that informed later representations including those by Dostoevsky and Sologub.

Zagoskin's "Concert of Demons" associates the holiday masquerade with infernal, supernatural forces and also links music with demonism, recalling the prohibition against skomorokhi performing publically in late medieval Russia. The story opens with a recounting of the "innumerable masquerades" that took place in Moscow during winter holidays. Its plot, however, revolves around a maslenitsa masquerade held in the Rotunda of the Petrovsky Theater in Moscow, an actual venue founded by the English entertainment impresario Michael Maddox in the late eighteenth century. The central character Zorin, once confined to an insane asylum, suffers from melancholy brought on by his unrequited love for an Italian opera singer, Lauretta. To lighten his mood, his friends advise him to attend every ball, masquerade, and theater performance in Moscow instead of relying on the doctors' pills.

Zorin learns that Lauretta is to perform at the Petrovsky masquerade and goes to the event dressed in a red domino and half-mask, the fiery color of which symbolizes romantic passion and demonic peril. Lauretta, wearing a seductive black domino, invites Zorin to a private concert, which is attended by the ghosts of famous dead composers including Mozart, Handel, and Gluck. The fantastic story of ghosts becomes macabre when the conductor tears off Zorin's right leg and plays its sinews as a violin. In addition to Zorin's dismemberment by the spectral performer, an assortment of supernatural musician-animals with freakishly mismatched body parts imbues the story with horror. Some figures have cranes' necks and dog snouts; one has a bull's torso but sparrow feet; there are roosters with goat legs and goats with human hands (again, satanic goats). After the physically rending concert and its frightful visions, Zorin awakes on the street in a sweat, leading the reader to wonder whether the character dreamed about the demonic masquerade of the dead or whether his former madness has returned. The masquerade is the setting for the uncanny, a category of frightful experience that Freud likened to insanity because it is marked by collapsing boundaries, blurring demarcations, and destabilized identities in alternate realms of consciousness.[7] As Freud concluded, fear such as that experienced by Zorin (and the reader) is the primary response to the uncanny: ontological uncertainty about the hybrid animals and ghosts poses an existential threat. Because masquerade costumes help overturn conventional categories (such as the living and the dead, for example) and create an uncanny atmosphere, the masquerade ball is an advantageous setting for introducing alternate realms of consciousness, such as insanity, into fiction.

Unlike Zagoskin's fearsome fantastic tale, Olin's "Strange Ball" colors the masquerade atmosphere ambiguously: the physical oddities of some maskers frighten, while the beauty of others delights. Amid the sumptuous décor and comely young women at a late-night masquerade, a character known as The General espies a menagerie of maskers including a horse leg, a windmill, a formless bat, a skeleton, a vampire, a gnome, and a horrific figure about whom the narrator says, "I swear to you, if this weren't only a masquerade, he could have been called Satan himself!"[8] The severed yet animated horse leg in particular bespeaks a violation of the natural laws that govern so-called reality and thus inspires dread. The formless bat also stands out for its disconcerting freakishness, while the skeleton, vampire, and satanic figure augur bodily and spiritual danger, as cultural myths dictate. These uncanny figures juxtaposed with the society ball's elegant young women create a confusing dissonance, which raises the specter of the distorted perception that typifies madness. Calling the masquerade hall a "temple of wonders," the narrator points to the striking contrasts: "life, flowers, and charms mixed with deformity (*bezobrazie*) and vileness."[9] Alternating between fear and delight, The General wonders if his extraordinary visions are hallucinations driven by the fever (*belaia goriachka*) from which he is recuperating. As in "Concert of Demons," "Strange Ball" does not dictate definitively whether the fantastic maskers are manifestations of a supernatural demonic force or phantasms of a sick mind.

The masquerade's illusoriness may also be a consequence of the exceptionally radiant milieu of the high-society costume ball. Sparkling and brilliant, the masquerade halls are decked out with candles, crystal chandeliers, mirrors and parquet floors, which create a luminosity (*svet*) that seems to reflect the dazzling nature of high society (*svet*) itself. As spaces of fantasy and wonder, the masquerade halls in Romantic-era stories are typically opulent in aristocratic style. While the magnificence of illumination signals wealth, the reflective surfaces of the mirrors and floors hint at the perceptual confusion that the masquerade can produce. Reflections of reflections blur the line between original and facsimile, while the diffuse masquerade lighting compromises clarity of vision and thus clarity of experience in "Concert of Demons." Bright rays also complicate apprehension in "Concert of Demons," where "blinding light from the crystal chandeliers" seemingly contributes to Zorin's otherworldly visions.[10] In "The Strange Ball" thousands of wax candles in the masquerade hall sparkle marvelously, brightening the already exceptional beauty of the women and fostering the illusion of uncanny maskers. According to the narrator, The General beholds in the flickering light "a dreamy gallery of fantastic guests," which resembles "an animated panorama of optical and ideal figures."[11] Are the eerie maskers supernatural demons, manifestations of mental illness, or illusions created by light and mirrors? More important than resolving the ambiguity in these stories is aligning the experience of the uncanny with the masquerade. Zagoskin and Olin inserted the demonic and fantastic into the society-tale masquerade, which extended Russian folk and religious beliefs about mumming and echoed the contemporary Romantic movement's fascination with sorcery and the supernatural.

The visual opulence in "Strange Ball" points to one more common feature of the literary society masquerade: events transpire in the rarified atmosphere of the beau monde, where lavishly decorated mansions and grand theaters are the stage for extravagant costumes and romantic intrigue. Sartorial elegance and beauty among women were code for sexual enticement, as in "Strange Ball," where a young lady dressed as an Andalusian boasts teeth that "shine like pearls." She wears a "white, sumptuous muslin skirt, lowered slightly below the knees, [which] freely and without envy allows ravenous eyes to see the slender and exquisitely turned calf that the black velvet slipper greedily enfolds."[12] The choice of dressing in Spanish costume hints at the lady's passionate hot-bloodedness, while the seemingly demure yet sumptuous muslin and velvet of the costume itself promise tactile delight. In similar fashion, the aging countess in Vladimir Sollogub's "High Society" (1840) wears a masquerade costume spangled with diamonds that beckon the social-climbing male officers to court her.

Romantic intrigue at the masquerade was a popular storyline that was even more piquant if the lovers were from different social classes, as is the case in "High Society." Safyev is a cynical dandy wearied and jaded by the petty intrigues and superficial concerns of the beau monde. He cautions the younger Leonin that a calculating desire for the affection and support of influential and powerful men motivates women's flirtation at the masquerade. Using the ladies' seductive black satin dresses as a metonym for the femme fatales themselves, Safyev indirectly warns his junior that feminine toilette is part of women's deceptive performance: "At the masquerade, one can attain the patronage of an important person through witty jokes and tender hints. Look at those black satin ladies who have latched on to the hands of those barons and are assuring them of their love: you better believe that their charm is nothing other than a consequence of their shrewdness."[13] Men also use the occasion of the masquerade to gain the favor of wealthy and powerful women. The low-ranking military officer Leonin romantically pursues the Countess, who was "one of the foremost ladies of Peters-burg, famous for her beauty and charm, enormous wealth, and her great importance in society." Although Leonin is at first surprised that the lavishly dressed Countess deigns to look at him, such a transgres-sion of social class barriers is common in society-tale masquerades. It also reflected historical experience. As the examples of Tsar Nikolai I, Grand Duke Mikhail Pavlovich, and Empress Alexandra Fyodorovna brought forth in the Introduction show, the escapist pleasure of sub-verting social hierarchy in the course of romantic flirtation at the masquerade appealed to all classes.

The disaffectedness of the dandy in "High Society" was a Romantic-era literary theme common in works of fine literature (Pushkin's *Eugene Onegin* and Lermontov's *Hero of Our Time*, for example) and in pulp society tales. In addition to Safyev, the Countess in "High Society" expresses weariness and disenchantment when she laments to Leonin that life in high society demands that every day she wear a mask, which she can never take off. She uses the mask as a metaphor for the superfi-cial role she feels compelled to play among her peers of the fashionable elite. Paradoxically, it is only when she dons an actual mask at the masquerade that she can speak openly about her life as a figurative masquerade.

While some of Sollogub's contemporary readers saw in the figure of Leonin biographical echoes of the writer Mikhail Lermontov, who was similarly from a noble family and served in the military, Lermontov himself disregarded this rumor.[14] Sollogub's story does, however, revive the cynicism of Lermontov's classical drama *Masquerade* (1835–36). The play's central character Arbenin, who has wearied of high-society's trivialities, proclaims that the masquerade is a place of libidinous excess, which is facilitated by masking social identity and rank: "All ranks are equal beneath the mask / The mask has no soul, no title—only a body. / And while the mask conceals the face, / Feelings are boldly unmasked." In these remarks, which foreshadow his own unjustified suspicions that his wife, Nina, is unfaithful, the aristocrat Arbenin links the masquer-ade with breaches of social class and romantic indiscretions.

Nina insists on attending a masquerade ball unescorted, despite Arbenin's admonition against it. When he sees the bracelet that his wife alleged to have lost at the masquerade in the hands of Prince Zvezdich, Arbenin assumes that she forged a romantic liaison with him and gave him the bangle as a souvenir. Not understanding that Nina accidentally dropped the bracelet and another female masker picked it up and later gave it to Zvezdich, Arbenin poisons Nina to punish her for her infidelity, the final consequence of which is his own descent into madness. Although Nina is a faithful wife, Arbenin's expectations about the masquerade kindling romantic infidelity inflame his suspicion. Nina does, however, engage in socially risky behavior by attending the masquerade unescorted by her husband.[15] Her dicey action is implicitly correlated to men's gambling, with which the play opens, and suggests that the high-society masquerade is as hazardous for women as the baize table is for men.

Unlike Sollogub's story, Lermontov's drama contains no breathless description of the masquerade's lavish costumes and milieu. Instead, the painful emotional and psychological reactions to an ostensible marital infidelity at a beau-monde masquerade constitute his play's focal point. Lermontov's weighty tragedy criticizes high-society's insidious machinations and ruinous intrigues, all of which were sensationalized in the era's popular society tales and which the writer claimed to have witnessed firsthand while living in Saint Petersburg.[16] The play satirizes corrupted aristocratic culture in general and the morally perilous masquerade in particular. Although Lermontov's drama polemically engages with the unseemly side of society life and thus contains a measure of realism, it also subtly evokes the Romantic fashion for the fantastic. An ominous black masker who likens himself to a nameless specter ("*kak prizrak, bez nazvan'ia*") presages Arbenin's impending demise. Although the identity of this stranger in a dark domino remains a mystery, his premonition of Arbenin's death is accurate and suggests that he possesses an otherworldly omniscience. Through his small role he perpetuates the masquerade's cultural and literary associations with supernaturalism and dark powers.

Lermontov's scathing satire of Petersburg high society demonstrates how the masquerade can operate in literature as a site of exposure: the writer uses anonymity and costumes to spur plot development, while the ensuing scandal unmasks social and individual shortcomings. Dostoevsky and Sologub adopted this tradition and incorporated the masquerade into their novelistic satires (*Demons* and *Petty Demon*, respectively) as a mechanism for exposing what they perceived as pernicious social trends. They reworked the masquerade motif in various ways, but one key trait links their representations with the nineteenth-century popular literature discussed above: the connection between disguise and demonism that is rooted in folk and religious beliefs. Both novels imply that there is a direct correlation between the physical and the spiritual, between aesthetics and ethics: disguise and distorted appearance symbolize actual or impending infernal possession. This essentialist paradigm differs markedly from the widespread modernist understanding of identity as a social construct and expresses enduring anxieties about the soul's vulnerability.

Dostoevsky's Demons

Dostoevsky aligned morality and aesthetics, each defined in religious terms by the conflict between *obraz* and *bezobrazie*. As Robert Louis Jackson has explained, "The moral-aesthetic spectrum of Dostoevsky begins with *obraz*—image, the form and embodiment of beauty—and ends with *bezobrazie*—literally that which is 'without image,' shapeless, disfigured, ugly."[17] Dostoevsky based his ideas about the spiritual centrality of the face on Orthodox conceptions of the beautiful ideal form (*obraz*) and its deformation (*bezobrazie*). The word *obraz* is used to signify an icon, "the visible symbol of the beauty of God," as well as the traditional focal point of early icons, the face.[18] *Bezobrazie*, which literally means without image but carries a standard lexical meaning of disorder, is the defilement of *obraz*. The beauty of God, symbolized by the icon, is a spiritual beauty; debasing that inner beauty results in spiritual depravity and corruption of the external image.

Dostoevsky manifested this opposition between beauty and depravity, *obraz* and *bezobrazie*, in the character of Stavrogin. His face is repeatedly described as being waxen and mask-like, which indicates his divorce from the divine. Strangely puppet-like yet charismatic, Stavrogin is a spiritually empty shell. When the student Shatov slaps Stavrogin because of the latter's mock marriage to the feebleminded Maria Lebiadkina, the narrator describes Stavrogin's face in terms of its fragmented features—cheek, nose, lips, and teeth—as if a porcelain mask has shattered. Prefiguring cubist portraits, which religious philosopher Sergei Bulgakov would call "black icons," Stavrogin's fractured face symptomatizes his moral depredation and capacity for dissimulation.[19] Religious philosopher Pavel Florensky pointed to Stavrogin as the quintessential example of how "sin possesses a personality" and "the face ceases to be a window through which God's radiance shines" in his 1922 essay "Ikonostasis."[20] Stavrogin's mask-like image, which lacks Christ's effulgence, symbolizes his moral fall.[21] His crimes (which include sexual assault and hiring Fedka the Convict to murder the

Lebiadkins) are manifestations of *bezobrazie*, the breakdown of Stavrogin's moral order, which is reflected in his fractured face. Stavrogin's individual corruption is also symptomatic of the political and social upset that plagued Russia in the 1860s.

Demons, Dostoevsky's most political novel, engages polemically with the ideological radicalism that roiled Russia beginning in the 1860s. Dostoevsky supported the monarchy and was among those for whom the attempted assassination by Dmitry Karakozov of Tsar Alexander II in 1866 ignited the fear of a new social phenomenon in Russia: conspiratorial violence aimed at effecting revolution. Terrorist organizations, such as The People's Reprisal (*Narodnaia rasprava*) led by Sergei Nechaev, became synonymous with the Nihilist movement, which disregarded the authority of existing institutions and sought their destruction, even through violent and immoral means. In 1869 Nechaev organized the murder of the troublesome group member Ivan Ivanov; this became known publically as the Nechaev Affair and inspired Dostoevsky's novel. Nechaev served as the prototype for Pyotr Stepanovich Verkhovensky, who likewise ordered the murder of a vacillating agent named Shatov. The conspiratorial activities of Verkhovensky and his fellow provocateurs in *Demons* thus reflect the political radicalism and disorder sweeping Russia in the 1860s (such as the strikes and acts of arson mentioned in the novel).

In portraying the grassroots terrorists, Dostoevsky repeatedly used the imagery of masks, costumes, and performance. The dissimulating and role-playing of Verkhovensky and his agitators initially mask their subversive plans, which they put into effect at the staged literary matinee and the costumed quadrille of literature. Dostoevsky thus mobilized the enduring cultural association of costume with corruption and menace. Verkhovensky's provocateurs seek to destabilize the political status quo, as embodied in the feeble Governor von Lembke: their disruptive behavior at the literary matinee and costume ball, both organized by the governor's wife Iuliia Mikhailovna, is part of their political action campaign.

Mrs. von Lembke's series of daytime literary readings (the "literary matinee"[22]) and evening ball, the crowning glory of which is to be a costumed "quadrille of literature" that features "masks and character costumes representing famous literary trends,"[23] are intended to raise money for the province's governesses. Her preliminary plans are extravagant: she wants the fête to be intellectually enlightening and refined. She hopes it will instill respect and awe, inspiring tales that will "go winging over all the provinces, arousing astonishment and imitation."[24] Such a grandiose event, she imagines, will be an expression of her social prominence and civic benevolence. The resulting success will bestow upon her a soft social power through which she can exert influence on the town's youth. The benefit ball thus serves as a source and symbol of political power and prominence, which the provocateurs contest.

The novel's townspeople anticipate that the benefit will exhibit the high-society glamour and sophistication typical of the historical and literary courtly masquerade. This provincial benefit "promised to be so magnificent, boundless; wonders were being told; rumors spread about visiting princes with lorgnettes, about ten ushers, all young cavaliers, with bows on their left shoulders."[25] The beginning of the literary matinee seemed poised to fulfill all hopes for a sumptuous affair, as "silks, velvets, diamonds shone and sparkled on all sides; fragrance permeated the air. The men were wearing all their decorations, and the old men were even wearing their uniforms."[26] Preparations for the second part of the benefit, the evening ball, also seemingly augured a stately affair, as "almost all the officials took an advance on their salaries, and some landowners sold much-needed cattle, and all this just so as to bring their young ladies looking like real marquises, and to be no worse than others. The magnificence of the costumes this time was, considering the place, unheard-of."[27] Even the venue, the White Hall, was breath-taking in its beauty. The elegant costumes and sparkling venue recall the milieu of courtly masquerades as represented in literature and in the historical experience of Russia's nobility.

However, the narrator ruefully observes that the "mood of society" was such that "there was among us something rather more serious than the mere thirst for scandal; there was a general irritation, something unappeasably spiteful."[28] Despite the officials taking payday loans to outfit their daughters for the evening ball, in the end none of the town's upper crust attended. Instead, local "scum" who were "in all but torn frock coats, in the most dubious and utterly un-ball-like outfits, who had obviously been sobered up with boundless effort and for a short time only" attended the ball.[29] Instead of wearing jewels and sumptuous fabrics, and instead of demonstrating good manners, these drunken guests were rumpled and boisterous. They beat up the musicians and vandalized the hall, thus defying expectations about proper social comportment. In addition, some "crop-haired" nihilist girls participated in the costumed quadrille of literature, their bold rejection of traditional feminine toilette signaling their social non-compliance and rebellion against the beau-monde masquerade's expectations of conventional beauty.

The costumed literary quadrille, the evening's anticipated climax, devolves into chaos and farce as one of Verkhovensky's provocateurs acts out. The quadrille's participants come dressed in "costume representing some tendency (*napravlenie*)," some "famous literary trends," by which Dostoevsky meant the ideological orientation of certain newspapers and their editors.[30] Several of the so-called costumes, however, represent a semantic riddle: "six pairs of pathetic maskers" were, in fact, "wearing the same clothes as everyone else."[31] The paltry costumes offer few hints at what it was they emblematize, a situation rendered most acute and literal by the maskers who wear algebraic variables pinned to their shirts. As the narrator puts it, "what the X and Z signified remained unclear."[32] The algebraic maskers and the maskers that "were almost not even maskers," so insignificant were their costumes, collectively comprise an unsolvable equation. Their indeterminacy and mysteriousness compromise the legibility of the allegorical costumes, resulting in a quadrille of unintelligible literature.

The nihilist provocateur Liamshin participates in the costumed quadrille and does so in proper allegorical fashion: he dresses as the publisher of a "formidable non-Petersburg publication." It has been suggested that this costume is an allusion to *The Moscow Gazette*, the two-time publisher of which, M. N. Katkov, wrote condemnatory articles about the progressive anti-tsarist press.[33] One of the other journals represented in the quadrille is the radical-democratic *Deed*, which stands for the type of press that Katkov reviled. At the quadrille, Liamshin, dressed as the Non-Petersburg Publication, suddenly begins to walk upside down on his hands ". . . to signify the constant turning upside down of common sense."[34] The political conspirator's representation of the figure of Katkov attacks the latter's conservatism. Turning Katkov and his newspaper upside down, Liamshin symbolically mocks what he perceives as *The Moscow Gazette's* muddleheaded support of the monarchy against which he and his fellow radicals rebel.

Liamshin's stunt riles the public at the literary quadrille and sparks the outbreak of scandal. However, this is not because of the antic's metaphorical and polemical value, which is lost on the audience. Rather, his gymnastic impropriety excites the public precisely because his carnivalesque behavior is alien to expectations of social decorum. Governor von Lembke roars in displeasure at this figurative attack on the supporters of the monarchy and status quo. His outburst of anger and humiliation physically and emotionally enfeebles him and forces him to leave the event in a state of incapacitation. With the governor's retreat, the provocateurs enjoy a symbolic political victory. The break-down of order at the ball mirrors the graver and more consequential social tumult concurrently roiling the provincial town. The narrator declares, "Into what was already the beginnings of a crush [at the ball], a bomb struck":[35] the guests at the ball learn that the part of town called Zarechye has been set afire, which turns out to be an attempt to cover up the murders of Captain Lebiadkin, his sister Maria, and their housekeeper.

The nihilists' subversion of the ball is part of their grassroots political activism, which is aimed at dismantling the very type of old order that the von Lembkes and the aristocratic tradition of the costume ball repre-sent. Under the cover of disguise, the secret agent Liamshin acts the buffoon and catalyzes mayhem. His mask paradoxically reveals his menacing intentions, demonstrating the intimate link between appear-ance and essence. As the aspiring revolutionaries strive to break down social order in the public sphere, they begin by travestying the conven-tions of the courtly masquerade. Their degradations of *obraz* into *bezo-brazie*, order into chaos, deform the normative Romantic-era image of high-society masquerade into a travestied masquerade.

For Sologub as for Dostoevsky, appearance mirrors essence, a corre-lation vividly expressed in the costume ball scene of *Petty Demon*. Solo-gub's essentialist view runs contrary to the relativistic understanding of identity that circulated around the turn of the last century and pivots on longstanding cultural beliefs about the spiritual dangers of disguise. He summarized his views in the essay "Immortal Flame," where he wrote, "ethics and aesthetics are kindred sisters. Offend one and the other is offended."[36] As in *Demons*, the degradation of *obraz* as an ethical or aesthetic phenomenon into *bezobrazie* finds expression in the imagery and dynamics of the novel's costume ball.

However, *Petty Demon* also differs in key ways from Dostoevsky's novel: Sologub did not engage polemically with political radicalism, but rather satirized the vulgarity that he saw corrupting provincial Russia.[37] He also wrote *Petty Demon* during the masquerade's renais-sance as a leisure-time activity in early twentieth-century Russia. Solo-gub himself hosted costume parties, and his personal knowledge of modernist masquerade culture differentiated his treatment of masquer-ade as a literary motif from that of his predecessors. In addition to travestying the nineteenth-century masquerade motifs of glamour and decorum that endured into the 1900s, *Petty Demon* parodies distinctive features of the leisure-time masquerades from the modernist period as part of its social satire. These features include the costume contest and its prizes, romantic escapades, and a carnivalesque spirit of play that sanctioned deviations from high-society decorousness. While the dominant cultural images of the society masquerade still centered on their sumptuousness, a parallel trend of measured deviations from the historical script is recorded in the period's press.

Transgressive Modernist Masquerades

Newspapers from around the turn of the last century actively chronicled balls and masquerades, and generously commended the elegance of the ladies in attendance (and especially of the hostess), as well as the refinement, tastefulness, or novelty of the furnishings and décor. Journalistic reports on the "magical scenes" of elegantly dressed ladies at fin-de-siécle costume parties and balls reinforced the earlier cultural image of the masquerade ball as a zone of rarified beauty, gentility, and social exceptionalism.[38] On February 18, 1899, *The Petersburg Gazette* rapturously described a ball held at the home of Princess Urusova, at which the ladies' collective toilette was deemed "the height of elegance." The costumes were effusively catalogued and praised: three ladies' costumes were described as "elegant," two as "sumptuous," and one as "lovely."[39] *The Petersburg Gazette* also effusively recorded the aesthetic delights of a costume ball held at the home of Madame Ignatyeva just two days later. Guests came "to marvel at a scene rare in its beauty" and costumes were likewise deemed "rare in their beauty"; even the auditory pleasure provided by the "enchanting sounds of music" merited praise.[40]

These reports identified the costume wearers by name, thereby enhancing the attendees' social prominence by trumpeting their exquisite taste. Such newspaper reports created a sort of cultural currency out of glamour and suggest that public admiration for the beautiful woman and her sartorial splendor was no longer the domain solely of actresses. The private domestic costume ball offered women of privilege and connection an opportunity to flaunt their access to a rarified world of aesthetic pleasures, as well as their copious leisure time. Attentively covered by newspapers, the events and their doyennes captivated the public's imagination and reinforced the class divide. Published in mainstream newspapers, the columns read as if directed at an aspirational audience, their awestruck tone exciting the middle-class reader's longing for and admiration of cosmopolitan glamour. While such individuals had access to public entrepreneurial masquerades, they could not purchase entrance to the exclusive costume parties of Saint Petersburg's elite.

Concurrent with the tradition of aristocratic refinement at the masquerade, a new tendency emerged in the early twentieth century. The growing spirit of individualism and the increasing range of masquerades organized among students, writers, and artists challenged conventional high-society strictures. Avant-garde by virtue of age, university and institute students began orchestrating spectacular masquerades that celebrated original costumes. Circles of artists and writers did the same. Public costume balls and domestic costume parties became opportunities for participants to test old-school practices, to engage in mildly carnivalesque behavior, and to flaunt their ingenuity, which sometimes verged on transgression.

A newspaper article reporting on a costume ball held on August 24, 1910, in Yalta recorded an unusual disruption that defied dominant assumptions about public masquerades as sites of decorousness and good taste. Certain unidentified individuals arrived at a public masquerade wearing costumes representing such ruinous phenomena as "Cholera," "Plague," and "Death." Recalling the biblical story about the four horsemen of the Apocalypse (Pestilence, Famine, War, and Death), whose arrival signals the impending Last Judgment, these maskers sought to darken the masquerade's lightness and perhaps menace its guests. The sinister figures were not admitted into the costume ball and were asked to leave the grounds.[41] These sartorial representations of disease and suffering flagrantly opposed the fashionable elegance and breeziness that typified earlier society masquerade costumes. They expressed an individualistic and highly polemical approach to costume design that was virtually unknown in the early nineteenth century. No longer did the costume disguise identity: instead, it allowed the individual to express herself and enabled her to construct a social identity based on ideas and beliefs. Such costume designs that articulated their wearers' opinions and beliefs established a resonance between physical appearance and intellectual ideas.

Another journalistic account of a modernist-era costume ball vividly expresses the reporter's delight in a carnivalesque disruption of order that agitated the hall. The masquerade, described under the heading

"A Nighttime Inspection of Petersburg," was held at the Maly Theater on the evening of January 5, 1913. According to the *Ogonek* journalist, "The gayest moment of the evening was the intermission, during which time an enormous ball was thrown into the crowd. A terrible ruckus arose. Bouncing on each and every person, the ball flew from one corner of the theater to the other. It even fell on the heads of esteemed social figures who, while trying to flee, nonetheless had to take part in the general merriment. Not insignificant was the suffering of ladies' hairdos because of the ball."[42] The reporter gleefully described the disturbance to order that the uncontained ball ignited, relishing the fact that the respected members of society were compelled to break their serious demeanor and that their lady companions' careful coifs were spoiled. The public's joy, evidenced by the "laughter that poured throughout the theater," was rooted in the frisson of pleasure that comes from such mild disruptions of decorous adult behavior. The wayward flying ball granted the guests freedom to play; even the most august figures engaged in the revelry under the cover of supposed self-protection. The unruly ball ricocheting around the hall, batted by unsuspecting guests, incited a type of play that was generally forbidden to adults in the public setting of the theater. The participants' childlike indulgence in spontaneous joy and delight in breaking out of controlled proper behavior did not deeply transgress social boundaries, but it did mildly test conventional strictures. Five years earlier in an article dated January 7, 1907, the editor of the journal *Theater and Art* complained in the pages of his periodical that certain actors were "fooling around in the most flagrant manner" and engaging in "hooliganism" at a benefit costume ball for the Theatrical Society's children's shelter. Grousing that actor V. N. Davydov, who dressed in women's clothing, and K. A. Varlamov, who "flew through the air," took money for their undignified behavior, the editor worried that their shenanigans compromised the social respectability of the purportedly civic-minded event.[43]

In addition to rejections of elegant costumes and proper high-society comportment, one recorded incident reveals how an inappropriate act of individual eccentricity spoiled the New Year's costume party held by Sologub and his wife, Anastasia Chebotarevskaia, on January 3, 1911. According to Chebotarevskaia, Aleksei Remizov made an egregious misstep in his disrespectful treatment of an animal hide that she had borrowed from an acquaintance for his use as a costume. In a letter voicing exasperation, she reproached him for allegedly severing the animal's tail from the rest of the hide: "To my great dismay, today I discovered that your tail came from my animal hide (actually not mine, someone else's—that's the problem!). Moreover, I cannot find the rear paws. Have they really been cut off? Where shall I look for them? I await your reply. I've taken the skin to be fixed,—but how ever can I return it [to its owner] with patches?"[44] Remizov wore the tail in question affixed to his rear, allowing it to poke out through a slit in his jacket.[45] In reply to Chebotarevskaia's indignation, Remizov claimed that the tail had already been severed when he found the hide lying around at the previous day's costume party hosted by writer Aleksei Tolstoy. Regardless of who severed the tail, the social damage was irreparable: Remizov and the Tolstoys would no longer be welcome at the Sologubs' frequent gatherings and costume parties.[46]

The Remizov monkey-tail incident with its literal and social rendings points to the role of individual eccentricity in revamping the early twentieth-century experience of masquerades as a leisure-time activity. As I discuss in chapter 6, the Russian avant-garde pushed this emergent trend of vestimentary eccentricity even further in the 1910s, and costumes worn at events hosted by high-society dames and students alike became increasingly experimental. A modernist individualism emerged, transforming costume balls into artistic spaces where imagination and fancy could freely play out. The wittiness of costumes emerged as an important trait, especially among men, and it was rewarded with prizes in the ubiquitous contests for best costume. *Petty Demon* parodies the modernist masquerade's premium on inventiveness (exemplified by the travestied costume contest) along with features of the Romantic-era courtly costume ball.

Sologub's *Petty Demon*

The savage assault, murder, and arson at the costume party in *Petty Demon* brutally amplifies the mildly transgressive spirit that marked some polemical costumes and eccentric behaviors at costume parties and balls in the early twentieth century. Sologub transformed the possibility for playful disobedience at modernist-era masquerades into an opening for grave transgressions. The moral crimes and aesthetic debasements in the novel's masquerade scene evoke ingrained cultural beliefs about masking, demonism, and the disruption of order that were mapped out in *Demons* and in certain early nineteenth-century society tales noted earlier. Other modernist writers also reworked the enduring cultural paradigm of demonic and impure powers intruding into the masquerade, but I have elected to focus on different aspects of their works in later chapters. Among the most noteworthy examples are Leonid Andreev's *Black Maskers* and Anna Akhmatova's *Poem without a Hero*. *Black Maskers* casts the uninvited masquerade guests as menacing figures from the underworld whose arrival signals an invasion of perilous, supernatural forces. In *Poem without a Hero*, the Yuletide mummers are ghosts of the dead who transform the opening scene into what the narrator calls a "midnight Hoffmanniana," terrifying in its macabre atmosphere. An important part of associating masks and costumes with the demonic is the conviction that appearance indexes essence: Russian folk and religious beliefs held that disguise either signaled or precipitated possession by infernal powers. The costume party in *Petty Demon* thus serves as an apt venue for exposing the defiled spirit that pervades the provincial town.

The central theme of vulgarity in Sologub's novel manifests itself in the spheres of aesthetics and ethics: paltry appearance bespeaks lowliness of spirit (and even criminality) among the town's residents, a correspondence that comes to the fore in the costume party scene. The atmosphere of paltriness runs contrary to the archetypal high-society masquerade's splendor and gentility and signals a social malignancy. It ramifies most vividly in the dirty venue, measly costumes, and violent behavior that characterize the scene. Unlike the magical milieu and extravagant décor that guests beheld at cosmopolitan masquerade balls, the hall that Sologub describes is filthy and dilapidated, with crooked chandeliers, sooty walls and ceilings, and discolored curtains that "looked as if they would be repulsive to the touch."[47] Bereft of sparkling mirrors and parquet, lush tropical plants and velvety carpet, the town hall where the costume ball takes place travesties the normative glamour of the masquerade trope. The location of the municipal building also points to the costume party's deviation from the high-society script: situated in the town's market square, the venue recalls the outdoor folk fair (*balagan*) that found its home in the public space.

The majority of participants in Sologub's fictional masquerade sport tasteless and uninspired costumes. Their grim appearance betokens their anti-aestheticism and correlative debasement of spirit. Grushina, for example, wears a Greek-goddess costume so flimsy it reveals almost all of her flea-bitten body, the coarseness of which is underscored by her "vulgar" movements and "unbearably uncouth" words.[48] The local notary's wife Gudaevskaia dresses as a sheaf of wheat, thereby according with the surrounding provincial landscape. And Varvara, the betrothed of anti-hero Peredonov, dresses as a cook whose forearms are made up to look ruddy from overexposure to the kitchen hearth. In contrast, at high-society masquerades women in particular aspired to sartorial elegance and eschewed impersonating members of the servant class.

Costume contests gained currency at the end of the nineteenth century and awarded prizes to exceptionally beautiful, imaginative, and witty costumes, a tradition that Sologub parodied. At the Academy of Arts in Saint Petersburg, costume contest prizes were typically paintings donated by teachers and students; for benefit balls held at the Saint Petersburg Noblemen's Assembly, the Society of Watercolor Painters donated their works to recognize the exceptional taste and creativity of select costumes. Individuals might also hope to win lottery tickets for the masquerade's *lotereia-allegro*, or to receive a gold, silver, or bronze medal along with the satisfaction of public recognition in local newspapers. In *Petty Demon*, the provincial town's tawdriness manifests itself in the costume contest and its utilitarian prizes, which differ sharply from the purely aesthetic prizes awarded at historical masquerades. Rumors about the kitty for best male and female costumes excite a competitive spirit among the townspeople: the men believe they will vie for a bicycle while women will compete for a cow. The actual prizes, a fan and a photo album, deepen the chasm between the banality of the provincial costume party and the artistry of urban high-society balls.

Another form of gratification inscribed in the cultural myth of masquerade that Sologub travestied is the convention of romantic intrigue. Pale, slender, and dressed as a Spaniard, Valeriia Rutilova mockingly flirts with Peredonov by whispering flattering doggerel in his ear. Calling him handsome and "wise like Solomon," Valeriia teases Peredonov, with whom she has no interest in establishing a romantic liaison.[49] Also at the costume party, the character Volodin receives an anonymous letter in a pink envelope summoning him to a romantic rendezvous at Soldier's Bath. Volodin decides against the tryst, however, because Soldier's Bath is located in a dangerous area, which threatens bodily harm and inverts the romantic escapade's promise of sensual pleasure.

The most memorable toppling of masquerade aestheticism, however, is manifested in the actual physical attack on beauty: the comely figure dressed as a geisha is assaulted and her costume torn in a barbaric display of jealousy and passion. Under the disguise of the geisha is the preadolescent, androgynous boy Sasha, whose very name bespeaks gender ambiguity and who embodies the beauty and sensual pleasure absent in the provincial community. Liudmila Rutilova, a young woman of marriageable age, befriends the younger Sasha after hearing rumors of his transvestitism. Inspired by Sasha's unspoiled spirit and body, Liudmila indulges herself and Sasha in all manner of sensual stimulation: she sprinkles him with exotic perfumes, treats him to sweets, coaxes him to kiss her naked feet, and dresses him in women's clothing. It is Liudmila who conceives the idea of sending Sasha to the town's costume party dressed as a geisha, in a costume that emblematizes the beauty and decorousness characteristic of the idealized masquerade.

The lovely and flirtatious geisha attracts the attention of the townsmen who shower her with admiration and vote hers the best costume. The townswomen, however, assume the promiscuous actress Kashtanova is dressed as the geisha and rail against the injustice of rewarding her for her coquetry: "She took someone else's husband away and they gave her the prize!" With this cry the costume ball devolves into chaos as the geisha becomes the object of a "savage persecution." Bitter and jealous women together with curious and aroused men "smashed the [geisha's] fan, tore it to pieces, threw it on the floor and stomped on it."[50] The violent rendings—tearing her fan, ripping her dress—recall carnivalistic sacrificial dismemberment and the frenzy of Dionysian ritual.[51] As the geisha is symbolically dismembered through the removal of her costume, her reign as the carnival queen (recipient of best costume) is overturned. The attack on the geisha, who symbolizes aesthetic beauty and embodies the innocence of the boy Sasha, unleashes disorder at the costume party. This desecration of beauty exposes the townspeople's spitefulness in a vivid illustration of the novel's correlation of aesthetics and ethics.

The actions of the novel's central character, Peredonov, also demonstrate how his inner debasement leads to the external desecration of beauty and order. Peredonov transforms all that enters his consciousness into "something vile and filthy. He was immediately taken with deformities in objects and he rejoiced over them. Whenever he passed an erect and pure column, he wanted to deform it or deface it. He laughed with joy when things were spoiled in his presence."[52] Peredonov's moral depravity compels him to desecrate order and beauty, as is the case when he, Varvara, and Volodin gleefully vandalize his apartment's decorative wallpaper in a destructive frenzy. His penchant for vandalism and defacement registers paradoxically in his efforts at enhancing his own physical appearance.

In the interest of securing professional advancement, the school-master insists on wearing rouge, lest people, as he puts it, "think that I'm decrepit and I won't be appointed inspector [of regional schools]."[53] Peredonov makes this display of cosmetic deception at his wedding to Varvara, an event that is itself a consequence of fraudulence: he agrees to marry Varvara only because of her false claims to having connections to an influential princess in Saint Petersburg. In addition to the rouge for his face, Peredonov wishes to wear one of Varvara's corsets for the wedding to trim his shape, also to appear more youthful. His experiments with feminine toilette underscore his implicit refusal to play the role of the husband: at his wedding, when custom would dictate that he accentuate his masculinity, he reaches for external markers of the opposite gender. Peredonov's travesty of masculine gender norms fails, however, to make him more becoming and instead constitutes another act of defacement.

Peredonov's decrepit appearance reflects his compromised virtue and mental breakdown, which catapults him into a full-time psychological masquerade detached from objectivity and marked by paranoia. Imagined denunciations, invisible informers, and hallucinations of changelings entrap him in a world that is marked by inconstancy and betrayal. The fundamental experience of alienation—from oneself and others, from humanity, spirit, and nature—characterizes both the masquerade's surreal, dissociative atmosphere and madness's divorce from reason. As is the case in Zagoskin's "Concert of Demons" and Olin's "Strange Ball," in *Petty Demon* masquerade (understood metaphorically as Peredonov's experience of estrangement and literally as the town's costume party) is paired with madness and demonism.[54]

Convinced that changelings surround him, Peredonov submits to the irrational belief that his friend Volodin, who resembles a ram (a satanic symbol) in Peredonov's eyes, wishes to usurp his identity in order to steal his future wife, Varvara. He suspects that Volodin is motivated by a desire to commandeer the coveted government position of school inspector, which Varvara promises to help him attain. In an effort to thwart Volodin's impersonation, Peredonov "smear[s] the letter 'P' in ink on his chest, his stomach, his elbows and on various other parts," an act intended to mark him as Varvara's rightful husband and governmental appointee.[55] This gesture recalls a historical tradition in Russia of using bodily markings, or "royal signs," to assert one's divine assignation to power. Historical pretenders to the Russian throne (such as the first False Dmitry, Timofei Akundinov, and Emelyian Pugachev) could point to birthmarks in the shape of a cross, an eagle, or the tsar's coat of arms to prove that they were divinely selected to serve as monarchs.[56] Peredonov's efforts to affirm his identity and therefore his claim to the position of school inspector through exterior markings resonate with Russia's history of impostors who wrongfully established their right to rule based on physical attributes. Peredonov follows a line of Russian pretenders illegitimately claiming power (but in his case it is power over the provincial school administration rather than over the nation).

A hallucinatory embodiment of Peredonov's fears and anxieties, the demonic *nedotykomka* fatally upends the town's costume party.[57] The nedotykomka, laughing and leaping about the hall, "relentlessly trie[s] to inspire Peredonov with the idea that he ought to light a match and set this fiery, but captive nedotykomka loose on these dreary, filthy walls [. . .]."[58] A symbolic welling of his neuroses, the infernal nedotykomka also incites Peredonov to murder Volodin. These criminal acts, which are maximal expressions of *bezobrazie*, epitomize the provincial town's spiritual malaise, and their occurrence at the costume party reinforces the novel's link between disguise and demonism that originated in Russian folk and religious beliefs.

Following Dostoevsky, Sologub travestied the high-society masquerade as a figurative violation of order and beauty (*obraz*) into disorder and defilement (*bezobrazie*). Both writers used the costume party scene as social satire to unmask their respective eras' social ills. In correlating appearance and essence, aesthetics and ethics, they perpetuated certain cultural beliefs that had influenced early nineteenth-century society-tale representations of the demonic masquerade. The implicit link between mask and menace, disguise and demonism, provides a counterpoint to the emergent understanding of identity as a temporary social construct. As the next two chapters demonstrate, modernist impersonations and self-stylizations depart from the essentialist model of identity that inextricably associates external appearance and internal essence.

2

The Political Masquerade

Impersonation, National Identity, and Power

In *Recollections of a Terrorist* (1909), Boris Savinkov describes how Yevno Azef, leader of the Combat Organization of the Party of Social Revolutionaries (PSR), to which both belonged, designated a nighttime masquerade at the Saint Petersburg Merchant's Club as the venue for their clandestine meeting. Savinkov writes, "Azef arranged for us to meet at none other than the masquerade out of, as he put it, conspiratorial considerations."[1] Azef's foremost "conspiratorial consideration" at this meeting to plot Minister of the Interior Viacheslav Konstantinovich von Plehve's assassination was discretion: he insisted that Organization members take maximal precautions to avert suspicion, including the upkeep of inconspicuous appearance. In this regard the masquerade was an ideal backdrop for their secretive preparations. Abuzz with petty intrigues and sensory pleasures that occupied the attention of the masked guests, the public masquerade was a maelstrom of commotion, din, and unrecognizable faces that effectively shielded the terrorists from scrutiny. At the masquerade, the costuming and role-playing that Azef, Savinkov, and fellow activists embraced as part of their defensive and offensive combat strategies were common practice among all those present. Through their literal and metaphorical masquerades, the terrorists demonstrated the political agency derived from practices of constructing social identity.

The meeting between Savinkov and Azef at the Merchant's Club masquerade highlights the interlacing of disguise and performance with acts aimed at subverting political order. Such late nineteenth- and early twentieth-century works of Russian literature as Dostoevsky's *Demons* (1872), Savinkov's *The Pale Horse* (1909), and Bely's *Petersburg* (1913) reflect this reality and the theatricality of dissident grassroots political action. This chapter examines the theme of masquerade to reveal the differences between the waves of terrorism in the 1860s and early years of the twentieth century. Whereas Dostoevsky used the costumed quadrille in *Demons* as part of his attempt to discredit the political radicalism of his day, Savinkov and company deliberately associated themselves with the masquerade as part of their covert operations. Within the historical context of political impersonations, as well as the sovereign's use of masquerade balls and costumes to affirm or challenge Russian statehood, the present chapter demonstrates the interconnectedness of national identity constructions in the public sphere and the struggle over political ideology around the year 1905.

Tsarist Masquerades

In Hannah Arendt's philosophical work *On Revolution* she presented the idea of a public persona as a constructed mask, which she deemed "legitimate artifice." For Arendt, the political player's mask serves an essential function: it presents a stabilized public representation of an individual's private selves, that is, the array of personae each individual manifests in private affairs. In Norma Moruzzi's study *Speaking through the Mask: Hannah Arendt and the Politics of Social Identity,* the political scientist argues that "masquerade is the leverage by which we can enact ourselves as political beings in an inevitably social world."[2] To put it another way, political agency hinges on an individual's ability to present a strategically stabilized image of self in the public sphere; a mask gives constancy to an otherwise protean self. In Moruzzi's reading of Arendt, she notes that, "The mask provides the private ego with a stable public representation that is artificial, enabling, and salutary."[3] The public mask enables its wearer to integrate his multifaceted selves and disparate social identities. It presents a consistent public image, which is suggestive of predictability and trustworthiness; by demonstrating such qualities, a political actor can establish and maintain legitimate power.

This twentieth-century western model of legitimate political agency does not correspond to the patterns of identity manipulation and fracturing displayed by certain rightful Russian tsars. Instead, Russian tsars engaged in public games of masking and participated in themed masquerade balls that aimed not to unify the monarchs' private selves in order to acquire public legitimacy and support, as Arendt's model would suggest. The tsars' actual and metaphorical acts of masking were intended to disrupt the illusion of a singular, stable identity, which paradoxically affirmed their indomitable authority. Historical instances of what Boris Uspensky has called the "game of tsar" (*igra v tsaria*), which involved forms of costumed play, exhibited the reigning tsar's authority and thereby solidified his position as monarch.[4] This game could take two different forms. In the first variation, individuals dressed up as tsar without the sovereign's permission intending to disturb existing order. In the second variation, the tsar commanded other individuals to impersonate him in order to affirm existing order.

The first type of "game of tsar" was considered blasphemous and often carried severe punishment if discovered: the nature of the play too closely resembled the practice of political imposture, which had unsettled Muscovy during the Time of Troubles.[5] After the death of Ivan IV, who had no surviving heir other than the feeble Fyodor, Boris Godunov assumed control of the throne with the help of Irina Godunova, his sister and Fyodor's wife. Suspicious of potential threats to his tenuous power, Godunov drove out opponents, including Grigory Otrepyev. After fleeing Moscow, Otrepyev sought refuge in the Polish-Lithuanian Commonwealth, where he gained the support of many Polish noblemen and princes. There were unconfirmed rumors that Otrepyev was an illegitimate son of Stefan Batory, who had reigned as king of Poland from 1575 to 1586. If true, this fact would explain Otrepyev's fluency in Russian and Polish, skills that enabled him to assume both national identities and garner the sympathies of noblemen from both nations. With the help of the Poles and others who joined his cause en route to Moscow, Otrepyev returned to the capital claiming to be Prince Dmitry (Ivan's youngest son, who had allegedly been murdered). Otrepyev/ "Dmitry" claimed that he had escaped rather than succumb to death at the hands of his father's enemies in 1591 in the town of Uglich, where he had been in exile with his mother. Otrepyev's ruse was crowned with temporary success as he ruled from 1605–06, until he was overthrown and killed by restive boyars. His impersonation earned him the moniker of False Dmitry.

This historically pivotal impersonation is only one of several instances in Otrepyev's life that displayed his propensity for costuming and disguise. Shortly after ascending to the role of tsar, he married the Polish Marina Mniszek as a way to secure cooperation with the Polish-Lithuanian Commonwealth. During their brief courtship, he visited his future father-in-law disguised in costume, on one occasion dressing as a Russian dandy and on another as a foreign hussar. At their wedding celebration there was a special costumed or masked dance (*pliaska v lichinakh*) orchestrated to satisfy the pretender's reported fondness for various forms of spectacle and entertainment. It has even been suggested that this costumed dance and others like it during his short-lived reign were Russia's first costume balls; the practice was allegedly unable to take root in Russian culture, however, because of his exceptionally brief tenure as sovereign.[6] According to Nikolai Karamzin's *History of the Russian State*, False Dmitry lost his worthiness of being a tsar in the eyes of his subjects because of his passion for such entertainments.[7] Although he enjoyed costuming, Otrepyev's model of political masquerade hinged on his false narrative of self as constituted through his public behavior more than on his vestimentary disguise.

The second "game of tsar" that Uspensky described, in which the tsar ordered someone else to dress as monarch, showed how the act of temporarily relinquishing one's identity could serve the seemingly contrary purpose of affirming it. This variation allowed the tsar to exercise his political agency and to show himself as a powerful actor by forcing another to role-play. Safely controlled by the tsar, such masquerades bespoke a curious mix of monarchic confidence and insecurity: to prove that his identity and corresponding power as tsar were unassailable, he would temporarily renounce the former in order to fortify the latter. For Ivan IV, compelling another whom he perceived as a political threat to play tsar served to discredit the other's legitimacy. In 1575 he crowned Simeon Bekbulatovich, a direct descendant of the Khans of the Golden Horde who had ruled Kievan Rus for over 240 years, Tsar of Moscovy, in what Uspensky interpreted as an act of self-affirmation. Wrote Uspensky, "The role of travesty, pretender-Tsar is played by one who would formerly have possessed the right to call himself Tsar and to rule over the Russian state; such a Tsar is now revealed as a false Tsar, a Tsar in outward appearance only—and by the same token, the previous Tatar Khans are also seen as false Tsars, not true ones."[8] By

showing Bekbulatovich as a role-player, Ivan IV affirmed himself as
the rightful tsar whom Bekbulatovich was trying to imitate. He cast
Bekbulatovich's pretending in direct opposition to his own authenticity.
Moreover, Ivan's demonstration of Bekbulatovich's political impotence
served to underscore the illegitimacy of the Golden Horde as a foreign
ruler of Russia.

Like Ivan IV, Peter the Great also temporarily inverted his identity to
become not-tsar in an effort to affirm his own leadership. In one instance,
Peter designated F. Iu. Romodanovsky "Prince-Caesar" (*kniaz'-kesar'*)
and called him "king" (*korol'*) while referring to himself as Romodanovsky's "serf and lowliest slave."[9] Both by submitting another to his will
and by using the unnaturalness of the "impostor" as a foil to his own
authenticity, the tsar affirmed his power and his right to rule. Peter's
wish to assert his legitimacy stemmed in part from a need to defend
himself against his detractors who called him "the pretender from
Stockholm." Suspicions about Peter's national identity and patriotism
were fueled by the fact that he traveled abroad under disguise in his
youth, which his opponents interpreted as a demonstration of his proclivity toward imposture. Other detractors interpreted his traveling
incognito differently: since they did not accept him as a rightful Russian
tsar, his layman's "disguise" was seen as a revelation of his true foreign
identity.

Temporarily renouncing his identity in a theatrical display of power
was in keeping with Peter's style of performative governance and
policies that turned native Russian cultural codes upside down in
carnivalesque fashion. At the beginning of the eighteenth century Peter
played the role of a theatrical director who dressed and orchestrated
the performance of his troupe: he introduced the Table of Ranks, which
assigned roles by elaborating a clear social hierarchy, and his vestimentary policy mandated that Russian nobility wear German dress. Uspensky observed that "by forcing his people to wear 'German,' i.e. European,
clothes, Peter had in the eyes of his contemporaries transformed his
entourage into mummers (just as Ivan's *oprichniki*[10] had appeared in
their time as mummers too)."[11] Like the holiday mummers in Russian
folk custom who selected their costume based on the antithesis of
native and alien (the adopted identity was supposed to oppose the
wearer's age, sex, ethnic, or professional identity), Peter relied on a
perception of identity in binary terms (tsar/not-tsar) that could be
inverted. And like the holiday mummers Peter disrupted order with
carnivalesque behavior, which went against the grain of convention or

otherwise defied expected norms of comportment. Ernest Zitser has argued that by showing his power to abolish convention through anti-behavior, Peter affirmed his right to rule.[12]

Games involving assertions of identity that affirm monarchial power evolved into more elaborate and structured social rituals, such as the masquerades that celebrated tsars' coronations, weddings, and military victories. Richard Wortman has argued that such public spectacles as parades and masquerades were expressions and validations of political power. This was especially true of the costume balls with a Russian national theme: they permitted the monarchs to assert visually their patriotism and to inscribe themselves in the course of Russian history. No longer employing the reverse psychology of renunciation as an act of affirmation, by the mid-eighteenth century tsars began embracing Russian military and historical costumes to proclaim their legitimacy and worthiness. Empresses Elizabeth (1741–1762) and Catherine the Great (1762–1796), for example, cross-dressed as a means of asserting not only their legitimate claims to the throne but also their capacity to play male military roles. The empresses frequently sponsored "vice versa" (*prevrashchennye*) court masquerades at which they relished the opportunity to don men's clothing. Both Elizabeth and Catherine demonstrated a fondness for sporting Russian military uniforms, which had the visual effect of affirming their status as national commanders-in-chief.[13] Elizabeth reportedly wore the uniforms of all Russian military regiments as masquerade costumes within the first four months of her reign.[14] By donning national military regalia, the empresses asserted their claim to a position traditionally held by men and validated their rule over the Russian empire, which was especially important for the German-born Catherine. For her, wearing Russian costume was a type of sartorial propaganda that symbolically enshrined her allegiance by showing her as a native daughter.[15]

Tsars also dressed in historical Russian costume to consolidate their leadership through the illusion of historical continuity, to affirm Russian statehood, and to demonstrate patriotism. At the costume ball accompanying Nikolai I's coronation celebration in 1826, Russian national attire dominated and was seen as an expression of native pride. Nikolai ordered that the masquerade be repeated the following day at the Moscow Noblemen's Assembly because the event constituted "an expression of the emotional bond between the Russian nation and their tsar"—an emotional bond reinforced through the shared style of costume.[16] Russian national costumes also starred at an 1849 masquerade organized by the Governor General of Moscow, Count Arseny Zakrevsky, to celebrate the opening of the Kremlin palace. The account of the masquerade appearing in *Moskvitianin* enumerated the Russian historical figures represented, including Ivan Susanin, Dmitry Pozharsky, Ermak Timofeevich, as well as the mythical hero Dobrynia.

Masquerades of Russianness, such as the national-historical-themed costume ball held in 1856 to celebrate Alexander II's coronation, were celebrations of native identity and tools of political expediency. The empress and duchesses wore traditional Russian dress, as did the ladies of the court who were adorned with Russian-style tiaras called *kokoshniki*. The emperor and the grand dukes wore military uniforms of the rifle guard that had been established only three years earlier. Their costumes effectively validated the corps while at the same time honoring Russian national style, with its distinctive wide trousers (*sharovary*) and Russian-style kaftan.[17] On January 25, 1883, Alexander III's brother, Grand Duke Vladimir Alexandrovich, hosted a costume ball at his palace, which was decorated in the old-Russian style that evoked an imagined historical stability.[18] While the grand duke and duchess were dressed as a boyar and boyar's wife, the tsar attended the festivities wearing his customary general's uniform of the Cavalry of the Artillery, which identified him as an observer of the pageantry rather than a participant.[19] This was a politically savvy move in light of the fact that some of the 250 guests came dressed as Scythians and Varangians, ancient tribes assimilated into Russia and thus suggestive of the complexity of Russian national identity. Such historical nuance was not productive in the tsar's political pageantry.

A particularly poignant example of a Russian emperor using masquerade costume as a tool of nation-building and affirmation of his political power is Nikolai II's sumptuous *Bal costumé au Palais d'Hiver* (also referred to as the *bal d'hiver*) of February 1903, at which he wore the coronation gown of Tsar Aleksei Mikhailovich (crowned in 1645) to help anchor his reign and Russia itself in national tradition by evoking a stylized version of a secure Muscovite past at a time of great present peril for the autocracy. The *bal d'hiver* took place when the country was on the brink of the first attempt at domestic revolution and armed conflict with Japan. The ball was held twice, first on February 7 in the Hermitage Theater, where it was preceded by a performance of *Boris Godunov*.[20] The choice of staging Pushkin's play about the Time of Troubles and the False Dmitry underscored Nikolai's anxieties about internal and external attacks on Russian statehood. The nationalist

Figure 8. Photo of Tsar Nikolai II dressed in the clothing of Tsar Aleksei Mikhailovich for the *Bal costumé au Palais d'Hiver* in 1903. (image courtesy of the New York Public Library)

Figure 9. Photo of a group of dancers at the *Bal costumé au Palais d'Hiver* in 1903. (image courtesy of the New York Public Library)

spirit of the event was undermined, however, by using the French name for the Winter Palace, a confounding choice given the overarching political agenda.

The patriotic spirit behind the Russian national costumes at the Bal costumé au Palais d'Hiver reflected the period's interest in traditional dress, one example of which was the concurrent International Exhibition of Costumes that took place in Saint Petersburg. In April 1903, art critic Vladimir Stasov published a review of "the first international exhibit of historical costumes" in the newspaper *Novosti i birzhevye vedomosti*.[21] Stasov boasted that this event, which was held at the Tavricheskii Palace, was the first such ambitious international exhibition of national dress anywhere. Conceived and organized by private initiative, the exhibition featured clothing, accessories, and articles of toilette hailing from countries all over the world and supplied by individual collectors and antique dealers.[22] Stasov indignantly grumbled that certain countries, namely England, Italy, Spain, The Netherlands, and Belgium, among others, did not respond to the exhibit organizer's request for donations representative of their respective national vestimentary traditions. Nonetheless, Stasov boldly claimed that the exhibition's scope and the

Figure 10. Advertising poster for "The First International Exhibition of Costumes" by Elena Samokish-Sudovskaia (1902). (reproduced from Eleanora Glinternik, *Reklama v Rossii XVIII-pervoi poloviny XX veka*)

ethnographic insights it offered put Russia in the vanguard of studying the development of nations' different aesthetic tastes as reflected in "one of the most interesting and individual manifestations of a nation's art," its costumes.

While the exceptionalism of the First International Exhibition of Costumes consisted in its international scope, the advertising poster created by book illustrator Elena Samokish-Sudovskaia placed Russian national costume front and center (figure 10). On the right-hand side is a pen-and-ink drawing of seven ladies, all of whom wear European-style ball gowns and whimsical millinery confections atop their heads, including one in the shape of a clipper ship. In contrast to the tumble of European frippery, a man and woman stand proudly on a platform in brightly colored Russian national costume on the poster's left-hand side. The Russian lady's kokoshnik and carmine cloak, along with her companion's traditional kaftan and tall boots, constitute the poster's visual focal point. The exhibition's dates are given as 1902–1903, indicating that the costume exhibition began before Nikolai's February 1903 bal d'hiver.

The coincidence of these prominent displays of ethnic costume points to the period's emerging interest in fashion as a distinctive marker of national identity. It also reveals a shared jingoistic wish to reinscribe symbolically Russia's statehood and assert its national superiority in the face of domestic and international threats through traditional dress. In May of 1903 Saint Petersburg enjoyed yet one more state-sponsored affirmational historical-national event, the "Week of Peter" held in the Summer Garden. On May 11, the opening day, there was "a grandiose historical procession," which was a reenactment of "the ethnographic masquerade organized by Peter the Great in Saint Petersburg and Moscow to celebrate the Nishtadt Peace Treaty [of 1721]."[23] After the Treaty, Peter declared that Russia would henceforth be known as the Russian Empire, and he introduced new state regalia to signal the expanded state.[24] Although Peter's "ethnographic masquerade" commemorated Russian national triumph, the new regalia marking the birth of a multiethnic empire differed from the nationalistic symbolism of historical Russian dress.

A mainstream revival of interest in national costumes accompanied the late imperial state's use of them for political ends. In the days before the "Week of Peter," several tailors from Berlin arrived in Saint Petersburg to study women's national Russian costumes, which had become fashionable in Germany.[25] This interesting fact shows that Russian vestimentary tradition enjoyed vogue in Europe nearly a full decade before the Ballets Russes ignited a craze in France for the oriental exoticism of Russian dress. New public policy was introduced in Russia at the end of 1902, concurrent with the First International Exhibition of Costumes, in response to the fashionability of national garb. State-owned theaters began working out a policy that would allow spectators dressed in national clothing, Russian or otherwise, to be admitted as spectators.[26] A newspaper article from 1911 announcing the formation of the society "Revival of National Clothing" in Moscow offers a probable explanation for what motivated this seemingly odd policy. In Petersburg several years earlier there had been a similar society popularizing old Russian national dress, "but its members very quickly lost the desire to wear ancient dress in light of the fact that many public places did not admit 'the boyars,' not to mention the numerous strange situations (*kur'ezy*) and misunderstandings that accompanied the revived boyars."[27] With new laws and organizations to promote national dress, the fashion grew in its social acceptance.

Terrorist Masquerades

Concurrent with the vogue for Russian-style costume, the tumultuous years surrounding 1905 witnessed political provocateurs adopting foreign national identities and costumes to disguise themselves in order to evade suspicion and arrest. In real life and literature from the period, treating national identity as a non-essential part of self was an integral part of perpetrating treasonous acts: renouncing one's Russian nationality, even temporarily, could be symbolic of renouncing one's loyalty to the fatherland.

It is important to note, however, that sporting foreign national costume in the context of the leisure-time masquerade ball did not necessarily have the same subversive implications that it did on the streets as part of political conspiracy. National dress endured as a favorite form of costuming at public and private masquerade balls, as is illustrated by newspaper accounts and features in women's fashion magazines. The January 8, 1904, issue of *Fashion World* (*Modnyi svet*) featured the costumes "Germany" and "France," which combined traditional costume with symbolic ready-made objects.[28] In 1911 the magazine *Women's Affair* (*Zhenskoe delo*) listed suggestions for 17 masquerade costumes, nine of which revolved around adopting a foreign national

№ 3.   № 4.

Figure 11. Illustration of the costumes "Alsatian" (*left*) and "Indian" (*right*).
From *Women's Affair* (issue no. 1, 1911). (image courtesy of the Russian National
Library)

Figure 12. Photo of masquerade participants in costumes, including a couple in Spanish national dress on the left (1912–1914). (from the studio of Carl Bulla; image courtesy of TsGAKFFD, Saint Petersburg)

identity: the magazine counseled readers to dress in Alsatian, Indian, Portuguese, Swiss, Chinese, American, or a variety of French costumes (figure 11).[29] While such costumes at society masquerades generally carried an apolitical air of cosmopolitan sophistication, the newspaper *Novosti dnia* reported on the infelicitous consequences of one gentleman's decision to wear Japanese national costume to a masquerade on the eve of the Russo-Japanese War. The so-called "comical incident" transpired on January 7, 1904, at the Saint Petersburg Merchant's Club. A certain nobleman V. dressed up as a samurai, which so inflamed the patriotic sentiment of fishmonger S. that he gave the former a good thrashing.[30] As this incident shows, national costume could be controversial or inflammatory if it touched on a sensitive political issue of the day.

In the years immediately after the tumult of 1905, newspaper articles reveal a trend for polemical costumes oriented toward domestic politics. The February 14, 1906, issue of *Russian Word* (*Russkoe slovo*) reported on an arrest that took place the previous day at a masquerade at the Saint Petersburg Noblemen's Assembly. A woman sported the polemical costume "Russia," which "depicted clearly and entirely correctly our fatherland in the days of riots and strikes." Regretfully, the journalist offers no description of how the costume achieved such an effect. The police accompanied the lady home and there "arrested the costume" (*[politsiia] kostium arestovala*).[31] In this instance, the "national" costume was not a return to a distant or idealized historic moment, but a documentation of contemporary ideological strife within the nation.

The same 1906 issue of *Russian Word* cited above reported on another arrest that took place at a private Saint Petersburg society masquerade only days later. A brave and inventive female masker donned the following politically themed costume: "on her back she sported two pig heads, on her head there were two machine guns fashioned out of red crepe-paper and tied in the shape of a bow, and there were also two ribbons with the inscriptions 'Don't begrudge the bullets, don't send out blank salvoes.'" On her torso hung portraits of prominent government officials and headlines cut out of satirical journals. For this brash condemnation of the violence endorsed by members of the Imperial regime in 1905, the police demanded that the unnamed woman take off her costume in the ladies' changing room, whereupon they also "arrested the costume." One more political protest through costume was documented in the "Day to Day" column of *Russian Word* on January 29, 1907. The Estonian Assembly in Saint Petersburg held a masquerade at which the most interesting costume, in the reporter's opinion, was also the most divisive. A young man wore a "costume that clearly illustrated the activity of 'The Black Hundred' generally and 'The Union of Russian People' in particular." While both groups generally supported the tsar, the costume's explicit political content proved controversial at the masquerade, which resulted in the wearer being arrested and put in jail.[32]

Terrorism and Masquerades of National Identity

As these examples suggest, masquerades of the modernist era afforded costume-wearers a forum for expressing personal opinion about political issues of the day, especially the fate of the Russian autocracy. The costume itself served as a tool of national discourse, a voice for personal opinion about public good. In contrast to individuals who conspicuously expressed political protest through their costumes, the period's provocateurs and agitators engaged in terrorist acts under the protective cover of disguises and false identities. In Boris Savinkov's own biography and in his fictionalized account of a terrorist's activities, entitled *The Pale Horse*, as well as in Bely's *Petersburg*, political provocateurs impersonate foreign nationals to renounce symbolically their allegiance to homeland and to deflect suspicion and arrest. The temporary masks that these renegades adopted offer a direct contrast to Hannah Arendt's model of rightful political agency, which depends on a stable projection of identity through a metaphorical mask. The terrorist's repertoire of constructed social identities, inspired by a wish to remain inconspicuous in order to achieve his subversive goals, illustrates the intimate relationship between public disguise and disruptive political agency.

The literary representation of grassroots terrorism in *Demons* served as a model for the real-life acts of Savinkov, as well as his fictionalized accounts thereof. Dostoevsky depicted a terrorist network of cells, each containing five individuals. This became a paradigm that Savinkov imitated as terrorist and author: he led a cell of five "English" fighters during his masquerade as a London merchant, and Zhorzh's cell in *Pale Horse* also had five individuals. Vadim Shkolnikov has suggested that Savinkov styled his real-life persona and the lyrical persona of Zhorzh on Stavrogin, while at the same time struggling against this model in an effort to avoid the fate of Stavrogin and the other provocateurs in *Demons*.[33] Although Stavrogin is not a nihilist operative, Maria Lebiadkina calls him Grishka Otrepyev, the name of the False Dmitry, thereby classifying him as a political pretender. Verkhovensky, too, alludes to the story of the False Dmitry when he beseeches Stavrogin to join his plan for political overthrow. Envisioning a kind of puppet regime in which the charismatic and mysterious Stavrogin would be the front to his power, Verkhovensky imagines Stavrogin in the role of "Tsarevich Ivan" (Ivan the Terrible's son and heir-apparent until the tsar murdered him in a fit of rage). Stavrogin would reenact the False Dmitry's strategy for claiming the throne: he would present himself as the rightful ruler who had been forced into hiding for many years and had been mistaken for dead.

Verkhovensky styles himself as both an inventor of roles and a theatrical director, thereby emphasizing the performative nature of political activism and grassroots terrorism. Throughout the novel the nihilist provocateurs' role-playing and acts of dissimulation are part of their subversion and confer upon them political agency.[34] Verkhovensky, for example, skillfully postures with the governor's wife Iuliia Mikhailovna to give her the false illusion that she controls him. In a performance resembling the historical "game of tsar," Verkhovensky feigns subservience to her with the ultimate goal of asserting his own authority. He "got the upper hand with her [. . .] by entering into her plans, devising them for her, acting through the crudest flattery," and thus "he entangled her from head to foot, and became as necessary to her as air."[35] Another member of the Group of Five, Liamshin, is described as a natural performer and imitation artist (he plays piano and imitates pigs, thunderstorms, and even a mother giving birth) and uses his thespian talent for subversive purposes at Iuliia Mikhailovna's benefit ball. As we saw in chapter 1, Liamshin participates in the costumed literary quadrille and precipitates the explosion of scandal when he begins walking upside down on his hands, a literal overturning of order. Dostoevsky uses the motif of costuming at the quadrille to discredit the provocateurs' antics as buffoonery, in accord with his personal antipathy for the political activism of the 1860s.

The attempted assassination of Tsar Alexander II in 1866 fueled rumors about a terrorist conspiracy threatening society at large. According to the conservative *Moscow Gazette* (*Moskovskie vedomosti*), "terror and indignation" were on everyone's minds as the public resisted the explanation that the assassin (Karakozov) was acting independently. The newspaper's editor, Mikhail Katkov, stirred anxiety about political conspiracy in Russia and called it a "tool of foreign [Polish] intrigue inside Russia."[36] (Katkov was among the figures representing literary tendencies at the costumed quadrille in *Demons*.) Nihilist Sergei Nechaev, leader of the terrorist organization People's Reprisal (*Narodnaia rasprava*), served as the model for Verkhovensky in *Demons*, and the group's tactics were adopted decades later by Savinkov and the Combat Organization (1902–1908) of the Party of Socialist Revolutionaries.

The Combat Organization was responsible for numerous high-profile assassinations, including Minister of the Interior Dmitry Sipiagin (1902), Grand Duke Sergei (uncle of Tsar Nikolai II and Governor General of Moscow, 1905) as well as von Plehve. The PSR's own records documented over 200 terrorist attacks in the years 1905–1907.[37] In Savinkov's memoirs he recounted how he and his coconspirators disguised themselves as railway porters, coachmen, and peddlers while conducting reconnaissance and executing their violent plans in Saint

Petersburg.³⁸ Savinkov and members of the Combat Organization used the conceit of role-playing as an essential tenet of their political activism. Playing the roles of street workers allowed the terrorists to map their victims' itineraries across the city and to suss out prospective sites for attack while blending into the milieu.³⁹ On other occasions the "fighters" (*boeviki*), as Savinkov called them, dressed and comported themselves as aristocrats, flaneurs, and statesmen for the sake of diversifying their roles and evincing an inconsistency that would make them hard to track. On the day of von Plehve's murder (July 15, 1904), Savinkov posed as a gentleman strolling through the city and was even ushered to safety by a nearby policeman after the attack.⁴⁰ Under the guise of an aristocrat, Savinkov deflected attention away from his true role.

In addition to changing his profession and social class, Savinkov adopted new national identities as part of his ruse to conceal his affiliation with a terrorist organization aiming to undermine the tsarist regime. Savinkov recollected how he assumed the alias of an English businessman named Arthur McCullough, who was purportedly in Russia as a representative of a London bicycle firm. A supporting cast of provocateurs playing his business assistants and family members accompanied him to stage a convincing performance amidst the unsuspecting residents of Saint Petersburg.⁴¹ When the expense of supporting the entire "English" entourage became too great for the PSR to bear, Savinkov refashioned himself as a Polish dentist named Konstantin Chernetsky. Savinkov's foreign impersonations functioned as social disguises and more poignantly, they functioned as symbolic articulations of his abandoned allegiance to his fatherland.

In *Pale Horse* adopting foreign national identity is similarly an important part of the terrorist Zhorzh (George) O'Brien's protective guise. Written as a diary, the novella is told from the terrorist's point of view. The reader never learns the Russian terrorist-narrator's given name: in part I he is Zhorzh, in part II he sheds his English identity for that of a Russian timber merchant Frol Semyonov Titov from the Urals, and in part III he becomes an engineer named Malinovsky. Among his co-conspirators is the former student Henrich, who is the closest ideologically to Zhorzh and who fittingly has a non-Russian name: his German roots are implicated in his lack of loyalty to the tsar. In a memorable scene Zhorzh, posing as an Englishman with a poor command of Russian, has a confrontation at the theater with a Russian man who spits out hostile national slurs against him because of England's suspected support for Japan in the Russo-Japanese War.⁴² In the suggestive context of the theater, Zhorzh impersonates an Englishman with such finesse that the theatergoer excoriates him because of his credible performance of national identity.

A 1904 journalistic account of a Russian war correspondent planning to adopt an Anglophone identity for his trip to Japan similarly highlights the potentially dangerous consequences of national identity in the wartime context. In December the newspaper *Russian Word* featured a story about sending its correspondent V. E. Kraevsky to Japan to observe firsthand what was transpiring. In preparation for his impersonation, Kraevsky traveled first to London and then to New York, where he fell in love with everything American, "from hats to boots, from suitcases to toothbrushes," and therefore decided to adopt an American identity for his journalistic operation in Japan. The newspaper editor writing the account stressed the importance of Kraevsky wearing non-Russian attire in Japan in order to evade suspicion successfully. The need for the costume to correspond visually to the role (in this case, the wish to be unnoticed) is self-evident; however, the editor took his justification one step further by positing that the labels inside the clothing or even the manufacturer's stamp on a button might give away Kraevsky's Russian nationality. Such close scrutiny of a suspicious individual's clothing was, according to the editor, "the first path the police will take!" The instruction followed, therefore, for Kraevsky to purchase an entirely new wardrobe in New York. But here one must be careful, too: the editor cautions that new garments can also give away one's impersonation precisely because newness is conspicuous. "New things—it's the same as wearing a domino. It is an indication that here we are staging a masquerade!"[43] In this context, the domino emblematizes not just the temporary renunciation of one's everyday identity, but a covert and transgressive operation.

For Zhorzh in *Pale Horse*, the anonymity afforded by wearing a domino and half-mask (typically worn together) corresponds to the terrorist's existential loss of self. Nechaev expounded this nihilist trait in his 1869 manifesto "Catechism of a Revolutionary." He declared, "The revolutionary is a doomed man. He has no personal interests, no business affairs, no emotions, no attachments, no property, and no name. Everything in him is wholly absorbed in the single thought and the single passion for revolution."[44] Zhorzh points to his inconstant identity and the resulting spiritual and psychological unmooring he experiences, which coincides with Nechaev's characterization of the revolutionary. Additionally, Zhorzh calls attention to his physical dislocation when he states, "I'm living as an invisible man (*nevidimka*)—without a name and without a home." He recalls this about when he lived in the north: "I lost my very own self. I was alien even to myself."[45] The nihilist-terrorist's eviscerated self is a theme that Zinaida Gippius hit on in her diary writings about the terrorist Savinkov. In the century's first decade Gippius had been Savinkov's literary mentor, but by December 1923 he had fallen out of favor with her.[46] Gippius condemned her former disciple in the harshest terms: "Savinkov is emptiness [. . .]. He doesn't exist, and, more importantly, he never did."[47] Gippius's assessment suggests, however, that he successfully fulfilled the role of the revolutionary as set out by Nechaev in "Catechism."

Zhorzh's revolutionary fervor is his guiding religion until the PSR attempts to rein in his activism. He rebelliously commands the terrorist operations according to his own wishes, not those of the Party, showing that he holds sacred only his own will. This demonstration of extreme egotism contradicts Nechaev's manifesto of the terrorist: Zhorzh asserts himself rather than erasing himself. The question of agency arises explicitly at the novella's end when Zhorzh likens himself and his comrades to characters in a puppet theater "in red capes and masks." He asks, "Is this a *balagan* or life?" Savinkov alludes to the title of Blok's play *The Fairground Booth* (*Balaganchik*), and the question he poses, "Is it cranberry juice or blood?," recalls Blok's clown who bleeds cranberry juice.[48] Implicit in Zhorzh's queries is a concern that his politically motivated theatrical role-playing is, in the end, nothing more than banal theatrical role-playing.

The half-mask and cape (synonymous with domino) that Zhorzh envisions himself wearing is at once performance costume in Blok's play and a symbolic representation of his nihilistic self-renunciation. Unlike figurative, polemical, or character costumes, the half-mask and domino efface identity rather than supplant it with a substitute.[49] The absence of a decipherable identity is the most epistemologically unsettling kind of mask: it is simultaneously a blank page on which anything can be written and a vacuum into which everything collapses. It contains all possibilities and none. The inarticulate domino expresses the wearer's menacing intentions by withholding a recognizable identity.

Terror and National Identity in *Petersburg*

Scholars Lynn Ellen Patyk, Olga Matich, Alexis Peri and Christine Evans have commented on the likelihood that Bely based the terrorist conspiracy in *Petersburg* on the Combat Organization's assassination of

Viacheslav Konstantinovich von Plehve. The novel's narrator implies a parallel between the plots to assassinate Minister of the Interior von Plehve and the fictional senator Apollon Apollonovich Ableukhov. Upon seeing a portrait, the narrator questions the identity of its subject: "Who? The senator? He? Apollon Apollonovich Ableukhov? Why, no: Viacheslav Konstantinovich."[50] Bely himself averred in his memoir *Between Two Revolutions* that he "portrayed the terrorist [Dudkin] based on Savinkov of late 1905 as described by the Remizovs."[51] Bely also modeled the terrorist ringleader and *agent provocateur* Lippanchenko on Azef, whose work as a double agent for the police and the Combat Organization was discovered in 1908, and which led to the Organization's disbanding.[52] As Matich has pointed out, long after Bely completed *Petersburg* he learned that Azef had been living in Berlin under the alias of Lipchenko at the same time that Bely was writing the novel.[53] Regardless of whether one believes Bely's account or not, the similarity of Lippanchenko to Lipchenko reinforces the idea that the fictional character was based on the notorious double agent. In addition to these real-life influences, Bely has acknowledged his debt to *Demons* in his portrait of the revolutionary spirit in *Petersburg*.[54]

The historical context that Bely evokes in the novel is that of the year 1905, a year of tumult and tension as the Russo-Japanese War ended in defeat for Russia and attempts at reforming the monarchy reached the level of revolutionary fervor. The conflict between the tsarist establishment and those seeking broader constitutional protection and rights is embodied in the novel's generational conflict between Senator Apollon Apollonovich and his son, Nikolai. The mood of anxiety gripping Saint Petersburg is personified in the figure of the domino, whose alleged antics are detailed in several supposed newspaper clippings. The menacing domino is described as a "strange spectacle" (*strannoe zrelishche*), "extremely mysterious" (*chrezvychaino zagadochnoe*), and evoking "confusion" (*smushchenie*). As a subject of journalistic reportage, the enigmatic domino is accepted by the public as a true phenomenon. It turns out, however, that the newspaper reports were mere fiction: the story of the domino "rapidly unraveled into a series of events that never happened."[55]

The Diary of Events (*Dnevnik proisshestvii*) column of the newspaper that reports on the domino in *Petersburg* reflects the prevalence of such columns chronicling daily events, usually titled Events (*Proisshestviia*) or Diary of Adventures (*Dnevnik prikliuchenii*) in Saint Petersburg's contemporary newspapers. As Mark Steinberg has observed, in the years around 1910 these columns were full of stories about swindles and confidence games that relied on false names and identities. Steinberg underscores the fact that in most cases, the perpetrators were "respectably dressed."[56] Their orderly and legible appearance, along with their politeness and good manners, inspired confidence. Donning a black half-mask and red domino, in contrast, bespeaks the erasure of respectability and the effacement of a readable identity, all of which creates the concomitant possibility of overturning public order.

When Nikolai Apollonovich appears at the Tsukatovs' costume ball wearing just such a red domino and black half-mask, as had been chronicled in the newspaper, he sends a wave of fear through the ballroom along with rumors that it was he who has been terrorizing the city.[57] Amplifying the atmosphere of anxiety is a group of maskers dancing around the red domino in black capuchins with skulls and crossbones embroidered on their hoods. The novel's ball is a politically coded space where opposing political inclinations define the guests. Apollon Apollonovich, for example, spends the evening "expounding his prohibitionist system to the [liberal] professor of statistics, the leader of a moderate party, and to the editor of the conservative newspaper, once the liberal son of a priest."[58] Within this zone of political discourse, the enigmatic domino takes on revolutionary implications, even triggering heart palpitations in the Senator because "red was emblematic of the chaos that was leading Russia to its doom."[59] Nikolai's domino costume is associated symbolically with the threat to order, a connection that becomes actual when the reader learns that Sofia Likhutina has handed Nikolai a letter that "invited him to throw some sort of bomb" at his father.[60]

Worn by a figure described in the press as terrorizing the streets of Saint Petersburg, and also donned by Nikolai Apollonovich, a budding revolutionary and possible patricide, the domino and half-mask represent the destabilization of public order. Despite being an open-ended signifier in terms of identity, the domino nonetheless portends a threat and bespeaks the danger of the unknown. Instead of blankness signaling innocence like pre-Lapsarian nudity, it conveys the menace of intentional withholding. Recalling Malevich's notorious *Black Square* (1915), a modernist icon condemned by many of the painter's contemporaries as blasphemous because it replaced the face of divinity with the gaping absence of a black hole, the black half-mask and domino subvert the conventional external markers of identity, the face and clothing. Just as religious philosopher Sergei Bulgakov interpreted Picasso's violent fragmentation and distortion of the human face as an act of desecration, calling his paintings "black icons" because they distorted the divine essence of the face and rendered it unrecognizable,[61] the black half-mask ascribes a similarly depraved spirit to its wearer. Edgar Allan Poe's "Masque of the Red Death," an intertext of *Petersburg*, equates the red domino and half-mask's blankness with the ominously silent figure of death. Dating back to his 1904 essay "The Mask," Bely associated the mask with the ontological frightfulness of the unknowable. He cautioned that "beings enigmatic and strange" do not merely wear masks, but their faces are masks, a fact that instills profound fear and horror as it removes all possibilities of a true authentic essence.[62] The dread forces behind the mask use it as a vehicle, as a mode of instantiation. Explained Bely, "From behind the mask (*lichina*) of the visible gapes the invisible. [. . .] We'll never be able to say who is looking at us from behind the mask, but it is terrifying (*strashno*) when we are being followed by masked ones."[63] The impossibility of knowing what or who is behind the mask kindles an existential terror, the likes of which the anonymous domino who haunts the streets of Petersburg instills in the newspaper-reading public.

Potential terrorist and patricide, Nikolai Apollonovich Ableukhov comes close to fulfilling the threat to Russia implied by his Mongol forebears. The novel's first chapter opens with an account of the Ableukhov family ancestry, revealing that they descended from the Kirghiz-Kaisak Horde. The narrator also references a "forgotten Mongolian expression" on Nikolai's face, linking him directly with the terrorist Lippanchenko, whose yellow face conferred upon him the look of a "mix between a Semite and a Mongol," recalled the "yellow-faced people" from the east (i.e., the descendants of Genghis Khan) and belied his Ukrainian nationality.[64] (An unidentified interlocutor observes, "Every Russian has some Tatar blood."[65]) Dressed in a Bukhara robe, Tatar slippers, and skullcap, Nikolai Apollonovich appropriates the Asiatic identity imputed by his face. Lippanchenko's yellow clothing stokes anxieties about the yellow menace stirred by the Russo-Japanese War. The terrorist is also referred to as "the yellow hunchbacked Pierrot"[66] because of his yellow jacket. This reference to the commedia dell'arte character Pierrot foregrounds the theatrical idiom that characterizes the role-playing of the terrorist in general.

Shishnarfiev, the terrorist Dudkin's destructive alter ego, is also associated with the Asiatic menace and represents a direct threat to the Russian state. From the Azeri town of Shemakha, a culturally and ethnically Persian region, Dudkin's double suggests that foreignness is an integral part of a terrorist's identity. Moreover, an anagram of the Persian's name, Enfranshish, triggers in Dudkin a destructive impulse, which crystallizes the link between terror and alien national identity. Like Savinkov and other Combat Organization "fighters," Dudkin's use of aliases bespeaks his annihilated essential self: he carries a false passport bearing the name Andrei Andreich Gorelsky and favors the pseudonym Dudkin, although his real name is Aleksei Alekseich Pogorelsky.

At the Tsukatovs' costume party Nikolai Apollonovich unwittingly reveals his identity when he raises his half-mask in order to read the note from Sofia Likhutina. Unmasking himself and exposing his face presages his inability to renounce his love for himself and father by committing an act of terror. In this respect he is different from the inveterate terrorists Savinkov and Zhorzh, who thoroughly erase themselves and abandon emotional attachments in their ongoing identity charades. The exposure of Nikolai's face and name anticipates his failure to overcome his essential self: unlike Nechaev's revolutionary who has "no name [. . .] no emotions, no attachments," Nikolai cannot renounce his identity, his love for father(land), or for Sofia.

Nikolai's inability to play the role of the terrorist-revolutionary is also foreshadowed by the fact that Sofia repeatedly calls him a buffoon (*shut*), implying his harmlessness. Whereas Zhorzh in *Pale Horse* can no longer tell if his metaphorical domino and half-mask are mere performance accessories ("is this a *balagan* or is it life?"), Nikolai's domino is a clownish costume, the removal of which heralds his inability to perform the role of the subversive terrorist.

The culture of prerevolutionary terrorism positioned the terrorist-provocateur outside of mainstream society by rejecting the conventional tenets of morality. The terrorist's self-isolation, his rejection of humanity and faith, and his abdication of hope for the future all connect him to the Decadent themes of apocalypse and the collapse of civilization. One demonstrable way the terrorist's consequent embrace of destruction and self-annihilation manifested itself socially was in treating identity and existence as contingent constructs. The terrorist-provocateur's penchant for role-playing aligns him with the theatrical idiom that pervaded Russian modernism, conspicuous examples of which are the Decadent self-stylizations, which I discuss in the following chapter. However, the performative identities of the two types differ in a key way: the terrorist wished to impersonate another in order to conceal himself "out of conspiratorial considerations," as Azef put it, or to efface his identity and obliterate himself to become Nechaev's ideal revolutionary. The Decadent aesthete, however, wished to stylize his or her appearance to create a new self-image as part of the art-life continuum. The terrorist's pragmatic approach to disguise had nothing in common with the Decadent's creative play and experimentation.

As the historical and literary examples brought forth in this chapter show, political agency can be a function of the social performance of national identity. Acts of reinscribing native national identity supported rightful Russian tsars, while impersonating foreign nationality was an important tool among terrorists for destabilizing the monarchy in the troubled years surrounding 1905. Among regular citizens, masquerade ball costumes articulating polemical positions vis-à-vis the tsarist regime demonstrated in yet another way that publicly constructed temporary identities were an indispensable component of national discourse in the early twentieth century. During those years of domestic and international crises, certain individuals expressed political opinion and agency through performances of national identity, which often required specific national dress along with stylized social behavior. In the next chapter, I examine another type of socially constructed image: masquerades of female identity among men and women on the stage, on the page, and in daily life.

3

>─┤─◆>─•─◯─•─<◆─┤─<

The Gender Masquerade
Constructions of Feminine Identity

Experiments in social constructions of female gender proliferated during the wave of changes sweeping Russia and the West at the turn of the last century. In many respects these experiments were a response to the female archetypes spawned by the period's dominant literary movements of Decadence and Symbolism. Far from being a uniform phenomenon, masquerades of female identity were highly individual and mixed in their polemical value: performances of femaleness undertaken by male writers, burlesque actors, and main-street rogues differed widely among themselves and in relation to those undertaken by women, which similarly varied. This chapter focuses on unique feminine masquerades enacted by two women writers, Zinaida Gippius and Elizaveta Dmitrieva. Whereas Gippius's masquerade was primarily performative and based upon the illusion of conspicuous artifice, Dmitrieva's lyrical masquerade as Cherubina de Gabriak relied on sustaining an illusion of authenticity. By engaging in masquerades of socially and artistically constructed feminine identity, Gippius and Dmitrieva transformed gender from a liability into a performance space for enacting polemics with dominant female archetypes of modernist literature.

Scrambling Gender Identity

Elaine Showalter has called the period of gender-role revaluation in
Europe at the end of the nineteenth century a time of "sexual anarchy,"
noting that assumptions about so-called normative sexual behavior
were being overturned in lockstep with conventional gender typologies.
Studies on sexuality such as Richard von Krafft-Ebing's "Psychopathia
Sexualis" (1886) and Havelock Ellis' influential study of homosexuality,
"Sexual Inversion" (1896), complicated the relationship among biological sex, sexual orientation, and gender identity. Once the concepts of
masculinity and femininity were freed from the bonds of biological
determinism and understood to be social constructs, gender emerged
as a main stage for experimentation in self-representation. At the turn
of the century, certain British, French, and Russian writers, as well as
other elite artists, increasingly treated gender identity as a performative
self-fashioning.

This trend was embodied prominently in the figure of the male
dandy, who devoted excessively careful attention to his wardrobe and
grooming, thereby overstepping the bounds of what was considered
acceptable for men at that time. Since concern with refined appearance
was viewed as a woman's preoccupation, the public interpreted the
dandy's donning of dapper dress and use of appearance-enhancing
cosmetics like pomade as feminine behavior. The dandy re-constellated
mainstream codes of gender identity by exhibiting aesthetic preferences
and engaging in actions that were considered effeminate, which was
thematized in Decadent and Aesthetic literature in France and Britain,
respectively. The fin de siècle's most notorious fictional aesthete-dandy
was Des Esseintes, the hero of Joris-Karl Huysmans's novel *Against
Nature* (1884), whose obsession with material and sensual pleasures
challenged perceptions of his masculinity. Des Esseintes's sexual encounter with Miss Urania, a muscular American circus performer whose
masculinity eclipses his, points to his inverted gender preference.[1]
Another French writer, the frequently powdered and rouged Jean
Lorrain, was deemed as much a dandy as the hero of his arch-Decadent
story "Monsieur de Phocas" (1901). In Britain, Oscar Wilde demonstrated
a predilection for sartorial elegance and aesthetic pleasures, which his
conservative detractors read as signs of his homosexuality, thereby reinforcing perceptions that the dandy was overturning conventional
gender roles. The titular hero of Wilde's *The Picture of Dorian Gray* (1890),
described in the novel as being under the influence of a dangerous

French novel (which Wilde acknowledged to be *Against Nature*), embodied male vanity and sensual hedonism.

In Russia, amid the growing political destabilization in the years bridging the nineteenth and twentieth centuries, gender roles and typologies were similarly undergoing radical revision. The figure of the dandy appeared among Saint Petersburg's literary and artistic elite, although the correlation with homosexuality was not as direct as in France and Britian. Nikolai Gumilev and Sergei Makovsky, along with other members of the editorial staff at the prominent journal *Apollon*, dressed the dandy's part, but their refinement was not perceived as a sign of so-called sexual inversion. Makovsky even contemplated introducing a policy that required visitors to the journal's editorial office to wear dinner jackets.[2] In the cases of writer Mikhail Kuzmin and the character Larion Stroop from his groundbreaking 1906 novella *Wings*, sartorial flair and aesthetic refinement encoded the men's homosexuality. Kuzmin reportedly painted his eyes and lips, a practice that members of the Russian avant-garde adopted in the 1910s as part of their program to parody the figure of the Saint Petersburg dandy.[3]

Alongside such high-profile members of the artistic elite and their literary representations of the "feminized" male dandy were images of cross-dressing and sexually ambivalent or aggressive women. The same year Huysmans's novel appeared, Marguerite Vallette-Eymery published *Monsieur Venus* under the nom de plume Rachilde. Her novel's main female character uses the male name Raoule, wears men's clothing, and is a master equestrian and fearsome fencer who asserts her masculinity through athletic dominance and forceful personality. The work opens with Raoule ordering the costume of a water nymph bedecked with flowers to wear to a masquerade. This feminine costume stands in marked contrast to her masculine personality, which is why it constitutes appropriate masquerade attire. In tandem with Raoule's gender inversion, she comes close to inverting her sexual orientation when she fetishizes Jacques, the effeminate tailor who was to sew the flowers for her nymph costume. Like her heroine, the novel's author sported men's clothing in public, an act for which she had to seek special permission, as it was illegal in France.[4] Other women writers and performers in the west such as Vernon Lee and Sarah Bernhardt also wore men's clothing and stirred public consternation.

Russian writers Poliksena Solovyova (who used the pen name Allegro, with a neuter ending) and Gippius likewise donned men's clothing on occasion. The pianist I. Miklashevskaia and artist Elizaveta

Kruglikova also flaunted a masculine fashion sensibility that included articles of the male toilette.[5] While the growing popularity among women of sports such as bicycling and tennis, which called for donning bloomers, corresponded chronologically to the adoption of male fashions by female members of the artistic elite, it was nonetheless sensational for the average woman to wear such apparel on the streets outside of the progressive capital cities. A 1911 newspaper chronicled the "wild scene" that took place when a lady appeared in bloomers (*sharovary*) in Odessa on April 25th during the evening hours. According to the reporter, "the situation of the lady who took the risk of wearing the stylish outfit" came to a head when she decided to seek refuge in the hotel Frantsiia. "The crowd literally besieged the hotel," which was forced to close its iron shutters and lock its doors to keep at bay the raging throng.[6] It seems fitting that she found protection in Frantsiia, or France, in light of the fact that the fashion trend of the so-called skirt-bloomers (*iubka-sharovary*), which resembled modern-day harem pants, began that year in Paris and is likely what comprised the endangered lady's "stylish outfit."

Amidst the challenges to gender essentialism through external appearance emerged a theorization of a "third sex," the androgyne. Central to religious philosopher Vladimir Solovyov's conception of divine love were androgyny, sanctified flesh, and godmanhood. As Olga Matich observes, Solovyov's androgyne was theorized as a new type of human "representing the free union of the masculine and feminine principles, whose androgynous wholeness will reestablish in him the image and likeness of God."[7] In the circle of Gippius and her husband, Dmitry Merezhkovsky, Solovyov's ideas about the spiritual union of the male and female essence were translated on the physical plane into the image of the androgynous body. Solovyov's *The Meaning of Love* (1892–93) prompted alternative models of love and reproduction, in which traditional gender roles and sexual norms were reconsidered. Matich, who considers the dichotomy between Decadents and Symbolists to be an unproductive distinction in *Erotic Utopia*, lucidly explains that certain modernist writers, including Gippius and Merezhkovsky, rejected the dominant procreative heterosexual order in favor of a spiritually enlightened "erotic utopia" as part of a quest to overcome the inevitability of death. For them, the immortality of art and artistic creation stood in contrast to the mortal fruits of sexual procreation and its inevitable cycle of birth and death. For certain writers, creating art and stylizing life became one interrelated enterprise governed by the philosophy retrospectively known in Russia as "life-creation" (*zhizne-tvorchestvo*). In addition to Solovyov's idealized figure of the androgyne, Otto Weininger proposed in *Sex and Character* (written in 1903 and translated into Russian in 1908) that men and women shared traits of both sexes. Out of a common androgynous primordium emerged men, women, and individuals in between who exhibited mixed gender traits, one manifestation of which was homosexual tendencies. Weininger's work ignited vigorous debates among women's rights advocates and coincided with the revaluation of gender roles and sexual practices stirred by Solovyovian ideas.[8]

In the manner of a cautionary tale, the 1911 newspaper article "Disorder Because of Bloomers" cited above highlighted for its readers the potentially humiliating or even perilous consequences of women violating vestimentary norms.[9] Women's fashion magazines also subtly and perhaps unwittingly reinforced conventional gender identity through the prescriptions that accompanied some of their featured masquerade costume ideas. *Fashion World* and *Women's Affair* featured costume design recommendations for women and children that were intended to complement the wearer's identity rather than disguise it. *Fashion World*, for example, noted the age and gender of the children for whom certain costumes were considered appropriate. The January 1, 1904, issue categorized the costume "Fredrick the Great" as befitting boys age six or seven, while the thematically gender-neutral (but grammatically feminine) costume "World History" is recommended for thirteen- to fifteen-year-old girls. One year earlier the same magazine instructed women to dress in accordance with their physical appearance and disposition. The reader was counseled that the ancient Egyptian "Sphinx" costume primarily suits "shapely and tall individuals with a matte complexion and fluid movements." In contrast, the journal advises that the costume "Queen of Bells" ought to be worn by "merry and playful young individuals."[10] This prescriptive strategy runs contrary to the two principles on which masquerade costumes were traditionally premised: either they promised anonymity or they allowed for a creative expression of fantasy.

Outside of Russia women's changing social roles stirred up anxiety and critics adopted scholarly and pseudo-scientific arguments to indict Decadence as the culprit. Dismayed by the period's changing attitudes toward family structure and procreation exemplified by the dandy's feminine traits and the androgyne's asexuality, physician and social theorist Max Nordau saw the increasingly blurry division between

№ 1 Древне-египетскій костюмъ „Сфинксъ" для костю-
мированныхъ баловъ и вечеровъ.

№ 2. Маскарадный костюмъ „Королева колокольчи-
ковъ".

Figure 13. Illustration of the costumes "Egyptian Sphinx" (*left*) and "Queen of Bells" (*right*). (from
Fashion World, January 22, 1903; image courtesy of the Russian National Library)

Figure 14. Photo of Olga and Alexandra Stolypina in masquerade costumes resembling "Egyptian Sphinx" and "Queen of Bells" illustrated in figure 13. (from the studio of Carl Bulla; image courtesy of TsGAKFFD, Saint Petersburg)

sexes that the Decadent movement ostensibly incited as tantamount to evolutionary regression, a sure sign of civilization's decline. Drawing on the research of E. Ray Lankester regarding zoological organisms in "Degeneration: A Chapter in Darwinism" (1880), Nordau used the former's corrupted principles of Darwinian evolution to predict society's downfall in his treatise "Degeneration" (1892). Both provocative essays pivoted on corrupted evolutionary logic, which the scientist-scholar Herbert Spencer used to advocate for the reinforcement of extant gender roles and typologies in the mid-nineteenth century. An influential Darwinist whose works were translated into Russian as early as 1866 and who became something of a cult figure in Russia toward the end of the nineteenth century, Spencer posited that the highest level of human evolution consisted in the maximum differentiation of the sexes.[11] If the human race is to thrive, he concluded, men must become more manly and women—more womanly. His unimaginative and hubristic interpretation of Darwin's theory supposed that humans had reached their final state of development, and polishing the most essential biological difference, sex, was the final step to reach incarnated perfection.

Cross-Dressing and Impersonation

Like the binary paradigm of gender and sex promulgated by degeneration theorists, imitative cross-dressing locates the categories of masculine and feminine at the opposing ends of a single axis. The practice of dressing as someone ontologically opposite oneself was a dominant principle of costume selection in medieval folk mumming. Donning the clothing of the opposite sex was a common inversion, as was imitating the dead or figures from the nether world. The binary inversions of such essential traits as sex or vitality were also common to ancient carnival celebrations and produced a special kind of laughter, which Bakhtin called "carnival laughter." This regenerative laughter restores order after it had been upended in the carnival revelry: carnival laughter acknowledges the contingency of its object (social identity, for example) and thereby affirms its opposite. The act of temporarily renouncing identity in order to affirm it could take place only in public arenas or during ritual festivities where carnival laughter validated the absurdity of the inversion.

In a similar fashion, the female impersonators who temporarily inverted their gender on public cabaret and vaudeville stages in fin-de-siècle Russia were not viewed as subversive because their performances were clearly coded as theatrical play. Female impersonators, so-called "transformators," were staples of middlebrow culture.[12] Ikar Barabanov, for example, masqueraded as Isadora Duncan at the Crooked Mirror, a small theater in Saint Petersburg, which specialized in performance parodies.[13] Dressed in a gauzy Grecian-style toga and whirling about stage, Barabanov achieved a level of success that came close to that of Duncan herself. Another highly popular female impersonator, Alexander Galinsky, was described on his advertising poster as "a comic dancer, a parodist, and a playwright."[14] These professional cross-dressers were early drag queens who parodied tropes of femininity for the purpose of entertaining the public. Viewed as a type of discourse, their performance of gender appropriated select traits of womanliness and radically reoriented them to mock the contemporary dancing woman's fashionably styled self. As Bakhtin explained, the parodist "may make use of someone else's discourse for his own purposes, by inserting a new semantic intention into a discourse which already has, and retains, an intention of its own."[15] The two voices within parody are antagonistic: one voice attempts to appropriate the other for radically different purposes and does so in a hostile fashion. Through their exaggerated toilette and mannerisms, which produced a comical incongruity with their known identity as men, Barabanov and Galinsky converted feminine identity into an amusing spectacle. These gender "transformators" projected femininity as a construct on stage and were able to parody it precisely because of its constructedness: femininity was a collection of garments, accessories, and mannerisms that could be appropriated at will and manipulated for artistic effect.

The popularity of cross-dressing as public entertainment helps explain the cavalier attitude expressed in a newspaper article that exposed a gender-bending scandal. On January 29, 1910, *Utro Rossii* reported from the provinces that an anonymous voluptuary who wished "to drink in the air of women" (*vdykhat' atmosferu zhenshchiny*) had attended public masquerades on multiple occasions disguised as a member of the fairer sex. Cloaked in a convincing costume and using his small stature to avoid detection, he penetrated the ladies' lounge, where he lingered among the primping and gossiping ladies.[16] The lighthearted tone of the article confers upon the incident an anecdotal quality. By keeping the perpetrator anonymous and omitting any discussion of punishment, the humorous sketch distances the reader from the transgression and casts upon the scandal an entertaining aura. This journalistic tale of cross-dressing is completely devoid of indignation. In fact, it validates the provincial rogue's cleverness with the observation that ". . . our [Moscow] Lovelaces hadn't yet concocted" such a scheme "because of their paucity of imagination."[17]

While this escapade's entertainment value aligns it with the drag shows at cabarets, the roguish Lovelace adopted the appearance and behavior of a woman in order to be inconspicuous. He cultivated a disguise that he hoped would be perceived as authentic. In order to achieve his voyeuristic goals, he needed to style himself as closely as possible after the ladies among whom he mingled in the lounge: he engaged in an imitation of female identity. Imitation, as Bakhtin described it, "takes the imitated material seriously, makes it its own, directly appropriates to itself someone else's discourse."[18] The impish Lovelace at the masquerade tried to and temporarily succeeded in imitating the sum of womanly traits, which was facilitated by the fact that gender and other identifying markers are intentionally scrambled and therefore imperfect at costume balls. In contrast, the female impersonators did not strive to create the illusion of authenticity; their burlesques parodied attributes of female stage performers like Duncan, and effectively reinforced the male identity of the performers through their camp aesthetic.

In his study of French Decadence Leonard Koos likens the disruptiveness of cross-dressing to that of the pseudonym: both challenge notions of an authentic, stable self by revealing that appearances and names are mere masks. Although cross-dressing is a binary exchange and in this important way differs from the unbounded creative range of the potential pseudonym, both acts of masquerading highlight the principle of rupturing the relationship between signifier and signified. Fin-de-siècle experiments in cross-dressing demonstrated the arbitrariness of fashion as a system of signifiers; like other symbols with subjective meaning, garments depended on human interpretation. Uncoupling gender from clothing was analogous to separating a word's sonic attributes from its lexical meaning, which is an example of how Decadent experiments with self-representation mirrored Symbolist challenges to the prevailing notion of absolute semantic value. Scrambling sartorial codes and the correlation of name to person echoed the theoretical premise of the Symbol: meaning is contingent, not inherent. Subjectivity and personal interpretation enjoyed privileged status in Symbolism, the aesthetic tenets of which held that surface representations are not semantically stable, that an image or a sound intimates meaning but does not define a referent. The poetic assonance of language trumped its communicative function for certain poets, including Konstantin Bal'mont, Valery Briusov and Andrei Bely, who regarded music as the most emotionally powerful art form. In regard to both the poetic word and self-representation, signifier-signified relationships could be ruptured for the sake of creating an artistic effect.

Symbolists and Decadents in France and Aesthetes in Britain experimented with the artistic effect that the slippage between signifier and signified produced when they enacted metaphorical masquerades such as cross-dressing and the use of pseudonyms and lyrical masks. In Russia, however, these playful acts frequently acquired programmatic seriousness as an extension of the religious-philosophical ideas espoused by Solovyov. While Matich and Jenifer Presto have productively examined Gippius's self-fashioning in the context of Russian Symbolism and its ideological tenets, this study examines her performances of gender identity as part of the broader trend of feminine masquerades enacted among men and women in France, England, and Russia. It also expands Gippius's polemical range by putting her in dialog with the literary archetype of the Decadent femme fatale.

Gippius's Feminine Masquerade

Like the overwrought spectacles of femininity enacted by the "transformators" Barabanov and Galinsky, Gippius's own theatricalized femininity was regarded as caricaturish by her contemporaries Sergei Makovsky, Vladimir Zlobin, and Nina Berberova. In his recollections, Makovsky observed that Gippius's uniquely unfashionable wardrobe and her blatantly rebellious styling of hair and makeup symptomatized her "clear intention of being noticed": "there was a time she dyed her hair red and applied cosmetics in an exaggerated fashion ('proper' ladies in Russia at that time abstained from 'maquillage')."[19] Gippius's personal secretary Zlobin also noted the estranging effect of her clownish toilette: "At times she seemed unreal, as often happens with people of very great beauty or excessive ugliness. Brick-red rouge covering her cheeks and dyed red hair which looked like a wig."[20] In Zlobin's description Gippius's painted artifice created such an effective mask that he was drawn into ontological wonderment: Is she real or not? One of her contemporaries likewise noted that "there is something unnatural in her [. . .] something about her—certainly not her beauty—reminds me of the young woman in [Gogol's fantastic tale of sorcery] 'Vii.'"[21] Nina Berberova, underscoring Gippius's intentional artifice, went so far as to assert that Gippius "manufactured" an illusion of femininity, the constructedness of which was clear because, as she put it, Gippius simply "was not a woman."[22]

Gippius's amplification of feminine artifice bespoke a transgressive spirit because it rendered her appearance outside socially accepted norms. Not simply artifice (the application of cosmetics) but the excess of artifice (cosmetics garishly applied) points to the ironic nature of her feminine masquerade. Her manipulation of self into a caricature, a spectacle of femininity, relied on appropriating and redefining the tropes of womanliness as objectified by representations of the Decadent femme fatale. Gippius adopted the archetype's seductive artifice but exaggerated it to the point of parody and thus invested feminine toilette with her own critical intentions. Moreover, her masquerade in effect parodied the male writers who purported in their fictions to reveal the femme fatale's arsenal of cosmetic devices. Like them, she uncovered the falsity of the womanly toilette; she also uncovered the falsity of the mythical archetype itself.

Presto has examined Gippius's gender masquerades as sartorial and lyrical code-scrambling within the program of Symbolist life-creation. Presto suggests that Gippius's feminine caricature parodies prevailing representations of women: her gaudy self-styling was a polemical response to the image of the poetess circulating in the press and a strategy of artistic differentiation from the mystically inspired Eternal Feminine idealized by certain Symbolists. Presto points to the problematic conflation of woman as writing subject with the figure of the Eternal Feminine as a programmatic tendency in Symbolism against which Gippius positioned herself.[23] Gippius's accentuation of her earthly, physical body through cosmetic travesty may indeed be productively read as a protest against Symbolism's privileging of the Eternal Feminine as a dominant female archetype and the male-dominated movement that created it. Whereas Presto's study focuses on Gippius's engagement with the Symbolist image of the Eternal Feminine, I foreground her polemic with Decadent aesthetics embodied in the femme fatale.

Gippius actively played with her appearance and understood the polemical power of her image, which had been demonstrated for her by the satirical press in the early years of her career. Even before Blok's obsession with the Eternal Feminine idealized in the cycle "Poems about a Beautiful Lady" (1901–1902), Gippius was caricatured as an ethereal, fairy-like *dekadentka-prozaik* on the cover of the journal *Shards* (*Oskolki*) in 1895 (figure 15). As an artistic genre, the caricature irreverently stylizes an individual's face and body, often with polemical intent, making it a visual analogue to literary parody. In the journal's anonymous caricature, Gippius's enlarged face is attached to a small body wearing a white dress, a flowing white cape, and white butterfly wings. She stands on a book entitled "Miss Fay," likely a reference to the renowned American spiritual medium and mentalist Anna Eva Fay, who it is believed to have been a student of Madame Blavatsky and an adherent to the Spiritualist faith.[24] The name Fay also evokes the Russian word for fairy, *feia*, thereby reinforcing a connection to other worlds both spiritual and imaginary. In the caricature Gippius is mounted on and holds the reins of a white Pegasus, a creature suggestive of mythmaking and perhaps an allusion to speculations about Gippius's own hybrid nature as a hermaphrodite. Although she and Merezhkovsky did not inaugurate the Religious-Philosophical Meetings until 1901, this satirical sketch evoking contemporary trends in mystical thought which appeared six years before suggests that in 1895 she already represented for her detractors the antisocial tendencies of Decadence.

The satirical journal injected Gippius's image into public currency as an artistic construct, and its sardonic tone imbued her feminized image with a polemical message. Not only was the quality of her writing subject to judgment, but her (male) detractors had also appropriated her very likeness as part of their effort to belittle "Our Lady Writers." On the cover of *Shards* Gippius's body served as a cracked mirror in which to reflect the message of others: the representation of her physical self had been visually distorted and correlated with her station as a writer, thereby insinuating a lack of respect for both. The publication of this caricature came early in Gippius's career, establishing a precedent for using her body and its styled representation as a public discursive space, in particular one available for polemical purpose.

Gippius's femininity was caricatured most famously in 1907 by Dmitry Togol'sky (a.k.a. Mitrich), who portrayed her in a long white dress with her voluminous hair swept up into a lavish bouffant. She did indeed have a penchant for the modest, virginally white gown, the extreme length of which Mitrich exaggerated by pooling its fabric around her feet. The artist emphasized her extraordinary thinness, a

Figure 15. Caricature of Zinaida Gippius titled "Decadent-Writer." From *Oskolki* (1895). (image courtesy of TsGAKFFD, Saint Petersburg)

token of her androgyny, and placed a symbolic cigarette in her mouth, as well as an unusually long-handled lorgnette in one hand and a spider dangling from the other. Next to the caricature of Gippius is a line from her 1902 poem "White Clothing," which reads, "The Lord said: 'white clothing I shall send to the victor.'" The masculine egotism of this line is alluded to by the phallic cigarette and lorgnette handle, and clashes with her ladylike dress. Implied in both caricatures is Gippius's violation of the accepted mold for women writers: her own breaks with convention triggered corresponding breaks from realistic portraits and incited distortions of her physical image. Like those who caricatured her, Gippius understood that mannered constructions of her femininity served as a public exhibition space and a proxy for her voice.

Gippius consciously cultivated temporary public personae that travestied femininity to such a degree that they began to serve as a commentary on such constructions. French feminist theorist Luce Irigaray has termed the self-conscious appropriation of an ultra-feminine style *mimétism*, or "female mimicry," which she defined as a strategy for reclaiming the particular devices that undermine woman's power. While the self-consciousness and purposefulness of Gippius's feminine masquerades resonate with Irigaray's "female mimicry," the poet did not imitate or mimic traditional feminine style; she travestied it.

The Decadent Femme Fatale

With her brashly applied maquillage and its theatricalizing effect, Gippius laid bare the feminine toilette as a set of artistic devices. By exposing her appearance as cosmetically constructed, she mirrored how male writers of the period unmasked the artifice they saw as inherent in the cosmetic practices of the femme fatale. Gippius revealed the art and artifice of manufactured images and identities, especially of archetypes, and in this way she anticipated the Futurists' aggressive manipulation of their physical appearance, which was motivated by a wish to mock the Petersburg dandy. Like members of the Russian avant-garde in the 1910s, Gippius flagrantly deployed cosmetics in a fashion that was completely at odds with their supposed purpose of constructing classical beauty. In chapter 6 I discuss further the connections between the aesthetics of Decadence and the avant-garde.

While women frequently figured as victims in Decadent literature, they also had an alternate role as dangerous seductresses whose sex appeal armed them with a destructive power over men. The biblical tale of Salome, which inspired numerous literary and artistic iterations in Russia and Europe, vividly emblematized this dynamic for the Decadents.[25] Salome's suggestive dancing beclouded the mind of Herod who, intoxicated by her sensuality and the promise of his own sensory gratification, relented to her demand for John the Baptist's decapitation. Salome stands as the archetypal femme fatale among Decadents because her physical beauty masks her treachery. Feminine beauty was portrayed as even more insidious when it was an artificial illusion created with cosmetics. Thematized in many literary works, the falsity of the woman's toilette (including the deceptive application of powders and bodily padding) is a key attribute of many Decadent sirens. The perception of cosmetics as a mask-like perpetration of artifice is etymologically rooted. The *Oxford English Dictionary* posits the probable etymology of "mascara" as deriving from the Spanish *máscara* or the Italian *maschera* (Italian regional *mascara*), all of which signify "mask."

Resonant with the idea of cosmetics as disguise are the comments of the fictional Thomas Edison in Villiers de l'Isle-Adam's *Tomorrow's Eve* (1886). Edison wishes to comfort his heartbroken friend Ewald: "the axiom which summarizes these female witches in their relation to man is that their morbid and fatal influence on their victim is in direct ratio to the quantity of moral and physical artifice with which they reinforce—or, rather—overwhelm—the very few natural seductive powers they seem to possess."[26] Artifice, he says, is a defining quality of femininity for the men whom it threatens. The overt correlation of cosmetically enhanced appearance to treachery is also cast in the terms of parody, where parody is defined as a violation of nature. The narrator twice describes the cacophonous, unnatural human-like vocalizations of the birds in Edison's Underground Eden as a parody "of Life and of Glory."[27] Edison's world of artifice is a freakish travesty of nature and a renunciation of godly wonders. Such a violation of nature and piety is likewise embodied in the beautifully painted and corseted woman, according to Edison, who as proof shows Ewald the "true" image of the comely lass who drove another friend, Edward Anderson, to his death. Without her cosmetic deceptions, the real Miss Evelyn turns out to be "a little bloodless creature, vaguely female of gender, with dwarfish limbs, hollow cheeks, toothless jaws with practically no lips, and almost bald skull, with dim and squinting eyes, flabby lids, and wrinkled features, all dark and skinny."[28] In response to Ewald's horrified surprise, Edison smugly proclaims, "I see you've never really taken a serious accounting of the improvements in the art of make-up during these modern times!"[29] Miss Evelyn and Edison's electric birds both parody nature, one with her arsenal of prosthetics and paints, the other through Edison's "invention" of the magical power of electricity. Like Miss Evelyn's powdered construction of femininity, Gippius transgresses nature to create an artificial illusion. Gippius, however, wielded her artifice as a polemical weapon, not a weapon of seduction.

Charles Baudelaire's essay "In Praise of Cosmetics" (1860) inaugurated the conversation among Decadents about artificial enhancement of appearance. With seeming sincerity Baudelaire lauded cosmetics as a way for women to transcend nature and achieve a superior state of being. English essayist and caricaturist Max Beerbohm authored a parodic response to Baudelaire's piece entitled "A Defense of Cosmetics" (also known as "The Pervasion of Rouge," 1894). Beerbohm archly extolled women's elaborate toilette, proclaiming that "Artifice is the strength of the world, and in that same mask of paint and powder, shadowed with vermeil tint and most trimly penciled, is woman's strength."[30] His ardent justification of cosmetic artifice is overwrought, and his pseudo-scholarly tone belies the levity of the subject matter. This exaggerated disconnect between content and manner reveals Beerbohm's irreverence and parodic intent. In this particular essay Beerbohm's writing style itself acts as a cosmetic, transforming the banal topic of makeup into the subject of a learned polemic. Like the cosmetically enhanced woman, his language enacts artifice, its external form incongruous with its inner content-meaning. Beerbohm used the discourse of parody to treat the subject of artifice, thereby demonstrating that the latter (artifice) is at the heart of the former (parody) in form as well as content.

The discourse of parody, whether literary or performative, is itself an example of the Decadent aesthetic of artifice. Some critics believe that Huysmans's *Against Nature* parodies the dandy-aesthete, so extreme is the sensualism and so mannered is the writing. British Aestheticism boasted a wittiness and satirical playfulness that contrasted sharply with the disturbing motifs of perversion and despair typifying much of French and Russian Decadent literature. Wilde's play *The Importance of Being Ernest, A Trivial Comedy for Serious People* (1895), in which two main characters create fictitious personae for themselves, satirizes Victorian social conventions. Aubrey Beardsley, known best for his black ink drawings, also produced caricatures that included one of fellow Aesthete James McNeill Whistler, in which the American-born painter's slender fingers, dainty shoes, lush curly hair, and swelling hips code him as an effete dandy.

Beerbohm's overwrought parody of Baudelaire's essay differs from the sincerity of Tolstoy's attack on the cosmetically enhanced, sartorially bedecked women in *Kreutzer Sonata* (1889). The novella's narrator, Podznyshev, blames his wife for the fact that he murdered her, citing her artificial beauty and duplicitous charm. He complains, "Women have made themselves such a weapon for attacking the sense of men that a man cannot be in a woman's company with any calmness. As soon as a man approaches a woman, he falls under the influence of her spell and grows foolish. [. . .] It is something dangerous for men and contrary to law. I feel almost a compulsion to call the police, to summon protection from the peril, to demand that the dangerous object be removed and put out of sight."[31] In his retrospective self-analysis, Pozdnyshev indicts the bedazzling woman, decorated with ribbons and rouge, as a seductress whose sole arena for action and power over men is built around her sexual allure.

The cosmetic artifice of a young woman similarly betokens mortal danger for men in Sologub's story "The Poisoned Garden" (1908). In her garden of unnaturally exotic flowers, the Beautiful Lady extinguishes young men's lives with her poisonous kiss. Like the "enormous and too brightly-colored" flowers that emit a poisonous resin in her father's garden, the Beautiful Lady's splendor is artificial and perilous.[32] A nameless young woman cautions the youth against succumbing to the Beautiful Lady, deducing from her cosmetically enhanced appearance her sinister power: "Her beauty [. . .] is merely the dead allure of decay and corruption. I dare say she uses powder and rouge. She smells like a poisonous flower; even her breath is scented, and that is repugnant."[33] Literalizing the role of the femme fatale, the Beautiful Lady links artifice and peril.

Gippius's feminine masquerade fashioned with her gaudy makeup and ostentatious hair played an analogous role to Beerbohm's rhetoric in "A Defense of Cosmetics": she used it to flaunt the artifice of her self-representation and to draw into question the intention motivating her constructed image. In her conspicuous application of cosmetics, Gippius sabotaged the dominant male discourse of feminine artifice as a hallmark of the femme fatale by showing the discourse itself to be constructed, a fiction, as it was in Beerbohm's essay. Gippius's powdered construction of femininity was not a weapon of seduction but rather a travesty thereof. Her theatricalized appearance wrought through cosmetics, the ostensible weaponry of seduction, was incongruent with the avowed chastity of her marriage, her professed desire to extinguish her inner voluptuary, and her clear preference for the spiritual over the

carnal in her poetry.[34] Her playful experimentation with a garish feminine toilette, one bordering on the socially unacceptable and so at odds
with her transcendental concerns, in the context of Decadent literary
tropes reads as a polemical response to the femme fatale's cosmetic
arsenal and the movement that perpetuated the typology, as well as its
fetishizing of the artificial and the transgressive. Intentionally or not,
Gippius demonstrated that the cosmetic mask could signal a role, but
not the expected role of the femme fatale. Instead of signifying promiscuity and sexual rapaciousness, her feminine artifice directed attention
to the very fiction of the femme fatale as a literary type.

Gippius's Masculine Masquerade

Adopting a masculine mask for lyrical personae was common among
women writers in the nineteenth century, and it was a tradition that
Gippius continued into the early twentieth century. As she explained,
readers were accustomed to a male poetic voice, and its normativity
rendered it an unmarked poetic form. She wished for her poetry to be
classified not as women's writing but more universally as human. She
published under an array of names, ranging from Z. Gippius and
Ropshin, which merely masked her gender, to overtly male names such
as Lev Pushchin, Comrade Herman, and Anton Krainy (Anton "The
Extreme"), the last of which was the name under which Gippius published criticism of contemporary literature. The masculine side of
Gippius was captured in Lev Bakst's 1906 portrait of Gippius in which
the writer is dressed as a male dandy reclining insouciantly in finely
tailored riding breeches and sheer gray tights.

Presto has observed that Gippius styled her voice as a literary critic
in a fashion that evoked the male dandy's causticity, sarcasm, and
vanity, noting the "hint of Wildean dandyism in Gippius's critical
voice."[35] Several of the biting essays published in *The Literary Diary*
(1903–05) under the name of Anton Krainy derogate Decadence and
Decadent literature for an excessive privileging of aesthetics and a
self-indulgent disconnectedness from others. In much the same way
that Gippius modified her appearance as a polemical response to the
Decadent femme fatale and Symbolist Eternal Feminine, she also
modulated her critical voice as an attack on Decadent degeneracy.

Krainy's most vociferous condemnation appeared in the essay
"Decadence and Society," which identified the Decadents' fatal flaw as
isolationism. She condemned them for lacking " . . . the most intrinsic

qualities of the human soul: an inarguable feeling, like a knowledge, that I am not alone in the world, but surrounded by people like me."[36] Voicing a populist view that literature and writers must engage with society, Krainy bemoaned the fact that "Almost all poetry and literature, in as much as it is Decadent—is outside the movement of history, humanity, outside the battle between 'we' and 'I'; neither does this literature have anything to do with the movement of life and thought, nor life with it."[37] Krainy disparaged the Decadents as worse than individualists: at least the latter engaged in a dialog with society by trying to differentiate themselves from the masses. In contrast, such heroes of Decadent literature as Huysmans's Des Esseintes placed themselves not merely outside of society, but above it as well.

Krainy berated Blok for his individualist fantasy of the idealized Eternal Feminine and condemned his imaginary muse for being too veiled in mystery. "Tender Blok among the newest poets just keeps singing to himself about a Tsaritsa, a Virgin, who comes to him and is seen by him alone. He sees himself and her, for himself and for her does he compose his poems. [...] Enough casted allusions, unproven images, half-incarnated movements of the soul, signs, almost not words; for that reason Decadent poetry—it's not that it isn't poetry but for all of its deep, almost holy sincerity—it is half-poetry, half-art. It is a half-manifested something or other (*poluproiavlennoe nechto*), it is a half-born child, a premature fetus in the vast majority of cases."[38] It is hard to locate any Wildean wit or sarcasm in Krainy's grotesque imagery, which sooner recalls the seaminess Krainy condemned in the work of Leonid Andreev.

Krainy attacked the stories "In The Fog" and "The Abyss" for their "reverse aestheticism," by which he meant violence and psychosis. He lamented the animalistic impulses that Andreev illuminated and bemoaned the fact that Andreev was degrading himself, his readers, and art by throwing his "Godly gift" into the mud.[39] Krainy also criticized formal style, in particular the ornately alliterative verse, which the self-proclaimed leader of Russian Decadence Valery Briusov admired. He pointed to the absurdity of favoring assonance over meaning in his parody of Konstantin Bal'mont's poem "Veter, veter, veter, veter," ("Wind, wind, wind, wind,"). Krainy wrote two faux encomia beginning with "Valery, Valery, Valery, Valery!" the purpose of which was to mock Briusov's role as the sorcerer (*mag*) leading the Moscow Decadents, whom he viewed as only slightly better than the westernized, dandified Decadents of Saint Petersburg.

Literary Stylizations and Narrative Masks

Classifying writing style and narrative voice as either masculine or feminine is a fraught task. While Hélène Cixous argued in 1975 for a distinctive genre of *l'écriture féminine*[40] through which women could realize what she imagined to be an essential writerly difference from men, writers at the fin de siècle practiced the opposite by actively concealing and inverting their genders with narrative masks and pseudonyms. Russian and French Decadents widely employed pseudonyms and created gender-masking lyrical personae as creative experiments.[41] In the context of socio-political shifts at the turn of the last century, their gender-bending games seem to acquire a polemical dimension. However, Decadents typically avoided topical themes and advocated art for art's sake, one aspect of which was the experimentation with artistic media as such (an attribute it shared with the Russian avant-garde of the early 1910s). Guillaume Apollinaire, Barbey d'Aurevilly, Jean Lorrain, and Stéphane Mallarmé all published under female names and adopted female lyrical personae on at least one occasion. Most impressively, Mallarmé took over the editorship of the ladies' fashion magazine *La Dernière Mode* and published eight issues in 1874 comprised exclusively of articles, reviews, and recipes that he penned under an array of pseudonyms. The fictional female contributors included society reporter Miss Satin, fashion and culture critic Marguerite de Ponty, and a Creole cook who signed her recipes "Olympe, negresse."[42] Rhonda Garelick has observed that the journal's "preciousness of tone and theatricality" make it "a precursor of a modern drag performance," suggesting that Mallarmé's overwrought spectacle of femininity amounted to a "deft parody" of the fashion magazine genre.[43] His playful textual "drag performance" elicited an amused admiration for his cleverness akin to that enjoyed by parodist-impersonators like Barabanov on Russian stages.

In another well-known instance, Guillaume Apollinaire published a review of Colette (then using the moniker Colette Willy[44]) in the literary journal *Les Marges* under the pseudonym of Louise Lalanne in March 1909. It was part of a series of articles on women's literature for which he wrote the introduction and other reviews under his own name (which was, in fact, an adopted name[45]). Apollinaire reportedly lifted much of the material for Lalanne's review from the notebook of his mistress Marie Laurencin. Like Mallarmé, Apollinaire created a female persona for dealing with presumptively female subjects (fashion and women writers), although his was not a parody. In aspiring to create a credible female narrative voice for Lalanne, Apollinaire objectified woman's discourse: he appropriated it and redeployed it without changing its message. Bakhtin noted that objectified discourse may sound original because the objectifier's "intention does not penetrate inside the objectified discourse," even though the objectifier has over-taken the utterance for his own purposes.[46] Apollinaire objectified Laurencin's writing by usurping her voice while still respecting her opinion and message.

The Stylized Persona of Cherubina de Gabriak

In November 1909 (the same year as Apollinaire's Louise Lalanne review), twelve poems by the fresh poetic sensation Cherubina de Gabriak appeared in *Apollon*, a journal dedicated to the visual and literary arts that served as an outlet first for Symbolist and later for Acmeist poetry. Cherubina was, in fact, a lyrical persona fashioned by poets Elizaveta Dmitrieva and Maksimilian Voloshin.[47] She possessed an exotic yet familiar voice, which burned with youthful passion and captivated her male readership—in particular, the male collaborators at *Apollon*. The artful manipulation of men's hearts (most notably that of the journal's chief editor, Sergei Makovsky) by this fabricated female persona whose appeal was predicated largely on tropes of femininity is a type of gender masquerade, although one quite distinct from Gippius's flamboyant parody. Whereas Gippius exposed the concept of manufactured identity by nurturing the conspicuous illusion of artifice, Dmitrieva wished to conceal her lyrical masquerade by perpetuating the illusion of authenticity. The success of Dmitrieva's ruse depended not on her ability to imitate a preexisting style or discourse, as was the case with the voyeuristic Lovelace who dressed as a woman to infiltrate the ladies' lounge, as reported in *Utro Rossii*. Rather, it required that she (together with Voloshin) craft a compelling voice that was stylized so as to resemble other female poets closely enough to feign credibility, and yet also to stimulate the journal editors' fantasies of their ideal female poet.

The lyrical voice of Cherubina was that of a half-Russian, half-French young woman of noble birth, sequestered in Spain at a Catholic monas-tery and torn between a lofty, transcendental life devoted to Christ, and the powerful stirrings of erotic passion. Cherubina was the archetypal dichotomy of Mary and Eve who simultaneously embodied exalted, virtuous purity and expressed sensual yearnings. In the poem "My dream brings me close to pride . . ." the lyrical self confesses to having "the temptations of sin" in her, and proclaims that she does "not know pure sanctity." She stands at the gate between heavenly and earthly love, and is on the verge of rejecting the call of her Heavenly Groom as her forbidden thoughts cause her vow of chastity to flicker like "a dimming icon lamp" before her holy duty. Her direct appeals to Christ's flesh, pain, passion, and blood draw attention to his carnality, which exerts the power of temptation and holds the promise of salvation. In the poem "Your Hands," Cherubina sensually describes her nighttime fantasy of wrapping Christ's hands in garlands of roses, an act she describes as both "gratifying" and "sweetly transgressive." Her focus on Christ's hands, his organs of touch, again emphasizes his physicality, in particular his Passion (the Crucifixion), in which his body suffers for his beliefs.

The poem "Retrato de una niña" similarly juxtaposes carnal sensuality with the religious injunctions against it. Gazing into a mirror, the lyrical persona describes the image she sees as strikingly Christ-like: the chestnut curls seem to be bathed in golden powder and to form a nimbus around the face. Blackening blood on the shoulder and the mouth contorted into a grimace evoke Christ's suffering on the cross. A muffled, mysterious voice rumbles and in it can be heard "The piety of blasphemous speeches, / The daring causticity of a barbed rebuke, / And all the possibilities of temptation and sin, / And all the shining of mystical candles." The conflict between piety and blasphemy, humility and daring, emerges full force in the final line, in which Cherubina addresses the image she sees in the mirror as "My sister in Christ and in Lucifer." (In other poems Cherubina speaks to her double, in an allusion both to her persona's inner struggle and to Cherubina's double identity as the penname of Dmitrieva.) Cherubina's poem "Crucifixion" portrays the lyrical persona as a supplicant to Christ, who ardently awaits his descent from the cross. She alludes to the dual nature of her devotion, confessing that "No one has yet guessed, / Why my look is so full of alarm, / Why I always return last, / From the Sunday Mass, / Why my lips tremble, / When the cloud of incense spreads / In a barely bluish lace." Despite the curses of monks and the pit of fire that awaits the fallen, the lyrical persona declares that she has purchased from the "sorceress" Astarte (a pagan goddess known by the Greeks as Aphrodite) "a bitter stone of love." The way Cherubina's devotional passion becomes conflated with erotic stirrings echoes distantly the Decadent treatment of religion: Huysmans, Wilde, and Walter Pater, among others, integrated the religious with the aesthetic and the erotic in their writings.[48] The Decadent religious experience was marked by hallucinations, visions, desire, fervor, and ecstasy—all of which closely resembled drug-induced rapture. Decadence valued the full range of intense bodily sensations, including pain: the self-flagellation, hair shirts, and practices of asceticism that the Catholic Church demanded coincided with the French Decadent sensibility.

It has been suggested that the eroticism of Cherubina's verse was influenced by the love poetry of Mirra Lokhvitskaia, dubbed the Russian Sappho, whose poetic career reached its height during the first decade of the twentieth century. Lokhvitskaia was the first female writer in Russia to have published poetry that gave voice to women's sexual desire.[49] Literary critic Tatiana Alexandrova asserts that "the mysterious Spanish beauty [Cherubina] was an image stylized to a high degree, but in that stylization much was appropriated from Lokhvitskaia and taken to the logical end."[50] Alexandrova and others have pointed to possible intertextual allusions, as between Cherubina's "My dream brings me close to pride . . ." and Lokhvitskaia's "Holy flame" (1902–1905), which begins, "In mad pride do they vainly blame my dream."[51] In her autobiography, Dmitrieva admits that "Mirra exerted a very strong influence on me—in childhood (13–15 years old) I considered her the unattainable ideal and I would tremble when reading her poetry."[52] By pointing out her adolescent fondness for Lokhvitskaia, Dmitrieva suggests that Lokhvitskaia's themes and style appealed to her romantic imagination when her creative consciousness was still forming.

Lokhvitskaia fashioned a stylized poetic discourse that Briusov described as full of "emotional passion, heroic egoism, [and] scorn for the crowd"; in short, he called it "poetry of true demonism."[53] In contrast to her claims of modesty and virtue, her poetic voice was one that hinted at an urgent sensuality. Her "Hymn to my beloved," in which she writes, "I rush to tear off the bracelet / unfasten my jewelry / My trembling breast yearns / For unknown happiness." The final stanza concludes, "I will enter your mysterious temple, / Prepare your conjugal caresses / My dear and only one / Quench my love!" Lokhvitskaia assiduously tried to distance what she maintained was her quiet domestic life from the intense, passionate verse for which she was known, once insisting that she was "the most chaste married woman in Petersburg," as if to counterbalance assumptions about her lasciviousness.[54]

The Madonna-Sappho opposition between Lokhvitskaia's personal life and her poetry highlights the constructedness of one or both identities (she was, after all, reputed to have been Briusov's lover). As has been noted elsewhere, "In her poetry she gave in to 'exaltations' and 'ecstasies'; however, the amorous passion in her poetry was, to a significant degree, conditional, decorative, smacking of literariness, and her 'Bacchic' element was contrived (naigrana)."[55] Lokhvitskaia intentionally crafted a shockingly libidinal lyrical voice, one that did not imitate any predecessor. She stylized the poetic discourse of Sappho's original ancient-Greek verse by adopting from it certain distinctive devices and using them to the same ends as Sappho herself. The distinctiveness of her lyrical persona in fin-de-siècle Russia left it vulnerable to parodies written by others, including ones that appeared in 1901 in The Star (issues 41, 43, 46) and New Times (Nov 5). Some lampoons were even published under Lokhvitskaia's own name.[56]

Cherubina was a uniquely stylized persona created to stir the romantic imagination of journal editor Makovsky and other male readers. Dmitrieva and Voloshin succeeded in surreptitiously eliciting Makovsky's fantasies about Cherubina, which they then incorporated into their realization of her, thereby making Makovsky a victim of his own clichéd romantic imagination. Voloshin stated in his memoirs that when it came to women, Makovsky had a well-known preference for glamorous high-society women and sylphlike ballerinas, implying that Dmitrieva—a plain schoolteacher with a chronic limp—lacked the sex appeal needed to capture his attention and compel him to publish her poems. In order to seduce Makovsky's editorial sympathy, Cherubina thus needed to be a self-assured beauty of noble birth with rare artistic gifts and unparalleled spiritual depth. Dmitrieva and Voloshin cleverly enlisted Makovsky's creative energy in fashioning Cherubina: it was he, for example, who decided that she was sequestered in a monastery in Toledo, and it was he who "divined" Cherubina's nationality based on her handwriting. These details were incorporated into Cherubina's biography. Makovsky quickly fell in love with his fantasy of Cherubina, his amorous feelings flamed by her poetic expressions of religious ecstasy that verged on, and at times were conflated with, sexual passion. Makovsky later confessed that "no other woman coincided so completely with my dream woman" as did Cherubina.[57] Makovsky's sincere efforts at courtship—he sent her lavish bouquets of flowers and persistently called her on the telephone—propelled the literary ruse into real life.

Dmitrieva penned poetic lampoons of Makovsky's naïve credulousness under her own name, the detached tenor of which suggested a playful insouciance. One such poem from November 1909, the same month that the Cherubina affair came to its climax, is "Spanish Sign" (*Ispanskii znak*), which chronicles some of the more embarrassing episodes for Makovsky in his relationship with Cherubina. It is the one surviving poem from a purported series of satirical poems and epigrams. The poem foregrounds moments when the myth of Cherubina as a literary and epistolary construct crossed over from art into life. For instance, Makovsky invited Cherubina to attend an exhibit of women's portraits organized by *Apollon* and sent her a ticket. Cherubina, however, sent her "cousin," Don Garpia di Mantilya, a Portuguese diplomatic attaché, in her place. The second stanza of the poem alludes to this incident in the lines "And next to her was Fernando, / A young Spanish attaché." On another occasion, Cherubina told Makovsky that she would be attending a certain ballet performance and that he would be able to find her there. Makovsky strained to pick out the most beautiful woman in attendance, sure that it would be his beloved; naturally, it was not. Cherubina mocked Makovsky by sending him a message the next day, "I'm sure that you liked that one [particular woman] . . ." (*Ia uverena, chto Vam ponravilas' takaia-to*).[58] The poem alludes to this event in the fourth stanza with a reference to the Countess Z (Makovsky had conferred upon her the title of countess, imagining her noble lineage) giving a "Spanish sign" to her admirer from the dark loge where she sat. Cherubina also breached the art-life divide by conversing with Makovsky on the phone, a practice alluded to in the poem's third stanza ("not infrequently did the telephone ring").[59]

The playfully mocking tone of "Spanish sign" locates Cherubina, and by extension Dmitrieva, in a position of power vis-à-vis the manipulated Makovsky. Joan Riviere theorized how such a stylized feminine mask garners power or authority for the female stylizer in her landmark 1929 essay "Womanliness as Masquerade." Riviere asserted that women perform their femininity in an accentuated way when they want to claim so-called masculine traits, such as intelligence and professional competence, but are afraid of public censure. The mask of femininity, typically constructed through flirtatious behavior and coquettish dress, mitigates an "inappropriate" display of male attributes and deflects accusations of the woman invading male territory.[60] Framed in terms of Riviere's theory, Cherubina could be viewed as Dmitrieva's feminine mask that enabled her to enter a man's world of poetry: were it not for her enticingly feminine lyrical front, Dmitrieva would not have had access to the male literary establishment. Poet Marina Tsvetaeva averred this theory in regard to Dmitrieva, whose "unattractiveness of face and life interfered with her [poetic] gift." According to Tsvetaeva, Dmitrieva was able to overcome those obstacles through the alluring persona of Cherubina.[61]

Maksimilian Voloshin's participation in the construction of Cherubina de Gabriak, however, complicates an argument about the lyrical persona serving as Dmitrieva's feminine mask to penetrate the male-dominated institution of literature. Voloshin was the mastermind behind the creation of a lyrical mask, and in "History of Cherubina" he claimed responsibility for coining the fictional poet's last name.[62] His main role in producing the performance of Cherubina consisted of penning frothy letters to Makovsky to accompany Dmitrieva's submissions of poetry. A member of Symbolist literary circles, Voloshin was an avid myth-maker who was known for donning ancient Greek costumes at his summer home in Koktebel'.[63] He favored a homespun orange mantel (*khlamida*) or a loose white canvas garment (*balakhon*) accessorized with a laurel-leaf crown, sandals, and a shepherd's staff. Voloshin encouraged his Koktebel' guests to dress in a similar fashion and he enjoyed organizing them into outdoor processions.[64]

Voloshin's penchant for theatricalization extended from his Crimean recreation to his literary mystifications. Tsvetaeva recalled how Voloshin proposed that she, too, adopt a pseudonym. Citing the fact that she wrote enough poems for two, he implored her to publish her poems about Russia under a nom de plume. According to Tsvetaeva, he relished the idea of collaborating with her to create the lyrical personae of "genius twins," brother and sister poets, but she resisted his proposal.[65] Because of Voloshin's well-known eccentricities, many suspected that it was he who wrote the Cherubina poems. He claimed that he never could have written them because the lyrical voice was not his, a comment that suggests an essentialist understanding of authorial voice that is at odds with the period's active narrative experimentations and Voloshin's own role-playing.

In the context of fin-de-siècle challenges to gender roles and sexual normativity, it is tempting to assign polemical value to Cherubina's stylized femininity. Solomon Volkov has noted that the hoax had elements of parody and suggested unconvincingly that it was intended to mock Petersburg's Symbolist establishment and its dream of "a new poetic female star."[66] To read Cherubina as a parody in the Bakhtinian sense would mean that Dmitrieva and Voloshin appropriated the poetic style of another and used it to express ideas that were contrary to the original utterance. Cherubina, however, was an original figure. Although her erotic poetry may have been influenced by Lokhvitskaia's, it was nevertheless uniquely stylized via the Decadent trope of sensualized Catholicism.

Cross-dressing, pseudonyms, and narrative and lyrical masks enabled men and women alike to enact masquerades of femininity for polemical or playful purposes at the beginning of the twentieth century. Amidst the roiling social upheavals taking place in Russia around the year 1905, issues of gender identity and sexual orientation became politicized and philosophical. The popularity of cross-dressers on middlebrow cabaret and vaudeville stages reflected the anxiety that the rampant challenges to gender roles provoked in the mainstream public. The camp aesthetic, which characterized drag queens then as now, signaled the parodic intent of the stage "transformators." On certain occasions at literary salons, Gippius similarly represented her femininity as a vulgar assembly of cosmetics and unfashionable clothing, thereby parodying the dominant discourse of cosmetic artifice that surrounded the Decadent femme fatale. Whereas Gippius's travesties of the feminine toilette's purpose of beautification resonated polemically, the stylized lyrical persona of Cherubina de Gabriak evinced playful fantasy fulfillment. Dmitrieva and Voloshin selectively adopted traits of the archetypal Mary and Eve to fashion a distinctively seductive persona. Absent an antagonistic wish to undermine either archetype, the voice of Cherubina resonates as a stylization of both discourses.

The feminine masquerades of Gippius and Dmitrieva foreground a defining element of Russian modernism: contingency. As paradigms in the social and physical sciences shifted from the static to the dynamic and relativistic, constructs formerly viewed as essential were recognized as conditional. Although gender categories remained intact, the destabilization of gender identity, especially among the artistic elite, was both a sign of the period's turbulent Zeitgeist and a manifestation of the artist's new experimental relationship to his material of craft. Symbolism encouraged a loose relationship between signifiers and the objects they denote, freeing garments of clothing, names, and narrative voices from the confines of strictly denotative meaning. The following chapter discusses how destabilized practices of signification and the period's emergent spirit of individualism produced a new interest in metaphorical costume designs at modernist masquerade balls.

Part II

Costume Design and Theatricality

4

⊱─┤─◆⟩─●─⟨◆─┤─⊰

Figurative Costumes
Metaphors in Text and Textile

The fundamental premises of costume design underwent a reconceptualization at the fin-de-siècle costume balls organized by students of the Russian Imperial Academy of Arts in Saint Petersburg. The result was a new artistic medium that combined elements of collage and theater to produce an innovative articulation of modernism's emergent individualism. In the eighteenth and early nineteenth centuries, masked balls emphasized personal disguise and anonymity. By the late nineteenth century, however, costume balls (balls at which guests wore costumes and occasionally masks) had eclipsed masked balls (balls at which guests primarily wore half-masks and formal attire) in popularity. At costume balls, the modernist approach to costume design was predicated on personal opinion and originality. The function of the modernist costume was to celebrate the individual of exceptional creativity, who would be awarded a public prize that would attest to her artistic sensibility and guarantee social recognition. Innovative approaches to costume design came about after the state's control of visual and performing arts in Russia weakened in the 1870s–1880s.[1] The unbridled experimentation in costume design represented a vital yet heretofore marginalized prelude to Russia's Silver Age cultural florescence.

At the Academy's 1907 Artists' Ball, the costume "Duma" took first prize for originality. A journalist reported that "the [costume-] wearer's legs were wrapped in a bag, in his hands he held a slice of bread and a bag of flour, and on his head stood the Duma building with the captions, 'Excessive confidence,' and 'There was no trace of evil intent.' Also on the Duma building waved two flags, and there were two arrows inscribed with [the names of popular newspapers] '*Novosti*,' '*Peterburgskii listok*,' '*Novoe vremia*,' and '*Peterburgskaia gazeta*.'"[2] What message did this costume wearer seek to convey with his ready-made props and textual excerpts, which defined the costume to a much greater degree than his actual garments of clothing? The verbal description alone reveals that this costume was not intended merely to represent the existence of the two-year-old Duma as a legislative body. The props—bread in hand, Duma building on the head—indicate that the wearer wished to disseminate a political message, which, as the bag around his legs suggests, was cloaked in allegory. More important than decoding this particular allegorical outfit is understanding how such costumes expressed meaning, and how this type of figurative, polemical costuming constituted a sharp split from the previous era's masquerade costumes.

The wearers of these costumes, which I call conceptual costumes, sought not to obfuscate or supplant their identity, as had been the goals of masquerade costume in eighteenth and early nineteenth centuries. Whereas the costume wearer's identity had formerly been the chief enigma at masquerades, it was the message of the fin-de-siècle conceptual costume wearer that now constituted the interpretive challenge. Unlike recognizable character costumes and unlike the black half-mask and domino, which operated via the complete effacement of identity, the conceptual costume was intensely personal: it frequently exhibited the individual's creativity, or expressed her opinion or beliefs. I characterize such costumes as conceptual or figurative because of their non-literal and non-linear construction: as artistic arrangements of garments, props, and pieces of text, these costumes approximated the collage in their modernist rejection of traditional representational art.

The Artists' Ball conceptual costumes, which relied on the wearer's and viewer's cognitive and imaginative engagement, resemble the allegorical costumes worn at the masquerade ball in Leonid Andreev's *Black Maskers* (1908). Both conceptual and allegorical costumes were hermeneutic puzzles. While such costumes were innovative, they risked narrative failure: the wearer's (and writer's) message was encoded in a portable fashion, while the beholder (and reader) played a key role in the reception and creation of meaning. This chapter examines how figurative costumes both rely on and problematize conventional practices of signification and interpretive strategies. Figurative costumes enjoyed a spike in popularity around the turn of the century, which corresponded to the rising influence of the Symbolist literary movement in Russia. The poetics of Symbolism, which were heavily reliant on metaphor and associative thinking, closely resembled the aesthetic principles governing the period's figurative costumes. The comparison of fin-de-siècle literary and sartorial poetics brings into sharper focus how the modernist's individualism ramified as a potential semiotic crisis arising out of subjectivity.

Artists' Balls

The Academy of Arts, founded in 1757, offered instruction in painting, sculpture, and architecture. By the mid-nineteenth century, the Academy's pedagogical institute was admitting all qualified students, regardless of their social class and financial circumstances. The students began organizing fund-raising events for their indigent peers in 1871. The benefit evenings, which would evolve into the lavish Artists' Balls, were initially comprised of concerts, literary readings, art exhibits, dancing, and tableaux vivants, in different combinations. The activities closely resembled those of the Academy's "watercolor Fridays" (*akvarel'nye piatnitsy*), which one program described as "an entertaining, humorous, fantastical, picturesque, [and] decorous evening of music and dance with games and costumes"[3] and which had enjoyed popularity since December 1861. A newspaper account of one such "Friday" in 1899 conveys a less carnivalesque event, with a refined, club-like atmosphere in which artists debated, played chess, sketched, and listened to live music.[4] In 1885, however, instead of the usual program, the students undertook to organize a costume ball, which was billed as an "artistic carnival" (*artisticheskii karnaval*). The costume ball, accompanied in the same evening by such earlier-established components as themed processions and tableaux vivants, enjoyed unprecedented success and thus became an annual event. Seven years later in 1892 students at L'École des Beaux-Arts in Paris began hosting similar evenings, called Bals des Quat'z-Arts. While the French balls did not have a philanthropic purpose, they did share with the Russian Artists' Balls the interweaving of artistic media in a theatrical framework, as underscored by their very name, a bastardized rendition of *quatre arts*, i.e., the "four arts" (painting, engraving, sculpture, and architecture) studied at L'École. The nature of costumes represented another important difference between balls at the Saint Petersburg Academy and those at L'École: whereas the Russian Artists' Balls distinguished themselves with ornate and fanciful costumes, the French balls subordinated sartorial innovation to a different kind of marked physical appearance—nudity.[5]

By 1892 the Artists' Balls had reached such a level of sophistication and refinement that organizer and secretary of the Aid Office Nikolai Tsirigoti could boast in a letter to the mayor: "Since 1889 our balls have been losing their resemblance to student events and becoming as good as other artistic-costume balls in Petersburg. . . . According to reviews in the newspapers, our ball is considered the best."[6] Such prominent artists as Ivan Aivazovsky, Lev Bakst, Vladimir Beklemishev, Alexander Benois, Dmitry Kardovsky, Arkhip Kuindzhi, Evgeny Lansere, Anna Ostroumova-Lebedeva, and Vasily Vereshchagin, among others, lent their talents, designing invitations, creating floats for the processions, decorating the halls, and donating paintings as lottery or best-costume prizes. Ostroumova-Lebedeva, for example, recalled making garlands of paper flowers out of colored cigarette paper.[7] Arkady Rylov, a former Academy student, recounted a similar experience in his memoirs, noting that it was "the female students" (*uchenitsy*) who made paper flowers and garlands with which to festoon the halls,[8] suggesting that there existed a gendered division of creative labor, with the more tedious work falling to the women. According to Rylov and Pyotr Neradovsky, also an Academy student at the time, everything from the invitations and poster designs to decorations for sets and kiosks was selected through competitions; thus was creativity spurred and top-quality work assured. Regarding the intensity of energy and imagination that the art students poured into preparing for these events, their professor Kuindzhi once lamented: "They exert so much effort; if only they painted pictures like that."[9]

The success of the costumes at the Artists' Balls was judged at the evenings' costume contests, in which prizes (principally works of art executed and donated by professors) were awarded "for the beauty, refinement, and [most importantly] wittiness," of their costumes.[10] During the heyday of the Artists' Balls, from the late 1880s to 1909, the costumes represented a form of innovative artistic expression.[11] Students, including Bakst, who helped validate fashion as an artistic enterprise in Russia, cherished the opportunity to immerse themselves in the

Figure 16. Advertising poster for the Artists' Ball "Fairytale Ball" by Nikolai Gerardov (1901). (State Russian Museum, Saint Petersburg; reproduced from Iuliia Demidenko, ed., *Veseliashchii-sia Peterburg*)

Figure 17. Advertising poster for the Artists' Ball "Ball of
Flowers" by E. A. Kiseleva (1903). (State Russian Museum,
Saint Petersburg; reproduced from Iuliia Demidenko, ed.,
Veseliashchiisia Peterburg)

Figure 18. Advertising poster for a Greek-themed Artists' Ball by unknown artist (1907). (State Russian Museum, Saint Petersburg; reproduced from Iuliia Demidenko, ed., *Veseliashchiisia Peterburg*)

Figure 19. Photo of artists and guests at an Artists' Ball at the Imperial Academy of Arts (1912). (image courtesy of TsGAKFFD, Saint Petersburg)

light-hearted, creative revelry, the likes of which was sanctioned by the notoriously conservative Academy of Arts only once a year. The student-creators thus used the Artists' Balls as an occasion on which to indulge their creative whimsy and express themselves freely, outside the constraining parameters of the Academy's classical mandate.

Conceptual Costumes

The novelty of costumes at the Artists' Balls emerges in vivid relief when contrasted with traditional costuming, the latter of which revolved around the mimicry of a person different from oneself in terms of gender, profession, nationality, or age. Costumes at the fin-de-siècle Artists' Balls, and those concurrently advertised in women's fashion magazines, however, began to popularize the practice of dressing as an idea, a polemical position, or a whimsical non-anthropomorphic object. Costumes representing intangible concepts and functional items implied that the body, the quintessential physical emblem of our humanity, could also serve as an instrument for temporarily displacing that most essential pillar of our identity. This practice is taken to the extreme in Andreev's play *Black Maskers*, in which the figurative costume is not merely a surrogate for the individual; it subsumes him.

The artists' costumes, which were often whimsical, highly complex, and ornate, demonstrated a new interest in using the body as an exhibition space in which imagination and polemic replaced character imitation. The avant-garde costumes at the Artists' Balls represented a departure from the traditional character costume's heavy reliance on textile signification in the form of national dress or professional uniform. The latter type of costume, which I address in the next chapter, was still ubiquitous at entrepreneurial masquerades attended by a mass audience, however. Examples of costumes at the Artists' Balls reported in the newspapers of the day include "Journalism" (*Pressa*), "Finnish Steam-Shipping" (*Finskoe parokhodstvo*), "The French Naval Squadron" (*Frantsuzskaia eskadra*), "Tobacco Factory" (*Tabachnaia fabrika*), and "The Duma," which is the lower house of parliament (*Duma*).[12] This shift in the conceptualization of public costuming bespeaks an interest in nonmimetic representation: the conceptual costume sought not to reproduce and thereby temporarily adopt the identity of another. Rather, its strategy for signification relied on the constructability of an original narrative and on the interpretive abilities of its beholder. The conceptual costume's capacity for polemic, its implied voice, distinguished it from other types of fanciful costumes and illustrated how sartorial semiotics could acquire a social agenda.

Whereas a character costume's visual iconicity evoked an established narrative or elicited an already-crystallized set of associations, the conceptual costume conveyed ideas and opinions, its rebus-like components constructing a narrative for the beholder without the assistance of linear arrangement. The fragmented nature of the Duma costume, the signifying parts of which had to be assembled in accord with the nonlinear human body, suggests the conceptual costume's formal affinity with collage, the appropriation and creative rearrangement of existing images and words. However, the medium of collage—born amongst the cubists and futurists—implies a juxtaposition of dissimilar elements undertaken with the subversive purpose, as art historian Christine Poggi explains, of either undermining "compositional and material unity" or underscoring "the arbitrary . . . character of representational signs."[13] Conceptual costume-makers, however, did not envision any subversive semiotic dissonance or divestment of meaning. On the contrary, they relied heavily upon, and reaffirmed the meanings of, ready-made objects as defined within a shared cultural imagination. Another key difference between visual collage and the assemblage of conceptual costumes is the fact that the latter were animated by their wearers, bringing to the fore a fourth dimension, time, and with it, action. Costumes that strove to convey a unique narrative message benefited from the power of a second semiotic system, the physical gestures of theater and pantomime.

Conceptual costumes were neither deliberately dissonant in their composition nor subversive in their formal deconstruction. Many actually aimed for narrative cohesiveness. Conceptual costumes did, however, occasionally display the wearer's irreverence in the form of parody and satire. The transgressiveness of parody relies on exaggeration and showiness—traits highly valued in the competitive masquerades of the Artists' Balls. Some tendentiously satirical costumes employed parody's mechanism of formal hyperbole as a visual articulation of subversion. Appearing at the ball in 1892 was a costume called "The 121st Aivazovsky Exhibit," which comprised numerous miniature copies of the titular artist's paintings pinned to the wearer. The proliferation of similar or identical signifiers (such as dozens of Aivazovsky reproductions) could, as Walter Benjamin theorized, eviscerate the content-meaning of the original. The ease of mechanically reproducing an original work of art at the turn of the century removed its aura; its value, both economic and semiotic, was diminished. With the "121st Aivazovsky Exhibit" costume, the multiplicity of copies of the artist's paintings usurped the voice and signifying power wielded by a singular original. The hyperbolic nature of the costume's overabundant reproductions of Aivazovsky's works signaled its status as satire, effectively lampooning the repetitiveness of this prolific waterscapist's subject matter and the excessive number (in the wearer's view) of his exhibitions.

Another such conceptual costume that relied on repetition to express a polemical position was entitled "The Wanderers' Exhibit" (*Peredvizhnaia vystavka*). The Wanderers (*Peredvizhniki*) was a group of civic-minded painters who held that art should serve a social function. They used the canvas to portray Russian life as it was, in its rural simplicity or urban cruelty, and inaugurated traveling exhibitions (hence their name) aimed at bringing art to the people. Because of their philosophical differences with the state-sponsored Academy of Arts (namely, their wish to portray specifically Russian scenes, which opposed the Academy's Classical mandate), the artists who would form the Society for Traveling Art Exhibitions (later shortened to "the Wanderers") severed their relationship with the Academy in 1870, thus forgoing valuable state patronage. This rebellion against the Academy's outdated Classicism proclaimed a spirit of independence and an avant-garde sensibility, if not aesthetic. However, after the Academy adopted a new charter in 1893, many of the old-guard professors were dismissed and replaced with such prominent Wanderers as Ilyia Repin and Ivan Shishkin, among others.[14] In light of the Academy's eventual embrace of the Wanderers, with their realism and advocacy of using art as a vehicle for social justice, the emergence of the polemical-satirical conceptual costume at the Artists' Balls appears to be a logical extension of their agenda. And while in the 1890s the Wanderers no longer represented the artistic avant-garde, their exuberant, democratic spirit of inclusiveness perhaps also helped nurture the Artists' Balls, which by 1900 were attracting crowds 4,000 to 5,000 strong.[15]

Describing the wearer of the "Wanderers' Exhibit" costume, a reporter for *The Petersburg Gazette* summarized concisely, "The lady was very effectively dressed in open letters."[16] The profusion of so-called "open letters" (a genre of public statement often submitted as a letter to the editor) can be read as a satire of the movement's tendentiousness and the cognitive basis of its artists' works. As Sergei Diaghilev, impresario of the Ballets Russes, once complained, the Wanderers "taught our viewers to 'think a picture' (*dumat' kartinu*) instead of feeling it."[17] The cognitive aspect of such artwork was underscored by the "Wanderers' Exhibit" costume's use of text, which would appeal to the intellect rather than emotions. Moreover, the voluminous editorializing letters suggested an ongoing public debate, an allusion to the Wanderers' civic mission and polemical pursuit.

The costume "Journalism," appearing at the 1907 Artists' Ball, likewise made use of repetitive text. The reporter's description of the 1907 costume, which comprised newspaper mastheads and headlines, does not reveal whether the clippings were united by a common theme. It is therefore unclear whether the headlines articulated a cohesive political message, as they did in the collages assembled by Italian Futurists who used the medium to voice protest against World War I.[18] Despite the lack of polemical orientation, the costume's compelling alignment of form and content bespeaks the wearer's cleverness. The assembly of newspaper headlines and mastheads points to the aggregating function of the newspaper itself: just as the costume brought together a range of headlines from different sources, so too does the newspaper aggregate information about events from different spheres of interest and locales.

This costume's form-function unity ostentatiously returns "text" to its etymological meaning of *something woven* (from the Latin *texere*, to weave), thereby evoking the structural affinity between text and textile. While not literally woven together, the costume's separate newspaper pieces are united through a collage-like assembly into a communicative whole whose semiotic value transcends that of each textual thread. A costume—or a story—is woven to produce a legible narrative. It was incumbent upon the costume wearer to find the right balance between cleverness and accessibility, between figurative and literal signification, lest the artistic enterprise be divested of its content-meaning.

Andreev's *Black Maskers*

Like the conceptual costumes at the Artists' Balls, the allegorical costumes in Andreev's *Black Maskers* communicate through metaphor and symbolic association. The play tells the story of Lorenzo, the Italian Duke of Spadaro, who hosts a masquerade ball that is crashed by uninvited guests, whose macabre costumes are imbued with allegorical meaning. Among the maskers is a figure dressed in red with a black snake wrapped around her, who identifies herself as Lorenzo's heart. Like the scaly black snake impugning Lorenzo's morality, the Hairy Black Spider and a nebulous Long Gray Thing (*Dlinnoe seroe*) sent by Death claim to be manifestations of that which lies within Lorenzo's heart. A shapeless and nameless creature (*Nechto*) possessing many arms and legs, speaking in many voices and in the grammatical plural, identifies itself as Lorenzo's contradictory thoughts.[19]

Chief among the allegorical maskers are the titular Black Maskers, who are grotesque hybrids of orangutans and insects, monstrous freaks of nature who are the progeny of an unnatural coupling (as is Lorenzo, a point to which I return). Embodying the gloom of night, the Black Maskers usher in an unbearable coldness and darkness as they unwittingly extinguish all the torches and lanterns, as if they were black holes that absorb oxygen, light, and heat. Despite the play's title, these so-called maskers are not wearing masks at all: they are living instantiations of nighttime darkness, a metaphor for turpitude. Although Lorenzo initially laughs at the wittiness of these maskers' "jokes," as he calls their allegorical costumes, he maintains that his heart and thoughts are pure. However, toward the end of the play when Lorenzo's vassals come to pay their final respects at his wake, the reader learns of his past brutish behavior and abuse of power, including the sexual violation of a young girl who later died.[20]

As the allegorical figures in *Black Maskers* arrive they announce their identity, thereby assisting the reader in the task of decoding their "costumes."[21] The reader must still engage in the act of interpretation, however, by making meaningful connections. The costumes draw on certain established cultural associations, between red and the heart, black and wickedness, and spiders and the underworld (from which they are emissaries). While each allegorical costume derives its communicative capacity from an entrenched cultural paradigm (rather than displaying original imagery), each does rely on the reader's ability to access and mobilize that paradigm. The reader must connect a visual impression to an intangible concept and translate symbols into meaningful messages that harmonize with what is stated explicitly. Confronted with the masker identifying itself as Lorenzo's "Thoughts," the reader thus interprets its multiple legs as a metaphor for the transitory, peripatetic nature of thinking, and its multiple arms as a metaphor for grasping new ideas. Andreev's imagery catalyzes associative rather than literal thinking.

In contrast to the Saint Petersburg Artists' Balls, at which the viewers read each costume as an independent narrative construct, at Andreev's literary masquerade ball the challenge is to read the costumes as part of an overarching, cohesive narrative. The hypothetical reader's hermeneutic task is to resolve the mystery of what the incursion of the uninvited and menacing allegorical maskers represents. This shift from micro- to macro-analysis (from the meaning of an individual costume to their collective value) happens because unlike actual masquerade balls, the masquerade in *Black Maskers* is a "masquerade-within-a-play," in which the characters are united by the dramatic script. Masquerades and theater share many formal and functional affinities: in both, the participants or actors can exchange identities temporarily, gratify their fantasies, and experience the pleasure of cathartic release. Theater and masquerades alike offer a momentary escape from the everyday, but masquerades are more spontaneous than the script-driven theater. Also, masquerade guests are not bound to one another by a plotline. This was particularly true at the Artists' Balls, where fanciful costumes were individualistic expressions of wit and artistry that often overshadowed conventional character costumes. Similar to the collage-like assembly of many costumes and the resulting absence of a linear narrative, the masquerade itself lacked an explicit narrative trajectory.

The allegorical maskers in Andreev's play reinforce Romantic ideas about the communicative power of symbols, which are based on the constancy and universality of certain associations. The masker identified as the Long Gray Thing, for example, trades in the fact that the color gray signifies indeterminacy, as does its ill-defined identity as a "thing." In contrast to allegorical costumes that underscore the principle of intelligibility, other maskings in the play rupture semantic stability and referential authority, thereby threatening the foundations of reality in Lorenzo's mind.

As the evening progresses, the masked guests are joined by masked sounds, masked words, and masked tastes. Lorenzo, who is a dilettante composer, instructs his musicians to perform a piece he has recently written. Not only are the notes sonically masked as false tones, which results in dissonance rather than harmony, but the music itself is masked at times by satanic laughter, wailing, and cries of despair. The lyrics, too, have put on masks. Instead of the words revealing a pious heart, Lorenzo's lyrics, mysteriously written in his forged handwriting, declare Satan the ruler of the world. Joining the auditory and lexical betrayals, Lorenzo's wine no longer tastes of sweet grapes but has soured, taking on the flavor of Satan's blood. Lorenzo's sensory perceptions no longer accord with his expectations. Semantic values have been corrupted and authenticity undermined, the effect of which is to produce an alarming disorientation that makes Lorenzo fear that he is going mad.

The act of masking veils or dislocates the referent, which in turn disrupts the stability of representation. This displacement opens up a space in which sensory perception may not be trusted and in which interpretation (analytical or imaginative) must compensate for the lack of certainty. This zone of dislocated codes does not compromise semiotic integrity, however. The systems of signification remain intact, only their values are inverted. Music is still sound, wine is still a drink. But rather than beauty and pleasure, they deliver dissonance and bitterness. Furthermore, and most significant to the reader, language itself remains an intelligible system. Nonetheless, the upending of semantic values creates a semiological labyrinth out of Lorenzo's castle, which complicates the play's narrative resolution and is a problem to which I will return.

Among the various forms of semantic attenuation, the most troubling for Lorenzo is his doppelgänger. Having retreated to his castle's tower to escape the hellish harlequinade, he is confronted there by a masker dressed as him. Both Lorenzo figures claim authenticity. They proceed to fight a duel and one fatally wounds the other. But which Lorenzo is victorious: the original Lorenzo or the Impostor? The play leaves this question open and thereby challenges the very idea of authenticity and knowability. For the first time amid the play's semantic dislocations and allegorical signifiers, the reader faces a cognitive impasse. The doppelgänger presents an uncanny obstacle to orderly narrative resolution. Lorenzo's body is the site of dual arrest: in addition to the fatal lancing, the body's doubleness disrupts legibility.

The doubling of Lorenzo's body takes place at the moment he discovers the truth of his paternity. Among old papers stored in his castle's tower, he finds a document that reveals he is the illegitimate son of a dishonorable stable boy, not the legitimate offspring of the virtuous, noble knight whose name he bears. The arrival of this second self literalizes the dawning of Lorenzo's new perception of himself, which he must reconcile with his former identity. The play foreshadows this revelation in an earlier scene when among the uninvited costumed guests appear a young queen embracing a half-drunken stable boy and a nanny carrying a small deformed child (*urodets*) that is half animal, half man. As they pass by, a masker asks Lorenzo, "Do you recognize yourself?" suggesting that he is the product of this unholy union. Like the monstrous Black Maskers who are half orangutan and half insect, Lorenzo is conceived in an unnatural coupling. Lorenzo's lowly lineage, which has been disguised by an honorable family name, is underscored by the kinship he feels with his hunchbacked jester, Ecco, whose very name hints at their biological doubling. The body's inability to communicate its genealogy is thus one more way that Andreev registers the body as the ultimate site of semantic slippage. Lorenzo's distorted sensory perception (noted earlier) reveals a similar anxiety about the limits to his control over his own body. Amidst this diabolical masquerade of the senses, the most distressing betrayal is perpetrated by sight. In an emotionally fraught moment, Lorenzo is unable to distinguish his wife's eyes from those belonging to the multiple figures dressed as her doubles. His eyes fail to identify his wife's, compounding the unreliability of the body's organs of vision.

Lorenzo's doppelgänger arrives at the costume ball and cannot be differentiated from the original, which suggests an eerie equivalency: the costume in effect becomes a surrogate for the person. Following nineteenth-century literary convention, Andreev refers to the masquerade participants as maskers, or literally "masks" (*maski*), identifying them through one element of their costume. Using a part to stand for the whole is the principle of synecdoche, a signifying strategy which I treat below in my discussion of mainstream masquerade costumes featured in women's fashion magazines. In the play, using the mask to stand for the individual renders the two linguistically indistinguishable; the mask subsumes the wearer's identity and challenges him ontologically by subordinating the wearer's animacy and gender to the mask's object status and grammatical femininity (*maska*). Identifying the wearer not just *by* the mask but *as* the mask problematizes conventional notions of selfhood and being. The play's allegorical "maskers" similarly highlight the collapsed boundary between costume and wearer: the maskers do not actually wear costumes at all, but rather are embodiments of Lorenzo's turpitude. His corrupt heart and monstrous thoughts are instantiated as masquerade costumes, which function not to disguise but to reveal. The masquerade, at first cloaked in mystery, turns out to serve as a site of unmasking, exposure, and discovery.

Fashionable Mainstream Costumes

In contrast to the use of the masquerade motif in high literature, and the elite costuming practices at the Artists' Balls, the promotion of costumes in mass fashion magazines for the attendees of commercial and domestic masquerades demonstrated a manner of creativity that was more literal. These widely circulated costume ideas offered little room for analytical or imaginative engagement, trapped as they were in their delimited status as representations of objects. Women's fashion magazines such as *Fashion World* and *Women's Affair*, for example, printed illustrated suggestions and patterns for masquerade costumes around Yuletide and Shrovetide, two holiday periods when folk celebrations included the practice of mumming and urban celebrations included costume balls. Issues from early January in particular offered a rich array of costumes, many of them highly imaginative, although traditional character costumes were also well represented. For example, Issue no. 1 (January 1) of *Fashion World* in 1903 included object costumes portraying such phenomena as "Night and Day," "Phonograph," and "Automobile," while *Women's Affair* in 1911 highlighted costumes such as "Dirigible" and "Love Letter" (figures 20 and 21). The instructions for the "Night and Day" costume advised the reader to sew or glue onto her dress pictures of the sun, clouds, moon, and stars. The "Dirigible" costume called for affixing little sandbags all around the wearer's waist, as well as sporting a model airship atop one's head. These costumes are united by their synecdochic use of objects to convey an identity of "thingness" typically divorced from any larger narrative. A minimal number of carefully selected parts represented the object as a whole, prompting the viewer to fill in the blanks based on common knowledge.

Despite their reliance on rather explicit signifying icons (the sun standing for day, or miniature sandbags around the dirigible's waist implying a hindrance to her skyward trajectory), such synecdochic costumes were incommunicative of anything beyond their self-contained object status. Like conceptual costumes at the Artists' Balls, synecdochic costumes enabled their wearers to escape the predictability of established roles prescribed by character costumes. However, in contrast to the conceptual costume's unique economy of signification, which constructed narrative in the name of expressing opinion, synecdochic costumes demonstrated the wearer's resourcefulness by cleverly breaking down sophisticated objects and rendering them through a minimal collection of constituent parts. Synecdochic costumes, while no less creative than their conceptual counterparts, were less cognitive and more impressionistic: instead of presenting a hermeneutic challenge, such costumes counted on the viewer's ability to apprehend and deduce simultaneously the whole from its pieces or symbols.

The imaginativeness of costumes depicted in mass-circulation fashion magazines was of course not that of the costume wearer. Armed with someone else's idea and assembly instructions, any woman reading the feature could create for herself the same costume as any other reader. The paradox of fashion magazines in general holds true for masquerade costumes as well: it was the job of fashion designers to express creativity and whimsy, while the magazine readers' role was to appropriate and execute another's creative vision for themselves. As noted in chapter 3, fashion magazines recommended particular costumes for certain types of individuals (the "Queen of Bells" costume, for example, should be worn by merry women). The mainstream use of masquerade costume as a mechanism for reinforcing the wearer's identity reflected an ambient anxiety about shifting gender roles at the turn of the century, which was discussed in the previous chapter. Fashion magazines—tools, after all, to create trends and ensure uniformity of

Figure 20. Illustration of the costumes "Automobile," "Star," and "Fantasy, 1813" (*left to right*). (from *Fashion World*, January 1, 1903; image courtesy of the Russian National Library)

taste—promoted costumes not as offering personal anonymity and escape from repressive social taboos, but, to the contrary, as a mechanism for maintaining social order.

Some of Russia's early fashion pioneers gained experience with sartorial innovation at the Artists' Balls. In the years leading up to World War I, parallel to the aesthetic wonder of the World of Art movement, fashion design in Russia was gaining respect as a "serious artistic endeavor."[22] Lev Bakst, whose opulent and exotic costume designs for the Ballets Russes garnered the admiration of Paris, began designing elaborate clothing as well as masquerade costumes for high-society women in the early 1910s. Employing his fashion designs for the purposes of courtship, fellow artist and Ballets Russes set-designer Sergei Sudeikin dressed his beloveds in outfits reminiscent of bygone epochs. Other members of the World of Art association such as Konstantin

Figure 21. Illustration of the costumes "Bazaar" (*left*) and "Love Letter" (*right*). (from *Women's Affair*, no. 1, 1911; image courtesy of the Russian National Library)

Somov and Anna Ostroumova-Lebedeva contributed their creative energies to prerevolutionary fashion magazines, although there is no evidence that they designed clothing.[23] It is noteworthy that Bakst, Somov, and Ostroumova-Lebedeva attended the Saint Petersburg Academy of Arts in the period when the Artists' Balls were at the height of their popularity and relevance. (Sudeikin, too, attended the Academy of Arts, but he enrolled only in 1909, the first year in which no elaborate costume ball was held.) The artists' experience of designing costumes for these events, of merging art and dress, would come to bear as they made their subsequent forays into fashion design and display.

The mass-market nature of fashion magazines raises again the specter of the duplicate costume and its ramifications for the individual and for semantic authority. While the wearer may don a temporary identity borrowed from the magazine that is new for her, the costume's success in the sphere of public opinion is threatened by its lack of uniqueness. Many women may wear the same costume to any given masquerade, thus revealing their costumes to be derivative. The problem of multiple iterations of a given costume also plagues Lorenzo's masquerade in *Black Maskers*, where the double poses the greatest challenge to semantic and narrative authority. Multiples of a masquerade costume compromise individuality and echo an essential characteristic of theater: the mask or costume is arbitrarily and temporarily connected to its wearer, creating a contingent relationship between the posited identity and the individual. No dramatic character is linked inseparably with a single performer. In addition to Lorenzo's doppelgänger, among the guests is an array of regular maskers dressed as the Italian commedia dell'arte characters, Harlequin and Pierrot, among others. Andreev's play thus enacts its central thematic dilemma: the plot raises the issues of compromised referential authority and indeterminacy, which are manifested anew in each stage performance through the revolving cast of human actors.

Theatricality and the Art-Life Continuum

Andreev's inclusion of the commedia dell'arte figures in the masquerade scene draws attention to the issues of agency and originality that he also thematizes in the plot. Although the Italian stock characters have a negligible role in *Black Maskers*, they evoke the period's fascination with self-referential theatrical gestures. From Chekhov's *Seagull* (1896) and

Blok's *The Fairground Booth* (1906) to Mayakovsky's *Vladimir Mayakovsky* (1913) and Andreev's own *He Who Gets Slapped* (1915), plays about plays, and plays about performers and other spectacles were in vogue. As Vsevolod Meierkhol'd argued in his essay inspired by his production of Blok's *The Fairground Booth*, the commedia dell'arte characters as well as other conspicuous masks emblematize the concept of artifice, which he saw as the defining essence of theater. Existing only in the world of creative arts, the purely fictional commedia characters lack extra-artistic referents: there is no real-world Pierrot on whom the character is based, which bespeaks the figure's fictional provenance.

While the commedia characters are the product of imagination, their reproduction is a form of referential promiscuity that devalues their originality, as was the case with the masquerade costumes in fashion magazines. Likewise, the "Aivazovsky exhibit" costume of which I spoke earlier (numerous copies of his paintings pinned to the wearer) exhibited how the unique value of the content-message becomes eviscerated as a result of reproduction. The commedia characters, burdened with established personalities, unchanging costumes, and cemented relationships, are confined to repetitive roles. Although they may symbolize the worlds of imagination and artistic creation for some, such as Meierkhol'd, their ready-made nature also consigns them to being like props on the stage, always disposed to remobilization. Blok's play *The Fairground Booth* calls attention to the commedia characters' puppet-like lack of agency and puts on stage the problematic relationship between author and stage performance in a more blatant fashion than *Black Maskers*. Chapter 6 treats Blok's play as a harbinger of avant-garde aesthetics and focuses on the symbolic material value of the maskers' costumes.

As *The Fairground Booth* and *Black Maskers* each suggests in its own way, the script, the textual cornerstone of dramatic play, lacks a permanent creative authority. Like Lorenzo's musical composition, the performance of which did not resemble what he composed, the playwright faces the prospect of stagings inconsistent with his artistic vision. The main character's inability to control the events at his masquerade, including the performance of music that he has composed, reflects an anxiety of authorial control that is met on the formal level by the work's status as a performance script. Each production of the play will differ from preceding performances; each director interprets the script in his own way, each actor imbues a new spirit into a given character. Both plays thematize the issues of authenticity and authorship, which are reiterated in the theatricalizing process of the play's staging. Each mis-en-scène varies in accordance with each director's unique vision and the acting style of different players.

The distance between the dramatic script and its realization on stage not only highlights the problem of duplicate costumes and referential inconstancy but also draws attention to the divide between the world of make-believe and so-called reality. Aspiring to dismantle the foot-lights, avant-garde theater theorist Nikolai Evreinov echoed the convic-tion popular among writers at the fin de siécle that art and life should merge into one creative enterprise. Contemplating the divide between fantasy and actuality, however, prompts epistemological questions about identity. Around the turn of the last century, the essentialist para-digms of biological and social identity waned and in their place arose an anxiety-provoking existential uncertainty. Andreev's *Black Maskers* draws attention to this destabilized worldview that privileged ambigu-ity, specifically regarding the individual's identity. In the play he re-worked a trope from Romantic-era society tales and used it to probe the existential dilemmas posed by masking and the unreliability of sensory apprehension (especially vision) as a means of knowing the world. At masquerades in society tales, masked characters frequently asked one another, "Do you know me?" as a flirtatious way of opening conversa-tion with a potential paramour. Like English, Russian does not have separate verbs for knowing a person and knowing a fact. In Andreev's play, Lorenzo moves from telling his guests that he doesn't recognize them (*ia vas ne uznaiu*), for which there is a distinct verb, to the more ontologically fraught "I don't know you," (*ia vas ne znaiu*), a phrase that seems to signify not just that the other person's identity is unknown, but that the masker is fundamentally alien.

As the play progresses, Lorenzo switches from striving to recognize his guests to grappling with the supernaturalism of their incursion. In his discussion of the fantastic as a literary genre, literary theorist Tzvetan Todorov juxtaposed supernatural events (which do not accord with natural laws) and uncanny events (which can be rationally under-stood or explained from an external point of view). The uncanny may be a manifestation of madness, hallucination, inebriation, dream, or allegory—all of which are types of imagined alterity. In contrast to the confused Lorenzo, the reader can see that the uncanny maskers in Act I are allegorical; according to Todorov's theory, this precludes the possibility of interpreting them as supernatural phenomena. Whereas Lorenzo experiences the incursion as an event that violates the natural laws as he knows them, the reader retains an external point of view that acknowledges their poetic meaning and thus their imaginary origin.[24] In order to resolve the tension between the supernatural and the uncanny, Andreev reveals in the final scene that Lorenzo is mad, although it remains unclear whether the events in Act I are the cause or consequence of Lorenzo's madness.

Andreev achieves this causal ambiguity by locating the final scene at the same time and in the same place as the first scene. Just as at the play's beginning, the servants illuminate lanterns and torches for the masquerade guests whom Lorenzo awaits at its end. However, this time there will be no masquerade; it only seems to Lorenzo that there will be because he has gone mad. With no references to the horrors that played out in the previous scenes except for those from Lorenzo, who repeats earlier phrases and who has the wound from where he was lanced in the duel with his double, it seems to the reader as if all that transpired might have been in Lorenzo's troubled imagination. The bloodstain on Lorenzo's shirt, however, is a visible trace that leaves open the possibility that the supernatural events really did occur. The circular structure of the play thus complicates its orderly narrative resolution. Differing from the standard linear progression of the traditional script-driven play, *Black Maskers* demonstrates a kind of masquerade chronology, in which time is shuffled and consecutive actions lose their cumulative meaning.

While the supernatural and the imaginary are posited as different ways to make sense of the fantastic in the play, they share a fundamental experience of alienation, an estrangement from logical thought and rational explanation. The masquerade is an apt venue in which to elaborate both the supernatural and the imaginary because it is governed by the principles of ambiguity and the attenuation of so-called "reality." Masquerade costumes possess a dissociative power that creates a dream-like atmosphere in which a masker's identity is estranged from her appearance, thereby undermining assumptions about the constancy of visual referentiality that purportedly abides in reality. The action in *Black Maskers* is set in an Italian Gothic castle, a geographically and temporally distant location that also amplifies the masquerade's characteristic power of dislocation for Andreev's contemporary Russian reader.

Compounding this mood of estrangement, traditional paradigms for reading social relations break down at the masquerade because organizing principles of cultural identity such as historical era and national origin are temporarily scrambled. The coalescing of all time and all space into one chronotope opens up a realm of unique possibilities for plot development, making masquerade an artistically productive motif. The following chapter explores the syncretism of the masquerade chronotope, which facilitates an incarnated intertextuality.

The figurative costumes of Andreev's allegorical maskers and of the Artists' Ball participants demonstrate how the costumed body serves as a legible yet hermeneutically challenging exhibition space. Enrobed in a sartorial code devised through associative, metaphorical thinking, the masker poses as a poetic puzzle. The figurative costume is a sartorial manifestation of the veiled, indirect nature of Symbolist discourse. The creatively constructed garments emblematize the split between the surface, which is visible but perhaps misleading or unintelligible, and that which is authentic and lies hidden, awaiting discovery—i.e., the costume's content message. While the figurative costume was capable of causing narrative arrest if it failed to speak intelligibly, and it was vulnerable to misinterpretation, it nonetheless proclaimed a unique and autonomous artistic vision. Freed from the demands of representative art and its accompanying anxieties of authenticity, the creators of figurative costumes in life and literature embraced modernism's spirit of individualism and the era's quest to expand the range of communicative possibilities.

5

> ─┤ ◆ ─ ◯ ─ ◆ ┤ ─

Character Costumes
Cultural Memory and the Philological Masquerade

ℵ newspaper account that appeared in *The Petersburg Gazette* on December 28, 1910, testified to an unnamed individual's wish to honor the recently deceased Russian literary giant Lev Tolstoy by dressing as him for a holiday masquerade. Instead of enjoying commendation for his sartorial tribute, however, the guest was forced to leave the event because his choice of costume, in the estimation of his hosts, showed too little respect for the writer who had passed away the previous month. Titled "The Profanation of The Memory of L. Tolstoy," the article showcases the ill social consequences of infelicitously appropriating the identity of a known cultural figure as masquerade costume.[1] While the unfortunate denouement of this incident points to the perils of wearing a character costume that resonated too deeply, such costumes that appropriate the identity of fictional, mythological, and historical figures performed an important cultural function, especially in the early years of the twentieth century, when Russia was on the threshold of revolutionary change. The specific symbolic value of character costumes is grounded in the reality of the country's cultural heritage;

this fact suggests how profitably we can examine these aliases as examples of what Viacheslav Ivanov called "Realistic Symbols." The character identities represented at Ivanov's real-life costumed salon gatherings, known as "Evenings of Hafiz," functioned as such Realistic Symbols, as did the figures in Anna Akhmatova's poetic portrait of a New Year's masquerade in *Poem without a Hero*.

Character costumes played an important role in preserving cultural memory: their assembly at balls and parties created a uniquely incarnated intertextuality. Drawing on the original meaning of the term philology, namely the love of learning and literature, I call costumed gatherings that draw on cultural patrimony philological masquerades.[2] The philological masquerade uniquely unifies life and art: its historicity and erudition differentiate it from the individualistic instances of self-stylizing discussed in chapters 3 and 6. The characters populating a philological masquerade may originate in diverse national traditions and historical epochs but they coalesce in the event's distinctively syncretic chronotope. The philological masquerade performs a museum-like function of evaluating cultural artifacts through careful curation and, like the art museum that perpetuates exclusivity by housing works by and for the elite, it is a public exhibition space for erudition and refined taste. Such events are the domain of the classically educated and culturally literate, among whom shared knowledge is the medium of communication.

Philological Masquerades

Certain nineteenth-century writers employed the philological masquerade as a literary motif in their fiction; this motif allowed for the evaluation of other works of literature in a way that calls to mind a discriminating museum curator. In Alexander Shakhovskoi's play *Mercury Again, or The Novelistic Masquerade* (1829), the main character Count Odashev orchestrates a masquerade party to entertain an unnamed princess by dressing her grandchildren and servants as characters from well-known (mostly European) novels. Of the 18 literary works represented, only two are Russian: Pushkin's "Count Nulin" and Faddei Bulgarin's *Ivan Vyzhigin* (the latter enjoyed fame as Russia's first best-seller, 6,000 copies of which were sold in 1829[3]). After remarking on the notable lack of quality Russian literature, Odashev and the princess handsomely praise Pushkin and Nulin, while dismissing Bulgarin's character Vyzhigin as "some simple Russian" to whom the folk (*narod*) might relate.[4] At Shakhovskoi's "novelistic masquerade," the titular literary characters stand as metonyms for their source texts: the writer transferred the liabilities or merits of the former onto the latter. Bulgarin's unsophisticated common man Vyzhigin thus embodied the novel's overall pedestrian appeal, which led Shakhovskoi to consider it inferior to Pushkin's narrative poem "Count Nulin."

In Ivan Panaev's feuilleton "A Literary Masquerade," which appeared in the January 1852 issue of the journal *The Contemporary*, costumed literary characters also serve as emissaries for their respective source texts.[5] From among the figures who "personified the remarkable works of Russian literature from 1851" and attended this fictional New Year's ball, Faust (from Heinrich Heine's ballad "Faust") and Marina (from Evdokiia Rastopchina's "Fortunate Woman") were crowned the literary victors of 1851 by the costume ball's organizer.[6] The masquerade takes place in the mansion of a "Petersburg Monte Cristo," who transformed his home into a natural wonderland for the festive occasion. Himself embodying an allusion to Alexandre Dumas's *The Count of Monte Cristo* (1844), the host combines his wealth and his artistic discernment to sponsor an event whose magnificence rivaled the imagination of the authors represented. The hall for the costume party "was not a hall at all, but the utmost charming and diverse array of gardens, forests, lakes, rivers and valleys," where "the wide stairs were covered with a downy velvet carpet and decked out with colossal banana trees and bright luxuriant flowers from some exotic place."[7] With the striking appearance of a theatrical stage set, this venue brings nature's wonders indoors with a spectacular display of manmade artifice masquerading as organic landscape; the setting foreshadows the lavishness and ingenuity that characterized the décor of modernist masquerades, which I discuss toward the end of this chapter.

A costume ball featured in an anonymous feuilleton entitled "The Literary Christmas Party: A Provincial Fantasy," which appeared on February 7, 1859, in the newspaper *Saint Petersburg News* (*Sankt-Peterburgskie vedomosti*), exchanged a population of costumed characters hailing from artistic literature for the symbolic personifications of contemporary periodicals. The journalistic theme of the holiday masquerade emerges in the costumes that exhibit the content of various magazines. The periodical maskers augment their illustrative costumes assembled from actual journal pages and other ready-made objects by calling out advertising slogans befitting their content. Among the maskers at this masquerade is the journal *Illustration*, who was "hung from head to toe with drawings, portraits, and maps primarily taken from foreign publications."[8] Although this "Literary Christmas Party" lacked the explicit contest that provided the narrative thread for the previous two examples, in which the most meritorious maskers were singled out, the feuilleton satirized certain periodicals (as by pointing out the foreign provenance of the features in *Illustration*) along with their noisy hawkers, thus expressing the author's low regard for certain journalistic organs. The literary quadrille in Dostoevsky's *Demons*, in which the maskers are dressed symbolically to invoke particular periodicals and their editors (analyzed in chapter 1), resembles this critical feuilleton in its satirical function.[9]

Character Costumes

In contrast to the figurative costumes discussed in the previous chapter, character costumes replace a reliance on the wearer's imagination and beholder's subjective interpretation with a dependence on shared cultural literacy for the communication of meaning. While whimsical, metaphorical costumes articulating ideas and representing intangible phenomena such as Spring, Summer, and Night grew in popularity around the turn of the century, costumes that reference a fictional or historical figure such as Tolstoy, which I call character costumes, enjoyed perennial vogue at masquerades. A character costume visually reproduces the physical appearance of an individual and metonymically represents a particular fictional or historical narrative in which the character lived. The character costume's symbolism is not a function of the garments themselves; rather, it stems from the character's original source text, be it a work of fiction, a stage production, a myth, or a historical episode. Because the character costume is imitative and exhibited little originality, costume-contest jurors and newspaper reporters around the turn of the century often considered it less praiseworthy than whimsical and figurative costumes.

Despite the relative dullness of dressing as a generic representative of a profession or nationality, the practice endured on the masquerade circuit. Such women's magazines as *Fashion World* and *Women's Affair* featured instructions for assembling costumes to resemble the national dress of an Alsatian Woman, Indian Woman, Swiss Woman, Noble Chinese Woman, Portuguese Man, a Sorceress, and a Shepherdess (figure 22).[10] These demographic costumes sometimes acquired symbolic meaning in works of modernist literature: in Sologub's *Petty Demon*, for

Figure 22. Illustration of the costumes "Swiss Woman" (*left*) and "Noble Chinese Woman" (*right*). (from *Women's Affair*, no. 1, 1911; image courtesy of the Russian National Library)

example, Valeriia Rutilova playfully adopts an ardent attitude toward Peredonov while wearing Spanish dress that evokes Iberian feistiness at the costume ball. At the masquerade that Sofia Likhutina attends with the journalist Neintelpfein in Bely's *Petersburg*, Lippanchenko dresses as a Spaniard from Grenada. His Grenadian masquerade costume and yellow face, a "mix between a Semite and a Mongol," establish Lippanchenko's symbolic link with the Jews and Moors who formerly inhabited Grenada.

A costume's symbolic significance becomes increasingly undecipherable in lockstep with the specificity and obscurity of the character's identity. Take for example the costumes portraying Mesdames de Pompadour and Récamier at a Saint Petersburg costume party on February 16, 1899.[11] Identifying the Pompadour costume as representing a particular eighteenth-century French courtesan requires a significantly higher level of cultural literacy than recognizing her nationality as French or her profession as a courtesan. Dressed as Madame de Pompadour, any masker temporarily adopts the courtesan's legendary narrative and its symbolism. Born Jeanne Antoinette Poisson, Pompadour was the chief mistress of Louis XV from 1745 until her death in 1764. She met the sovereign at a masquerade ball where she earned his affection through her beauty and coquetry. For those familiar with her story, she represents feminine seduction and the romantic intrigue endemic to masquerade.[12] Costumes that did not index a unique identity but which aspired to great historical specificity problematized the seeming simplicity of the generic costume. Figures dressed as "A Parisian Milliner from 1800" or wearing "A Costume from the Era of Louis the XVI" would confound all but the savviest historians of French fashion.[13] The legibility of such costumes depends not only on how effectively they iconicize the original through dress, but also on shared cultural knowledge.

Evenings of Hafiz

Viacheslav Ivanov and the guests attending his exclusive evening gatherings known as the "Evenings of Hafiz" dressed in costume as part of their neo-Platonic exploration of the link between aestheticism and eroticism. The first Evening was on May 2, 1906, and hosted by Ivanov and his wife Lidiia Zinovyeva-Annibal at their apartment (which enjoyed its own nominal disguise, having been dubbed "The Tower"). In contrast to their popular "Wednesdays" salon, which was open to a wide circle of artists, musicians, philosophers, and writers (including Akhmatova), the Evenings of Hafiz were limited to a coterie of seven male guests: philosopher Nikolai Berdiaev; artists Lev Bakst and Konstantin Somov; music impresario and *World of Art* journal editor Val'ter Nuvel' (Walter Nouvel); and writers Sergei Auslender, Sergei Gorodetsky, and Mikhail Kuzmin.[14] Ivanov envisioned the Evenings as a blend of performance art and spontaneous interactions. He specified in his diary that the gatherings should have a carefully crafted program of "poems, songs, music, dance, fairytales, and speeches, which could serve as the topics for discussion," and should include certain "collective acts" (*kollektyvnie deistviia*) that Ivanov himself intended to compose and direct. He stipulated that the programmed performances should alternate with breaks to allow the guests to socialize freely.[15] This was intended to introduce a zone of spontaneity into his script. In a letter to an acquaintance, Zinovyeva-Annibal described the "Persian, Hafizian" Evenings as "very intimate, very bold, in costumes, on carpets, philo-sophical, artistic and erotic."[16] She noted the spirit of liberation and resulting intimacy that emerged when they donned their costumes: "We dress in costumes, some of us have made wonderful ones, we are completely transformed [. . .] we recline in conversation . . . and in kisses, using names that we thought up for each other."[17] In his recollec-tions about the Evenings, Kuzmin described the rarified ambiance and feeling of emancipation inspired by the special décor, the participants' unusual dress, and mannered behavior: "The costumes, the flowers, sitting on the floor, the semispherical window in the distance, and candles below, it all created a particular freedom of speech, gestures, feelings."[18] Kuzmin remarked that "Everyone used '*ty*' [the informal mode of address], like at a masquerade," underscoring the Hafizites' release from conventional social mores and creating an atmosphere conducive to aesthetic and erotic experimentation.[19]

The Evenings were named in honor of the fourteenth-century Persian poet Hafiz (also spelled Hafez) and were modeled on Plato's *Symposium*, in which tippling men debated the meaning of love. Blending the artistic and the sensual, the Evenings of Hafiz pivoted on the promise of philo-sophical enlightenment. In "Thoughts on Symbolism" (1912) Ivanov explained the relationship between erotic love and Symbolism, offering retrospective illumination of the Evenings he hosted six years earlier. "According to Plato, the goal of love is 'to give birth in beauty.' Plato's depiction of the paths of love is a definition of Symbolism. In its growth the soul ascends from a state of attraction to a beautiful body up to the love of God. When an aesthetic phenomenon is experienced erotically, the artistic creation becomes symbolic."[20] Wedding aestheticism and eroticism in a philosophical program, Ivanov's circle attempted to create its own "erotic utopia," not so different from that of earlier Russian Decadent and Symbolist writers, such as Gippius, Merezhkovsky, and Bely. On May 8, 1906, Kuzmin detailed his erotic encounters at the Evening in his diary: "V[iachelsav] I[vanov] read his poem, Gorodetsky improvised. Everyone was kissing. The only ones I didn't kiss were Somov and the Berdiaevs. We played flutes, drank, it was noisy and a little confused, it smelled of rose oil, the clothing was diverse. I was in all pink with some white and pale green."[21] With their senses fully engaged by music, fragrance, the flavor of wine, and the visual and tactile delights of costume, the Hafizites tested Plato's philosophy that beauty experienced erotically could spiritually elevate a soul: their artistic Evenings ostensibly enabled them to "give birth in beauty" as a symbolic expression of divine creation.

The philosophical purposefulness of the Hafizites' role-playing and costuming (namely, using the aestheticized body as a channel through which to reach a transcendental state) raised the level of the salon: what was once entertainment had become an art form that approximated the idealized ritual significance of Symbolist theater. Although the Evenings of Hafiz were partially scripted performances and thus differed from conventional plays, their pretensions to mysticism aligned them with reigning Symbolist theories of theater, including Ivanov's own. Ivanov viewed the ideal theatrical experience as one that recreated the mystical power of ancient rites through collective action. Analogously, the Hafizites' full and equal participation in the Evenings united the players in the common quest for mystical experience.

Ivanov and his guests adopted aliases that bespoke the circle's cultural elitism. Ranging from demi-gods and statesmen to philosophers, artists, and literary characters out of Persian, Greco-Roman, and European traditions, the Hafizites' assumed identities were not part of a single, overarching, historical or fictional narrative script. With the exception of Ivanov and his wife playing the roles of the correspondents in Friedrich Hölderlin's epistolary novel *Hyperion or The Hermit in Greece* (1799), the character identities adopted by the Hafizites bore no clear link to one another. The personae hailed from disparate sources and national traditions, enacting at the Evenings the intertextuality that permeated Ivanov's poetry. His dialogs with cultural history mirror those of Goethe, whom Ivanov deeply admired. One particular collection of the German Romantic's lyrical poems entitled *The West-Eastern Divan*

(*West-östlicher Diwan*, 1827) was influenced by the poetry of Hafiz, and indicates whence Ivanov took the name for his Evenings.[22] As the title suggests, the poems in this collection allude to cultural traditions from the Occident and Orient; Goethe considered these references obscure enough to warrant extensive commentary on them. Writing the poems of *Divan* helped shape the poet's conviction that the world's rich cultural patrimony was shared and that there were no borders between national cultures.[23] Ivanov, who was deeply steeped in German Romantic literature, including Goethe, laced his poetry and essays with allusions to figures and texts from Classical antiquity to European Romanticism, thereby echoing the German master's philological range. As a translator of Aeschylus, Sappho, Goethe, Novalis, Byron, Baudelaire, Dante, and Petrarch, Ivanov acquired a formidable command of western civilization's literary core, one legacy of which was the multilingual epigraphs to certain of his poems.

Costumes, Roles, and Ivanov's "Realistic Symbols"

In the previous chapter I discussed the epistemological and narrative challenges that Lorenzo's double poses in Andreev's *Black Maskers*. The duplicate costume foregrounds the contingent relationship between the individual and his masquerade apparel in the same way that the actor bears no permanent link to the dramatic character he plays. However, the costume-ball masker may select an alias that has personal relevance and that thereby extends or expands the wearer's self-image: the costume's symbolism exhibits a metonymic relationship to the person wearing it. The character identities of certain Hafizites coincided with or amplified one or more of the wearer's roles in so-called real life. Bakst, for example, took on the character of fourth-century BC Greek painter Apelles, whose profession as an artist symbolically reinscribed Bakst's own. Kuzmin assumed the alias of Antinous, the youth from the ancient Roman empire whose masculine beauty and status as the emperor Hadrian's beloved reverberated with Kuzmin's dandyism and homosexuality. Bakst's and Kuzmin's personae for the Evenings were the opposite of disguises: they were proclamations of self.[24] Their temporary aliases enabled them to lay claim to resonant narratives and to amplify what they felt to be key traits of their identity.

A costume could also have a metaphorical relationship to its wearer, a point that Ivanov made using the example of the sun and its hypostases in "Two Elements in Contemporary Symbolism" (1908). Over the millennia world cultures have called the sun by different names and envisaged the sun in various hypostases, each of which strives to convey through the power of metaphor and personification the sun's essence. Explained Ivanov:

> In ancient times a man called the sun the Titan Hyperion or radiant Helios, not to adorn the concept of the sun or to color its perception in a certain way, but rather to signify it more accurately and truly than if it had been depicted as a bright disk that did not resemble man. By representing the sun as an indefatigable Titan or young god with a cup in his hands, ancient man asserted that it was something more real than a visible disk. Subsequently, another mythopoet came along and, disagreeing with his predecessor, argued that the sun was not Helios and Hyperion together but only Helios, while Hyperion was his father. Then new mythopoets appeared, saying that Helios was Phoebus. Finally, still later, the Orphics and mystics came and declared that Helios was that very Dionysus who had hitherto been known only as Niktelios, the night sun. These researchers of the hidden essence of a single *res* quarreled over all this, each seeking to say about this same *res* something more profound and real than his predecessor, each ascending in this fashion from less to more substantial knowledge of the divine thing.[25]

Ivanov imputed the epistemological quest of these ancient "researchers of the hidden essence of a single *res*" to the poet, who has the gift of communicating symbolically. One person who values above all the sun's ineluctable power over life on earth imagines it as an omnipotent Titan god. Another person who perceives the sun's luminosity as its most distinguishing trait envisions it as Helios or Phoebus. Translated into the context of the Evenings of Hafiz, the sun's symbolic hypostasis parallels a costume's metaphorical relationship to its wearer: each participant may adopt multiple character costumes, each of which functions metaphorically to reveal essential yet disparate qualities of the wearer. For example, Ivanov assumed the aliases of Hyperion and "al-Rumi," or Jalal Al-Din Rumi, a thirteenth-century Afghani Muslim mystic, philosopher, and poet. Such identities exposed Ivanov's wish to claim for himself certain attributes of each figure, one a character from fiction, the other an exotic writer. Gorodetsky, too, played the roles of both a mythic figure and a man of letters: he was Hermes, the shape-shifting Greek god, and the Iranian-born writer Zain.[26] Similarly, Nuvel' dressed alternately as the Roman writer Petronius, the Byronic literary hero Corsair, and nineteenth-century French philosopher Charles Renouvier. Like a secret knock or handshake, the abstruse cultural allusions and symbolisms embodied in the character identities assumed by Ivanov and his fellow Hafizites were intelligible to a closed society of initiates.

The flipside of a person or object having multiple identities, a signified with many signifiers (Ivanov as Hyperion and al-Rumi), is the name that has many referents, the signifier with many signifieds (the name Hyperion points to two source texts). An alias may thus have multiple symbolisms grounded in the reality of cultural history. Ivanov's role as Hyperion alluded to the Titan god identified with the sun and the writer's own place at the center of his salon's solar system. It also signaled the title character in Hölderlin's novel, which was based on the fictional correspondence between Hyperion and Diotima: the latter's teachings on the philosophy of love in *Symposium* (namely, that earthly love roused by beauty brings one closer to the divine) guided the Hafizites' program.[27] With Zinovyeva-Annibal starring as Diotima, Ivanov assigned himself the role of her lover, the eighteenth-century Greek philosopher-poet Hyperion, according to Hölderlin's novel.

The expansive web of associations emanating from Nuvel's alias Corsair highlights vividly the symbolic richness of a polyvalent identity.[28] The original Corsair was the hero of Byron's exceedingly popular 1814 eponymous poem about a pirate's battle against a Turkish pasha—and the romantic tragedy that ensued. The story of the pirate-rake, whom Byron suggested was a partially autobiographical figure, inspired the opera *Il Corsaro* by Giuseppe Verdi, the overture *Le Corsaire* by Hector Berlioz, and the ballet *Le Corsaire* by Marius Petipa, as well as at least six other pirate-themed performance pieces in the early- to mid-nineteenth century. Byron's Corsair thus migrated out of his literary context and into dance and music: such a translation between media would be meaningful for Nuvel', who was a connoisseur of classical music. The name also draws attention to the contingent relationship between actors and their roles. Each artistic transposition increased the number of Corsairs in the European repertoire, a number that is further multiplied by the plethora of actors, dancers, and singers who could fill the roles. While the name Corsair signaled a Byronic character type (the heartless adventurer and seducer), it also acquired new nuances in each artistic iteration. As Ivanov explained in "Two Elements in Contemporary Symbolism," a "symbol cuts through all planes of being and all spheres of consciousness, signifying different essences in each plane, performing a different function in each sphere."[29] Like a symbol passing through different planes, the name Corsair ramifies variously; however, all iterations remain "united in the great cosmogonic myth" that comprises his identity.[30]

The aliases and accompanying character costumes worn at the Evenings of Hafiz are analogous to Ivanov's concept of the Realistic Symbol grounded in the external reality of common cultural heritage. In contrast to the relativism of the "Idealistic Symbol" expressive of individual experience, the externally anchored Realistic Symbol evinces universal meanings. As Realistic Symbols, the costumes of fictional and historical figures enabled the wearer to reveal an even more "real" self, i.e., one that says "something more profound" about his person and "ascend[s] in this fashion from less to more substantial knowledge of the divine thing," in Ivanov's words.[31] As the poet showed using the example of Hyperion in his essay, each hypostasis of an object (such as the sun)—or by extension, an individual—helps transform the real into the more real, *a realibus ad realiora*, by exposing its many facets.

The esoteric character identities drawn from the narratives and myths of diverse epochs and nations, and adopted for the Evenings of Hafiz, constituted a philological masquerade, a performance of inter-textuality that dismantled temporal and spatial boundaries. As an enact-ment of cultural memory, the philological masquerade incorporates the past into the present and the epic into the lyric. It also affords a performa-tive model for the integration of art and life, but one that differs from the earlier instances of self-stylizing undertaken among modernist writers. Unlike the aesthetic practices that transformed quotidian life into a performance (such as those of Gippius or the Futurists), the philological approach that Ivanov practiced assimilated extant works of art into the costume-wearers' present-moment narratives of self. The Hafizites' orientation toward cultural memory and its preservation are integral to the philological masquerade. While the Evenings resembled general masquerades in their quasi-improvisation, and in the collective costuming that created an atmosphere of exoticism and a space for play that was distanced from daily life, their grounding in historical and literary realia defined them as philological masquerades.

Akhmatova's "Midnight Harlequinade"

Scholar and literary theorist Renate Lachmann has characterized the Acmeist dialog with world culture in terms of intertextuality: Akhmatova and Mandel'shtam mastered the polyphonic lyric, in which one finds "the construction and reconstruction of cultural space accomplished through appropriation, preservation and re-encoding" of previous texts.[32] Their "polyphonic lyrics," typified by Akhmatova's *Poem without a Hero* (1940–62), intermingle the voices of literature, performance, myth, personal biography, and national history. In this long poem composed over the course of twenty-two years, Akhmatova encoded personal experience in literary and political history, and vice versa. Like Ivanov and the Hafizites, who drew on established narratives to articulate more fully their self-myths, Akhmatova appropriated symbolic figures to act in the plot of her literary harlequinade, which is at the center of the plot in part one of *Poem without a Hero*. That Akhmatova called the costume party a harlequinade is significant: the term derives from the name of the commedia dell'arte figure Harlequin, whose colorful clownish dress made his costume popular at masquerades throughout the centuries and across national borders. It underscores the distinctively syncretic chronotope of the philological masquerade: the maskers are dressed as figures from world culture, such as Harlequin from the Italian commedia dell'arte, and function as Ivanovian Realistic Symbols.

Akhmatova engaged in a variety of indirect citational strategies in *Poem without a Hero*, including the use of quotations that have more than one referent text and quotations that "have already acquired dialogical echoes in other texts, so that there, too, more than one foreign text is evoked."[33] Such ambiguous allusions recall the polyvalent names of Hyperion and Corsair that also have multiple referents and dialogic echoes. Set in the Mirror Hall at the Fontanka House in Saint Petersburg, the poem thematizes doubling and employs it as an intertextual device. Akhmatova flaunted the poem's mystifications, admitting her use of "invisible ink" (*simpaticheskie chernila*) and "mirror writing" (*zerkal'noe pis'mo*); she also likened the poem's complexity of meanings to a "triple-bottomed box" (*u shkatulki zhe troinoe dno*). The abundant literary and cultural references and citations in *Poem without a Hero* make it a palimpsest. The first dedication, which is to the poet Vsevolod Kniazev, whose "Sonnet" is the draft upon which Akhmatova-the-narrator claims to be writing, establishes the practice of cultural recuperation that reigns throughout.[34]

Despite her initial refusal to offer an explanatory key to the poem, Akhmatova offered up *Prose about the Poem* ostensibly as a reader's guide, acknowledging that "The Poema will be incomprehensible and

uninteresting to the one who doesn't know certain 'Petersburg circumstances.'"[35] The purportedly explanatory *Prose*, however, is a hybrid of
fact and fiction, offering little resolution for the befuddled reader. The
polyvalency of her "mirror writing" opposed the early Acmeist poetic
mandate of returning the law of identity to poetry: "A=A what a fine
poetic theme," Mandel'shtam wrote in his 1912 manifesto "Morning of
Acmeism." Departing from Mandel'shtam's so-called theme and the
principle of "fine clarity" (to borrow the title of Kuzmin's 1910 article),
the poetics of *Poem without a Hero* adhere more closely to the Realistic
Symbolism of Ivanov, where reality comprises world culture.

Set on New Year's Eve, part one of the poem begins with a parade of
mummers whom the narrator identifies as ghosts from the past dressed
as literary characters, including Dapertutto, Don Juan, Faust, John the
Baptist, Thomas Glahn, and Dorian Gray.[36] As we saw earlier in the
case of Corsair, some of the mummers' identities display a semantic
overabundance, or "a polyphony of information," a phrase that Barthes
used to define the concept of theatricality.[37] Dapertutto, for example,
indexes multiple figures, all of which signify narratives or historical
personages that bear relevance for Akhmatova. Dapertutto is a character
in E. T. A. Hoffmann's "Adventures on New Year's Eve," the supernatural atmosphere of which Akhmatova mirrored in the poem with
the terrifying incursion of the holiday mummers. Dapertutto was also
the pseudonym under which theater director Vsevolod Meierkhol'd
published his writings in the journal *The Love for Three Oranges* (1914–
1916), to which Akhmatova contributed.[38] As a figurehead of theater
and theatrical role-playing, Meierkhol'd catalyzes a string of associations linked to stage performance, many of which are also woven into
the poem (figures of the commedia dell'arte, Sergei and Olga Sudeikina,
Alexander Golovin and Mikhail Lermontov, to name only a few).[39]

Another multivalent figure in the philological masquerade of part
one is Don Juan, who similarly unites the literary and performance
traditions. The epigraph on the title page of the poem, "Di rider finirai /
Pria dell'aurora" ("You will stop laughing / Before the dawn"), is from
Mozart's opera *Don Giovanni*. The third epigraph to chapter 1 alludes
to Byron's "Don Juan," and the line "Meierkhol'd's slave boys"
(*Meierkhol'dovy arapchata*) in chapter 2 points to Meierkhol'd's 1910
production of Molière's play *Don Juan*. Unlike the proliferation of similar
or identical images that could, as Walter Benjamin theorized, eviscerate
the content-meaning of the original, an amplitude of textual allusions
expands on the Don Juan myth. The multiple artistic iterations of Don

Juan function like the multiple Corsairs discussed earlier: each instantiation expands the name's symbolic significance and derives its meaning from established cultural narratives.

The opening scene of the New Year's harlequinade is simultaneously a philological masquerade that preserves cultural heritage through its character allusions and a condensation of autobiographical memory. Roman Timenchik has decoded many of Akhmatova's allusions to reveal how the mummer-ghosts instantiate her memories of her fellow poets and artists during the first decade of the 1900s.[40] The spectral return of Akhmatova's contemporaries disguised as literary characters intertwines the planes of personal and cultural memory. The mummer-memories suggest the act of psychological condensation and recall Freud's model of memory and dream formation. In describing how repressed memories merge together in dreams, Freud hypothesized that the mind may create composite figures and scenarios. The mummer-memories are such composite figures, but ones that differ from the Freudian model because they unite autobiography and philology. Akhmatova also engaged a more Freudian (i.e., personal-psychological) approach to condensation on at least one occasion: she condensed the figures of Vsevolod Kniazev and Osip Mandel'shtam, contemporaries and literary colleagues, by intermingling their words. Although the First Dedication is explicitly to Kniazev, the reference to the dark eyelashes befits Mandel'shtam, and the date ascribed to the dedication, December 27, is the officially reported date of Mandel'shtam's death.[41] The nearly coinciding birthdays of Kniazev (January 25, 1891) and Mandel'shtam (January 15, 1891) suggest an astrological twinning, both poets born under an unlucky star and destined to premature deaths. Most significantly, toward the end of chapter 1 and before the Intermedia, the line rendered in italics as a metapoetic aside speaks of Kniazev and Mandel'shtam as "the two merged ghosts." The whispered words the poem's narrator hears uttered in that digression echo those of the Dragoon (Kniazev) in chapter 4 of the poem, while the final line of the digression, "I am ready for death," was attributed by Nadezhda Mandel'shtam to her husband.[42] This composite figure's complex identity expands his symbolic value beyond that of either poet alone; it also brings forth intimate details of each poet's life instead of alluding solely to their poetry.

The idiom of performance pervades *Poem without a Hero* and comprises a substantial component of the work's intertextuality (the references to dance, opera, and theater number no fewer than 32[43]). The special role of the performer as an agent of cultural memory becomes clear in the figure of Olga Sudeikina. The dancer embodies cultural syncretism through her valence of performance roles (including a faun in Ilyia Satz's ballet *Dance of the Fauns* and Confusion-Psyche from Beliaev's *Confusion, or 1840*): her diverse roles converged on the space of her body and accumulate in palimpsestic fashion. In addition to these roles Akhmatova cast Sudeikina as her double, thereby spotlighting her own identity as a preserver of world culture: whereas Sudeikina fulfilled this role by embodying a palimpsest of performance, Akhmatova realized it through the intertextuality of her poetry.

Theatricality and the Masquerade Chronotope

Iurii Lotman characterized theater as a "translator code" (*promezhutochnyi kod*), a vital link between life and art. In "Iconic Rhetoric," he explained that a constant semiotic exchange transpires between life and theater, and between painting and theater, which establishes theater as the "translator code," or intermediary semiotic system, between life and art. Lotman asserted that "[t]heater occupies an interstitial place between the indiscrete flow of life and the division of discrete 'suspended' moments characteristic of representational arts."[44] The temporal continuity and forward-moving trajectory of the theatrical performance mimics the chronological arrow of life, and yet the division of life into discrete episodes or periods resembles the framed finitude of a painted canvas. Masquerade occupies a similar interstitial place between life and visual art, embodying qualities of each: like theater, masquerade assimilates the flow and punctuation of time. However, heterogeneity, spontaneity, and the implied lack of divide between actor and audience distinguish the masquerade from theater and align it more closely with life itself.[45] Unbounded by stage or script, the freedom and unpredictability of masquerade differentiate it from planned performance.

While Lotman's view of artistic media as systems of communication distinct from life and from one another facilitates an understanding of the unique expressive possibilities of each, it obstructs an appreciation for the creative richness born in their combination. The performance stage may conjoin the dramatic text, visual arts, fashion, and architectural design, as well as music and dance. Richard Wagner celebrated this artistic complementariness in his operas, which realized his ideal of the *Gesamtkunstwerk*, or "total artwork." Masquerade balls, too,

enveloped participants in a totalizing artistic experience and extin-
guished the figurative footlights. The Artists' Balls at the Saint Petersburg Academy of Arts, which I discuss in chapter 4, exemplify the
artistic collaboration that produced the events' legendary magnificence.
In addition to the elaborate costumes populating the masquerade's
performance space, decorations for the halls wherein the balls took
place were remarkably elaborate, transcending in ornamentation and
lavishness the typical stage décor and props used by the imperial theaters. Architectural in scope, the decoration of the halls often involved
the construction of kiosks, columns, pools, and fountains. The tableaux
vivants and processions with which the Artists' Balls would begin were
often governed by a theme, which in turn dictated the decorative style
of the halls.[46] (Note that multiple halls were involved: the evening's
events were too varied and the guests too numerous to be contained in
a single room.) In February 1900, a reporter for *Novoe vremia* rapturously
described the Artists' Ball venue, the Tauride Palace, arrayed according
to the theme of ancient Greece:

> In the first hall was built a lovely veranda decorated with pyramids
> of greenery, and next to it, a pavilion bedecked in grape leaves. . . .
> In the middle of the hall an enormous palm tree unfurled its
> branches. A white colonnade, separating the first hall from the
> second, was decorated with artificial pyramids of flowers and
> greenery on which were perched beetles, butterflies, and grass-
> hoppers. In the second hall was the Tsar's loge, guarded by Greek
> warriors in shining helmets; it was outfitted with tropical plants
> and illuminated from above the cornice by the colored rays of
> electric lamps. . . . In the third hall was a garden, and the sur-
> rounding walls were covered with decorations and pictures of
> nature from an earlier era with ancient structures. In the center of
> the hall amid pools of water was a fountain; to the sides stood
> statues of Venus and Apollo. Decorations on a dais portrayed the
> sea, and along its sides were white kiosks with blue trim where
> refreshing beverages were sold.[47]

The elaborate decoration of several halls for the evening's events not
only outdid the typical theater's attention to detail, but also far exceeded
the spatial bounds of the theater stage. Participants could wander freely
about, immersed in a totalizing aesthetic experience that included
detailed sets, costumes, music, dance, and theatrical sketches.

Many turn-of-the-century masquerades synthesized artistic media, but it was the philological masquerades that epitomized the masquerade chronotope as one of cultural conjunction. The free interplay among literary, historical, and mythic figures represented through aliases and costumes, demonstrates the combinatory dynamics of intertextuality. The syncretism of the philological masquerade positions it as a productive metaphor for memory and a tool for inscribing historical experience into personal biography, or writing oneself into cultural tradition. Ivanov merged his own autobiographical experience with world heritage through costumed role-playing at the Evenings of Hafiz as part of his neo-Platonic investigation of aestheticism and eroticism. Akhmatova mobilized the philological masquerade as a literary device that enabled her to cast her autobiographical memories (the ghosts from the year 1913) as cultural mummer-memories (characters from literature and performance), thereby underscoring the interconnectedness of her personal life and Russia's patrimony. The inconsistent narrative perspective and voice in *Poem without a Hero* reflect the particularity of the philological masquerade chronotope, wherein the convergence of epochs and national traditions contrasts with the cohesiveness and unity of the theatrical script.

Whereas certain modernist writers such as Gippius and Dmitrieva (discussed in chapter 3) merged life with art by intentionally fashioning their behavior and appearance as a project, Ivanov and Akhmatova took a philological approach to bridging the realms. Instead of transforming present life into an entirely new artistic creation according to a unique vision, the poets studied in this chapter used the philological masquerade as a strategy for appropriating artifacts of cultural history and intertwining them with personal experience. Character aliases based on fictional or historical figures served as Realistic Symbols that could function metonymically (Kuzmin as Antinous, Sudeikina as a seductive faun) or metaphorically (Ivanov as Hyperion, Akhmatova as Sudeikina). Casting personal experience in terms of cultural patrimony, the philological model of uniting art and life, gave way in the early 1910s to the irreverent costumes of the avant-garde, which signaled their rebellion against cultural tradition, as I demonstrate in the next chapter.

6

>─┼─◆>─•─◯─•─<◆─┼─≺

ʠvant-ʛarde Costumes
Estranging Practices of Masquerade

ʠfter the premier of Alexander Blok's *The Fairground Booth* on December 30, 1906, the play's cast and a coterie of Petersburg's cultural elite participated in "The Evening of Paper Ladies" at the apartment of actress Vera Ivanova on Torgovaia Street, not far from Vera Komissarzhevskaia's experimental Dramatic Theater, where the play was performed.[1] While the men wore standard black half-masks, actress Valentina Verigina and other actresses "decided to put on dresses made of colored crepe paper and to make headdresses out of the same paper."[2] The invitations to what became known as the Paper Ball stirred anticipation by announcing the evening's imaginative premise in terms bordering on science fiction: "Paper ladies on an airship of invention flew in from the moon. Would you care to attend their ball?"[3] Put in a metonymic relationship to their crepe-paper dresses, these paper ladies were emissaries from the world of sartorial imagination, their lunar adventure a metaphor for the flight of fancy that their unusual costumes betokened.

The cosmic trope's appeal for the ball's organizers lay in its suggestion of strangeness through formal novelty, a principle that Russian Formalist Viktor Shklovsky elaborated a decade later in regard to the practice of writing literature. Shklovsky's term *ostranenie,* translated as estrangement or alienation, applies to the costuming practices on stage and in life among avant-garde writers and artists. Speaking of costumes in terms intended for literary analysis assumes certain parallels in the way the semiotic systems signify, namely, that rupturing or overturning an artistic convention of any kind complicates or prolongs apprehension, causing authentic rather than automatized perception and enabling a more genuine or profound aesthetic experience. In the 1917 essay "Art as Device" Shklovsky articulated the idea that artistic literature produces a defamiliarizing effect on the reader. While avant-garde artists consciously strove for an estranging effect, *ostranenie* was also an important principle in more representative art and literature. As Shklovsky demonstrated in his analysis of works by the writer Lev Tolstoy, unconventional approaches to representation that complicated apperception were an important feature of classical literature as well. Shklovsky observed that formal strategies including unusual narrative perspective and unexpected metaphors could render the object of representation strange or alien to the reader, thereby renewing his perception and understanding of it. Avant-garde writers, most notably Russia's Futurists, engaged in literary practices that went far beyond the goal of awakening the reader from his perceptual coma, however. With their violent rhetoric of overthrowing the past, they complicated comprehension as much as apprehension by destroying words and syntax and replacing them with neologisms and, in the case of Velimir Khlebnikov and Aleksei Kruchenykh, fabricating an entirely new transrational language called *zaum* (the contraction of two words that translate literally as "beyond sense": *za um*).

In the same way that the Futurists aggressively reworked the purpose of literary language, severing it from its representational responsibilities and freeing it from symbolic signification, avant-garde artists overturned assumptions about clothing and cosmetics. No longer would gender and bourgeois notions of good taste dictate appearance, and no longer would appearance be configured to serve solely classical notions of beauty. The socially disruptive costuming and face-painting practiced in the early 1910s by such figures as Mikhail Larionov, Ilyia Zdanevich, Vladimir Mayakovsky, David Burliuk, and Kruchenykh evinced a renegade attitude toward the materials and craft of visual art similar to that of the Futurists toward language. The interest of modernists throughout Europe in expanding the limits of an artistic medium, literary or visual, as well as making conspicuous the very materiality and plasticity of that medium, characterized the Russian avant-garde's attitude toward dress as well. Their practices of épatage designed to shock and scandalize the bourgeoisie were fundamentally defamiliarizing. This chapter examines the avant-garde's unconventional, at times outlandish and subversive, strategies of representing, clothing, and adorning the human body. These strategies were on display in daily life, on the theater stage, and at costume balls of the period. I argue that the avant-garde reconceptualization of physical appearance and treatment of the body as an artistic canvas relied on the principle of applying or using materials unexpectedly, thereby disrupting traditional, culturally determined assumptions about aesthetics and form-function relationships. This avant-garde strategy for rebelliously stylizing the body's appearance penetrated into the public sphere and influenced mainstream costume balls and parties, the themes and dress for which became increasingly experimental in the early 1910s.

The Paper Ball

Verigina recounts in her memoirs how, only two or three days before *The Fairground Booth*'s premiere, the cast decided to celebrate its opening with an after party. It was on the advice of actor Boris Pronin (the future proprietor of the Stray Dog Cabaret, where costume parties were not uncommon) that they resolved to organize a costume party (*vecher masok*). This real-life, extratheatrical event, which became known as the Paper Ball or Evening of Paper Ladies, presented the production's cast with an opportunity for collective play during which their interactions and dialogue were unbounded by an overarching dramatic storyline. The Paper Ball was, however, sartorially circumscribed by a governing theme, or more accurately, a governing medium, that formally and thus visually unified the participants in a unique kind of performance. All of the costumes were made of crepe paper and fashioned in a single style. Each actress wore a gown and headdress of matching color, the choice of which was dictated by personal preference.[4] The uniformity of style directed attention away from the costumes' cut and toward the material from which they were constructed. The use of crepe paper instead of a woven fabric differentiated the costumes from everyday dress: lightweight and fragile, the paper gowns would neither warm nor protect the body. Their lack of functionality demonstrated the essence of fashion as art, the triumph of style over practicality.

Designing a costume out of paper was not, however, a new idea. The January 15, 1895, issue of the Russian women's magazine *Fashion World* featured instructions for making a masquerade costume in the likeness of a carnation from crepe paper. The reader was counseled to place an upper skirt made from dark red paper over an inexpensive satin skirt of the same color, and to weave a wreath of four matching paper carnations for the head.[5] What was new in the 1906 Paper Ball was the collective engagement in wearing identical nonrepresentational costumes: the actresses did not aspire to portray an individual or object such as a carnation. Rather, they reveled in the material alterity of their costumes as an homage to and perpetuation of the aesthetics that reigned in Blok's play, the debut of which they were celebrating. Significantly, the Paper Ball reiterated two key features of the play. As a costume party it recapitulated the play's central masquerade scene; and the material novelty of the costumes, the ladies' paper dresses, evoked the unexpected use of cardboard for the Mystics' costumes in avant-garde theatrical director Vsevolod Meierkhol'd's production. However, whereas Blok satirized the masquerade as an arch-Symbolist topos of mystery and enigma in *The Fairground Booth*, the playful but unironic Paper Ball costumes introduced an aesthetic sensibility dependent on the principle of estrangement, which would come to characterize the Futurist and Rayonist vestimentary and cosmetic travesties in the 1910s.

The ladies' paper gowns and headdresses problematized the inter-relation among objects (dress), their materials of construction (paper versus cloth), and the culturally determined assumptions about their value and function. In substituting paper for cloth, one cotton fiber for another, the actresses' costumes defied expectations about vestimentary construction and wearability, thereby revealing a manufactured relation-ship between material or object and its function. Much the same way cross-dressers disrupt assumptions about the correlation between gender and clothing, dressers who engage in games of material substitu-tion demonstrate the contingency of certain form-function relation-ships. The costumes of the alien "paper ladies" predicated their estrange-ment from convention on altering form, that is, substituting paper for cloth, and rupturing the conditional, culturally defined relationship between material and function. This artistic strategy of divorcing a material or object from its accustomed use, an act of Shklovskian es-trangement in its emphasis on pure form, resembled the non-Realist costuming and stage sets in *The Fairground Booth* and anticipated the avant-garde's experimentation with the formal components of physical appearance. In "The Construction of Story and Novel" Shklovsky encoded his ideas on poetic disjuncture, the slippage between signifier and signified in literary language, in terms of a word donning new clothing. "The poet makes a semantic shift," wrote Shklovsky. "He tears a concept out of the realm of meaning in which it had been located and transfers it with the help of the word (a trope) into a different one. Through this act we experience novelty, the presence of the subject in a new semantic zone. A new word sits on a subject like a new dress."[6] The avant-garde attitude toward self-representation resonates with Shklovsky's literary theory: redefining the relationship between object and function, construction material and purpose, is akin to rupturing the relationship between the word and its referent, signifier and signified. The dress, renewed perceptually through its novel form, resembles the poetic word that signifies metaphorically.

Avant-Garde Aesthetics of The Fairground Booth

Blok's watershed play is frequently discussed in terms of the Symbolist religious-philosophical program it satirizes. However, these discussions seldom fully acknowledge the play's pioneering articulation of the aesthetics of estrangement. This is in part because the continuity between the Symbolist and avant-garde attitudes toward signification is underappreciated. Decoupling signifier and signified, liberating the word from the responsibility of singularly literal denotation is a fundamental trait of literary language. Symbolists valued the artistic opportunity presented by semantic slippage and the accompanying subtleties of connotation it afforded. Some poets, such as Konstantin Bal'mont, separated the word from its literal meaning because they privileged such nonsemantic features of a word as its sonic shape (in the name of poetic assonance) and because they celebrated subjective, associative strategies of interpretation. The literary and artistic avant-garde also abandoned conventional, socially constructed paradigms that dictated meaning, but they did so in the name of épatage and a self-conscious quest for newness. The contingent relationship between signifier and signified championed by Symbolism migrated into the material world of the avant-garde as a contingent relationship between form and function.

The unusual set and costume designs in *The Fairground Booth* that divorced the physical materials of construction from their expected purposes evinced a Shklovskian strangeness. In addition to its own aesthetic merits, the resulting defamiliarization advanced Blok's satire of Symbolism's mystical strain, to which he himself formerly subscribed. The Symbolists' overemphasis on the spiritual and ineffable at the expense of the physical plane manifests itself in the play's central conflict: the Mystics mistake their meeting of Colombina, a fictional character from the Italian folk-theater tradition of commedia dell'arte, for a spiritually momentous, transcendental encounter with the personification of Death. They mistake her cardboard paleness for Death's ethereal pallor, and her braid for a scythe, punning on the fact that the words are homonyms (*kosa*) in Russian. Blok and Meierkhol'd thus expressed the Mystics' estrangement from the physical world through the use of material substitutions in the staging, most notably the Mystics' cardboard costumes, to which I shall return.

The conflict between the spiritual and the physical is also borne out in the incongruent performance genres alluded to in the play. The Mystics' religious striving evokes the medieval mystery play and its heavy influence on Symbolist drama, while the commedia dell'arte characters represent the spirited and earthy folk *balagan*, a type of unscripted performance at outdoor carnivals and town fairs. Viacheslav Ivanov, one of the most active theoreticians of Symbolist theater during the first decade of the twentieth century, envisioned the theater as a forum for collective inquiry into metaphysical questions.[7] Inspired by Friedrich Nietzsche's *The Birth of Tragedy* (1872) and by his own studies in classical philology, Ivanov insisted on the importance of dissolving the boundary between performers and audience as it had been in ancient Greek drama and Dionysian ritual. Nietzsche asserted that "the audience of Attic tragedy discovered itself in the chorus of the orchestra. Audience and chorus were never fundamentally set over against each other: all was one grand chorus of dancing, singing satyrs, and of those who let themselves be represented by them."[8] Ivanov accordingly aspired to create a modern theatrical experience that would unite audience and performers in a modern-day iteration, which Ivanov couched in the Eastern Orthodox conception of *sobornost'*, a perfect union of all believers that enabled transcendental experience.[9] In the essay "Presentiments and Portents," which appeared the same year as *The Fairground Booth*, Ivanov called for theater to overcome the narrow confines of pure spectacle in order to unify all participants in collective metaphysical investigation. "The spectator must become an actor, a co-participant in the rite," he declared. "The crowd of viewers must merge into a choral body similar to the mystical community of the ancient 'orgies' and 'mysteries.'"[10] In Ivanov's view, collective theatrical acting resembled collective ritual acts in its ability to transport participants beyond the boundaries of the earthly stage.

Fyodor Sologub subscribed to similar mystical ideals in theater, authoring in 1907 a mystery play, *A Liturgy to Myself*, and issuing a year later a theoretical formulation of his ideas entitled "Theater of One Will."[11] Sologub, however, questioned Ivanov's ideal of communal interaction, fearing that such an erasure of the divisions between actor and audience would "transform spectacle into masquerade, which is in fact a combination of play and spectacle."[12] The gravitas of theater as a solemn artistic and spiritual experience, Sologub suggested, would be compromised by universal participation, as at a masquerade. The maskers' persistent awareness that their quasi-performance is play, and the masquerade's improvisational interactions and resulting unruliness, tied it to earthly experience. Moreover, the anonymity of masquerade disguise offered the possibility of transgressing and violating social and ethical taboos, all of which compromised the ascent to pure, mystical heights. In this view, masquerade's levity and unpredictability aligned it more closely with the folksy balagan, the antithesis of Symbolist theater.

Blok's play thus brings into conflict the differing theories of theater advocated by Ivanov and Sologub. Mocking the quasi-religious ideals of Ivanov's Symbolist theater and sympathizing with Sologub's designation of such acts of collective play as masquerade-like, Blok mobilized the masquerade topos, a master trope of Symbolism, to satirize the movement's obsessive interest in ambiguity and enigma, as well as its feigned gravitas and mystical pretensions. *The Fairground Booth* collides the Mystics' solemn quest for transcendence through communal rite with the light-hearted and earthy, potentially bawdy and rowdy, interactive and improvisational balagan. The balagan opposed the high-minded quest for religious communion that was at the center of Symbolist theories about theater.

Born in the town square and folk festivals, the balagan was an informal act such as a puppet show, clown performance, or other slapstick comedy routine dependent on physical gimmicks, overacting, bright colors, and sonic ebullience (by way of rhyme and meter) to attract an audience and hold its attention. The puppet's mechanical movements and the clown's exaggerated facial features and vivid costume underscored not only their physicality but also the constructed artifice that differentiates these figures from the actors of mimetic theater. The town square balagan also featured acts of physical derring-do alongside circus-style shows boasting freaks of nature. Attractions might include the "fish-man," the "Negro-Hercules" who possessed "inhuman dental strength," the man with a stomach of iron who could down a shot of turpentine and chase it with the very glass from which he drank, and other "wondrous wonders" (*chudo-chudnoe*) such as a two-headed calf and a "spider lady."[13] Amusing in their deviance from the ordinary, such balagan performances represented a lowbrow tradition of folk entertainment at odds with the transcendental concerns of Symbolist theater.

In the case of the cardboard Colombina, Blok's play capitalizes on the balagan's affinity for estranging acts and performance surrogates (puppets, marionettes) to create a foil for the Mystic-Symbolists' obsessive focus on the spiritual and ineffable. By calling attention to the cardboard from which Colombina is constructed, Blok placed an emphasis on her physical presence in a way that also distinguished the premier's after party, the Paper Ball, at which the crepe-paper dresses extended the play's spirit of aesthetic alienation. In harnessing the balagan's reputation for featuring "wondrous wonders" of physical strength and bodily deformations wrought by genetic accident, and in the metonymically named Paper Ladies' implied exchange of flesh for fiber, the play and its celebration anticipated the avant-garde's rejection of Symbolism's preference for disembodied abstraction. The avant-garde embraced the physical, material world in pursuit of new ideas about the purpose of art, and in the desire to push the limits of any given artistic medium.

In the informal folk balagan performance, the performer frequently engaged with the audience, thereby bridging the actor-spectator divide. However, instead of the audience becoming the ancient Greek dramatic chorus or participants in Dionysian-like ritual, and experiencing the cathartic or spiritualizing performance sought by Symbolist dramaturges, the audience of the balagan interacted superficially with the entertainers. As is made clear in Blok's five-stanza eponymous poem from 1905 on which he based the play, the divide between performance and extra-performative reality is easily breached at the balagan.[14] Whereas the clown in the poem transgresses the implicit divide between actor and audience by crossing over the footlights, it is the author figure in the play who bridges the distance between performance space and extra-theatrical reality through his metadramatic interventions.

The disagreement between the Chairman of the Mystics and Pierrot, Colombina's fiancé, about her identity satirizes the Symbolists' insistent attempts to find metaphysical meaning in all earthly figures and events. The Mystics' mistaking Colombina for Death grants her a second, contingent identity, effectively creating for her an otherworldly doppelgänger. In the eyes of the Mystics, the two-dimensional Colombina is transformed into an animate incarnation of Death, in accordance with the Symbolists' tendency to divest the concrete object of its own value in pursuit of high-minded metaphysics. The play satirizes the Symbolists' blindness, their failure to see physical reality for what it was, as they stubbornly aspired to apprehend transcendental significance in the quotidian. The Mystic-Symbolists' unwavering conviction that the female performance figure is Death recalls Blok's own insistence that his wife, Liubov', was the earthly manifestation of his mystical ideal, the Eternal Feminine. With his acolytes, Blok relentlessly followed Liubov', observing her actions and awaiting divine revelation. In much the same way the play's Mystics pursue Colombina out of the misguided belief that she represents a spiritual apotheosis.[15] Like the Blokites' misreading of Liubov', the Mystics' misreading of Colombina is illustrative of their tentative, conditional relationship to the material world; of their alienation from the earthly realm; and of their treatment of physicality as something symbolic. The satire of the Mystics' religious philosophy, which recalls that of Blok's fellow Symbolists, reveals how the Mystic-Symbolists' penchant for associative and metaphorical thinking comedically distanced them from the physical world. The play's satire revolves primarily around the fact that the Mystics in their religious zeal mistake the fictional, cardboard Colombina for the embodiment of an ineffable state. The act of misidentification creates a false double, as if Death wore the mask of Colombina, the esoteric masquerading as the prosaic. Perhaps not coincidentally, the identical cut of the ladies' dresses at the Paper Ball likewise created an optical illusion of multiple doublings, thereby highlighting the fact that the dresses stemmed from a singular sewing pattern—also made from paper.

The play's Mystics participate in a masquerade, the guests at which were dressed in iconic half-masks and dominos in Meierkhol'd's production, according to Verigina's memoirs. Following nineteenth-century literary convention, Blok referred to the masquerade participants as "masks" (*maski*), synecdochally identifying them through one element of their dress, which has been singled out for its central symbolic significance ("The masks are spinning to the soft sounds of dancing").[16] The half-mask and domino represent the generalized ideas of concealment and costume, as they refuse to posit a new identity. Because it represents effacement, the obfuscation of all identity, the blank half-mask, the barest, most reduced form of disguise at a masquerade, is a signifier that lacks a signified. It is a symbol, an icon of disguise and anonymity. The half-mask symbolizes the very idea of the Symbol, which both conceals and reveals, offering a physical intimation of a secret that awaits discovery. The Mystics are thus connected to Symbolism both by their insistence on reading Colombina as an instantiation of Death, and by their wearing masks, which were quintessential Symbols and a widespread trope of the Symbolist movement. The mask was also a potent trope because of its dissociative powers, its ability to effect an existential strangeness. Echoing the opinion of the play's knight that the masquerade disguises make his rendezvous with his beloved more wondrous, Verigina recollected, "When we [the actors and actresses in the performance] put on the half-masks, when the music started up—music that was charming, as if leading into a bewitched circle—something happened that forced each of us to renounce (*otreshit'sia*) his or her essence."[17] The mask could fundamentally alter perception, defamiliarize the familiar, or—in the case of Verigina's experience at the Paper Ball—defamiliarize the unfamiliar by making it falsely familiar. Verigina described how all participants were required to use the informal second-person pronoun "ty," which was particularly awkward given their customary politeness with one another. She complained, "it was strange to use '*ty*,' despite the mask," suggesting that she expected the disguise to dismantle the commonplaces of social propriety.[18] Instead, the mask made everything more strange by distancing the individual from her self-defined identity and from normative social relations. Verigina's experience reinforces how the masquerade topos was linked to Symbolism's obsessive interest in the enigmatic and transcendental, and thus served as a target of Blok's satire.

The three pairs of lovers in the masquerade scene read as parodies of different worldviews within Decadence and Symbolism. *The Fairground Booth*'s satire of mystical Symbolism arises from Blok's renunciation of the movement's self-absorption and subjectivity. The political turmoil and attempted revolution of 1905 convinced him of the need to move away from transcendental abstraction in order to address timely civic-historical themes in his poetry. The first pair of lovers, dressed in blue and pink costumes, acts as if they are in a church, gazing upward toward an imagined dome. The exalted tenor of the couple's exchange, which takes place in an illusory church, evokes the Symbolists' mystical agenda that transported them beyond the physical confines of earthly existence.

The second pair of lovers is dressed in red and black, and the female masker's sexual aggressiveness aligns her with the early Symbolist/ Decadent trope of the femme fatale, which was diametrically opposed to Blok's former idealization of the Eternal Feminine. In the third pair, the male masker is dressed as a medieval knight, a sardonic nod to the Symbolists' fascination with the Middle Ages.[19] His female companion echoes the final word of his every sentence, a mockery of his arch solemnity that is also suggestive of the way that the figure of the Eternal Feminine was a mere reflection of what was projected onto her. The knight's chivalric idealization of his female companion recalls Blok's own former idolization of the Eternal Feminine, a mystical conception of divine wisdom. Blok adopted the conception from philosopher and poet Vladimir Solovyov, whose poem "Three Meetings" (*Tri svidaniia*) tells of the Eternal Feminine arriving as a ghost. In *The Fairground Booth* this moment of anticipated arrival is satirized when the Mystics mistake Colombina for the spectral figure of Death.

Another way Blok signaled that the play is satirical was through the use of material proxies, the falseness and artifice of which contributed to an ironic tone. Rendered artistically in cardboard, Colombina's body bespeaks her fictional provenance: her body is the work of human hands. As noted earlier, the fact that the Mystics mistake Colombina for Death, misinterpret artificial surface for authentic, transcendental essence, is the play's satirical lynchpin. The act of material substitution, using cardboard instead of flesh, communicates irony by inventively deviating from formal expectations. In a move that recalled Colombina's cardboard body and the Paper Ladies' crepe dresses, Meierkhol'd dressed the Mystics in cardboard costumes, the rigidity of which corresponded to their insistent belief in Death's visitation. In addition to literalizing their estrangement from the material world, the Mystics' cardboard costumes exposed them as the subject of satire by further associating them with the parodic imitation produced by material substitution. Moreover, the cardboard figure and costumes put on display the play's status as art. In their blatant exposure of formal construction, the cardboard proxies are instances of "laying bare the device" (*obnazhenie priema*), as Shklovsky termed it. The cardboard costumes served not only to cover the actors' bodies, but also to reveal the constructedness of the theatrical world.

Similarly, certain stage props and elements of the set are false replicas or artificial proxies, ironic doubles created through the act of substitution.

The accessories belonging to the knight from the third pair of lovers are materially divorced from their conventional construction: his helmet is cardboard, his sword—wood. The knight's falsity and pretension, qualities frequently derided by critics of the Symbolist movement, are made manifest in his phony props. The material substitution is a distorted doubling of an original that signals playfulness, irreverence, and polemical intent. The critical distance created by the distorted double, which is wrought by an unexpected material substitution, is an essential ingredient of parody. The substitute-doubles in this case are suggestive of toys and children's play. This association undermines and thereby mocks the knight's solemnity; it also reminds the viewers that the events on stage are, in fact, just play and not mystical rite. Recalling the knight, Verigina pointed out that he spoke in an excessively mannered fashion at Meierkhol'd's insistence, "so that the author's irony was immediately evident."[20] In addition to the visual and material substitutions, vocal stylization was another strategy of distancing that contributed to the estrangement of events on stage. Recollecting Meierkhol'd's own performance as Pierrot, Verigina also observed that his voice was eerily plaintive, sounding at some moments almost like a musical instrument and at others " . . . as if someone was pressing on a spring in the wooden heart of a puppet (*kukla*) and it emitted a moan."[21] Pierrot's inhuman wooden-puppet voice expressed his artifice, as did his white face that resembled a blank canvas.

Like the fake helmet and sword, which emblematize stagecraft and performative artifice, the clown's cranberry-juice blood reminds the viewer that theater's goal for Blok and Meierkhol'd was not mimesis, but rather creative artistry: artifice constitutes art. Further distancing the play from theatrical realism are the conspicuously artificial stage sets. When Harlequin jumps through the window, his body punctures the painted paper facsimile of an outdoor view. Following that, the stage directions indicate that the decorations suddenly shoot up and fly off stage. When the artistic devices of stagecraft are laid bare, the audience's attention is drawn to the production's status as performance art. The material substitutes for "reality" artistically fashioned for the stage expose the theatrical illusions as such. The play's author figure, who periodically "interrupts" the action on stage to bemoan in scripted asides that his "most realistic" drama has been hijacked and no longer resembles what he wrote, further contributes to the viewer's mindfulness of the spectacle as performance art.

Material Estrangement in Futurist Theater

The Fairground Booth not only represented a rejection of Symbolist and Realist theater; it was also a bellwether of the avant-garde aesthetics and parodic temperament that would reign in the early 1910s. In the 1912 essay "Balagan," which articulated his artistic philosophy governing the production of Blok's play, Meierkhol'd emphasized the importance of saving theater from dull mimetic representation. He celebrated a production style that joyfully reveled in its artistry and honored the director's creative license. He proclaimed that stage art (*iskusstvo cheloveka na stsene*) is "about expertly picking a mask, picking a decorative costume, and putting on a show for the public with the sparkle of technique—like the dancer, or the intriguer at a masquerade ball, or the simpleton from the old Italian comedy [commedia dell'arte], or the juggler."[22] He viewed the mask as an iconic manifestation of creativity, an expression of imagination, which he valued over bland "truthfulness." Like the English theater visionary Edward Gordon Craig, who favored the marionette over the human actor on stage in order to emphasize the artifice of stage art and to expand the range of theatrical possibilities, the Russian director embraced the use of human surrogates on stage.

Meierkhol'd prized commedia dell'arte characters because of their capacity for constant reinvention, their range of "faces." For him, they were endlessly regenerative and nuanced artistic devices. As he explained in "Balagan," "Harlequin is both a powerful magician and a representative of infernal powers. . . . He has two faces (*dva lika*), which represent his two poles, but there are also many nuanced faces in between."[23] The director likewise celebrated the commedia characters' centuries-long tradition because the spectator could "see [on stage] not only a given Harlequin, but all the Harlequins that remain in his memory."[24] Like the Ivanovian Realistic Symbols discussed in the previous chapter, the commedia characters were instruments of intertextuality, threads that could be traced through the fabric of European performance history, from sixteenth-century Venice to fin-de-siècle Russia, eliciting a chain of associations and thus broadening the spectator's experience.[25] Meierkhol'd focused on the commedia characters' transcendence of time and place, their universality and openness to endless creative appropriation and reinvention. Originally called *commedia dell'arte all'improviso*, or "comedy of the art of improvisation," the stock characters' established personalities and conflicts loosely guided the actors' spontaneous interactions at town fairs and other informal entertainment venues.

In addition to the creative possibilities inherent in masks and in such performance figures as puppets and marionettes, Meierkhol'd relished the shock-value and symbolism of using them on stage alongside live actors. In the staging of another watershed modernist play, Mayakovsky's 1913 *Vladimir Mayakovsky: A Tragedy*, such predilection for nonhuman actors coalesced with the trope of material substitution under the directorship of the playwright himself. In this play the girlfriend of the eponymous hero is a towering thirteen-foot-tall Amazon, who was constructed three-dimensionally of papier-mâché in the original production.[26] Unlike Colombina's satirically doubled cardboard body, the sculptural heft of Mayakovsky's papier-mâché woman is an unabashedly aggressive confrontation with bourgeois theatrical mimetism.

In other instances as well, Mayakovsky's play treats the body abjectly, magnifying its ungainly physicality by subjecting it to the same violent fracturing that characterized Futurist attitudes toward language, typography, and social norms. Several of the play's characters are named according to their missing body parts: The Man without an Ear, The Man without an Eye and a Leg, and The Man without a Head. In a play that speaks to the possibility of liberation from Old World constraints, including those of the ruling class and social convention (a possibility that can be realized only by the revolutionary, Mayakovsky), the characters' physical disintegration bespeaks their social dejection. Their grotesque bodies amplify their social alienation by physically distinguishing them from the mainstream, and they also create an unsettling effect on the spectators. One observer, actor Alexander Mgebrov, recalled: "A semi-mysterious light lit the stage around which cotton or calico had been stretched with a high backdrop of black cardboard, which basically constituted all the scenery. What this cardboard was meant to represent—I, as well as others, did not understand, but the strange fact of the matter was—it made an impression; . . . From behind the curtains those taking part in the play filed out one after the other. The participants were cardboard; live dolls. The public tried laughing, but the laughter died . . . and when in that first moment the laughter died . . . immediately one sensed that the audience was strangely alert."[27] The audience's "strange alertness" was, as Shklovsky theorized, the result of unexpected manipulations of form. The nonrepresentational scenery and boxy costumes jolted the spectators out of their passive role, the oddness of the former stimulating the attentiveness of the latter. By describing the actors as "live dolls," alienating them from their humanness, Mgebrov made clear that the cardboard garments subsumed the wearers, creating a powerful estranging effect. Avant-garde artist Pavel Filonov drew the characters' costumes on cardboard, which the actors carried in front of themselves on stage for the first production.[28] The cardboard costumes at once recall the Mystics' cardboard costumes in *The Fairground Booth* and evoke the paper dresses from the 1906 Paper Ball. Just as the unusual construction of the dresses at the Paper Ball earned the maskers the moniker "Paper Ladies," the cardboard costumes in *Vladimir Mayakovsky: A Tragedy* prompted Mgebrov to liken them to paper dolls. The abstract cotton and cardboard stage sets, along with the defamiliarized costumes, bespoke a conscious attempt to create for the viewers an experience of strangeness that corresponded to the characters' social alienation. Mayakovsky aligned the play's formal aesthetics, which pivoted on their intentional deviation from conventional imagery and strategies of representation, with the play's central ideas about forging a progressive future freed from bourgeois limitations.

Like the defamiliarizing cardboard costumes in *Vladimir Mayakovsky: A Tragedy*, the costumes designed by Kazimir Malevich for the Futurist opera *Victory over the Sun* stunned viewers with their daring departure from the aesthetics of theatrical realism. The opera was a collaboration among Malevich, Kruchenykh, and Mikhail Matiushin, and it was staged together with Mayakovsky's play in early December 1913 at the Luna Park Theater in Saint Petersburg. Malevich's Suprematist costumes, which Benedikt Livshits characterized as "artistic zaum," abstracted the actors' bodies into an amalgamation of geometric shapes and machine parts. One particular costume sketch, that of the "Reciter" (*chtets*), features a capital letter A and what appears to be an apostrophe on the left leg. Malevich replaced the conventional cloth costume with paper, a fact that he accentuated by adorning it with print (which also announced the declamatory role of the "Reciter"). Made from cardboard and wire, the costumes conferred upon their wearers a similarity to "moving machines," in the estimation of Kruchenykh.[29] Fittingly, a photograph of the three creators of *Victory over the Sun* was doctored to reflect the defamiliarization of the human body and the trope of material substitution that characterized the play's costumes. Whereas the original photo showed Kruchenykh reclining across the other two men's laps, the altered photo replaces Kruchenykh with a Primitivist paper cutout of Venus done by Larionov. It appears that Matiushin and

Malevich hold the life-size nude horizontally across their laps, as if the woman was a rigid, two-dimensional cardboard cutout. Upon closer inspection, however, one can see a penned outline of the mens' hands where they grasp the body, which exposes the image's inauthenticity. The substitution of the Primitivist paper figure for Kruchenykh mirrors the opera's use of cardboard for costumes: like the stylized, two-dimensional Venus, the flat, rigid costumes produced an illusion of anatomical transformation.[30]

A year before both performances premiered, their creators, Mayakovsky and Kruchenykh, together with Burliuk and Khlebnikov, penned the infamous Futurist manifesto, "A Slap in The Face of Public Taste." The manifesto demands to know, "Who would be so cowardly as to fear tearing off the paper armor from Briusov the Warrior's black tuxedo?"[31] The figurative paper armor they attributed to Valery Briusov, Symbolism's self-proclaimed leader, repeats the trope of paper substitution established by Blok in *The Fairground Booth* and featured in the two Futurist stage performances. Just as the knight's cardboard helmet points to Symbolism's fervor for substitute signifiers, Briusov's paper armor indexes the frailty of Symbolism's transcendental vision and its vulnerability to the Futurists' attack. The falsely protective helmet and armor offer as much bodily defense as the ladies' paper dresses at the 1906 costume party. Under the paper armor Briusov sports a black tux, a vestimentary detail which reads in this manifesto as a gibe at the figure of the Decadent dandy whom the Futurists frequently parodied. As is suggested by their mocking the aristocratic refinement of the Symbolist aesthete's clothing, the Futurists reveled in sartorial travesties.

Rebellious Dress of the Futurists

Mayakovsky's famous yellow blouse, which he claimed to have fashioned for himself out of his sister's ribbons because all of his shirts were too "disgusting" to continue wearing, became iconic. The color yellow had already acquired connotations of eccentricity and even deviance thanks to the English journal *The Yellow Book* (1894–97), an outlet of Aestheticism, the movement with which Oscar Wilde was associated. Wilde's fondness for a golden sunflower boutonniere further crystallized the color's social symbolism. In Russia, the tango craze that swept the country in 1913–14 was associated with the fiery colors of yellow and orange, which consequently became popular in fashionable circles. Perhaps the most deep-rooted Russian cultural association was, however, with the so-called "yellow house," a euphemism for the insane asylum. The color yellow thus both corresponded with and helped create the Futurists' reputation for outlandishness, eccentricity, unconventionality, and daring, as other avant-gardists incorporated it into their wardrobes. Burliuk and Vadim Shershenevich followed Mayakovsky's example with their own yellow and orange garments, Vasily Kamensky sported a jacket with yellow detailing on at least one occasion (for his appearance at the Polytechnical Museum in 1913), and Aristarkh Lentulov portrayed himself wearing yellow in his self-portrait (ironically titled "Le grand peintre").[32] Part of their rebelliousness in wearing yellow came from the irony with which they related to the color's associations with Aestheticism and Wilde, as well as the color's feminine connotations arising from the tango dance craze. The yellow clothing, along with other acts of eccentric dress and bodily ornamentation, were part of a larger quest to shock the bourgeoisie by flouting convention and to parody the snobbish figure of the dandy, which was frequently associated with Saint Petersburg and the pretensions of Western refinement. The lyrical self in Mayakovsky's 1914 poem "Fop's Blouse" (*Kofta fata*) ironically declaims his intentions of donning the yellow blouse to go promenading down "the Nevskii Prospect of the world" as a foppish flâneur.

The dandy's love of elegance, typified by his sporting a boutonniere, was a favorite target for the Futurists' irreverence. Mayakovsky famously substituted a bunch of radishes for the traditional flower, Kruchenykh opted for a carrot (its orange color recalling Wilde's iconic sunflower), while Malevich, Burliuk, and Aleksei Morgunov pushed the trope even further toward absurdity by tucking wooden spoons into their lapels. Having displaced the flower from the buttonhole, some Futurists put green carnations behind their ears and in their hair.[33] Through their substitutions, the Futurists played with subverting the customary functions of objects and the cultural paradigms of which they were a part. In the lapels of the Futurists, comestibles like vegetables and serviceable spoons were suddenly as decorative and non-utilitarian as flowers. Just as the crepe paper and cardboard costumes discussed earlier disassociated the compositional materials from their native visual-arts context and transacted a semiotic exchange, the Futurists' unexpected boutonnieres separated the objects from their culturally determined roles and assigned them new social values. By establishing their own sartorial protocol, members of the avant-garde inaugurated a new, irreverent relationship to certain physical objects, to their outward appearance, and to acts of self-representation. By distancing the spoon from its utilitarian purpose, estranging it from the dining table and valuing it for its formal qualities over its functionality, Burliuk and Malevich renewed perception of the object as such. The principle of defamiliarization that undergirded their aesthetic repurposing of functional, physical objects likewise reverberated in Futurist poetry and graphic arts.

In addition to the Futurists' sartorial travesties, which disrupted the conventional symbolic or compositional use of an object or material, their rebellious spirit found expression in their flamboyant application of cosmetics. Using the face and other parts of the body as a canvas for decorative painting, certain Futurists displayed a renegade attitude toward makeup that distanced it from the traditional aim of enhancing beauty by concealing flaws. They viewed makeup as paint to be applied to the face, which would beautify the wearer with decorative designs. No longer bound to accentuating facial features, the artist used face paint to express himself creatively. Larionov, considered the innovator behind avant-garde face-painting, applied the abstracting principles of his Rayonist style to decorating the body. In an anonymous article entitled "The Painted Larionov," which appeared in *The Moscow Gazette* on September 9, 1913, the reporter announced that the artist would be appearing at the first meeting of a group called "Aesthetics" with a "rayonist landscape" drawn in blue, yellow, and green on his face.[34] Larionov divulged to the reporter that this so-called landscape would consist of "circles on his cheeks and a net of rays all over his face."[35] Other face-painting Futurists, including Mayakovsky, Burliuk, Kruchenykh, and Kamensky, decorated their visages with whimsical imagery: zigzag lines, trees and birds, "a cubist portrait of a ballerina," and in the case of the pilot Kamensky, an airplane.[36] In yet one more example of *The Fairground Booth*'s celebratory Paper Ball exhibiting avant-garde aesthetic tendencies, Blok himself appeared with penciled eyebrows and eyes painted in carmine by actress Natalyia Volokhova, a cosmetic estrangement that anticipated the Futurists' and Rayonists' trademark face-painting.[37]

Later that year Larionov and Zdanevich composed the manifesto "Why We Paint Ourselves," in which the artists declared that the unadorned face is "vile," and that face- and body-painting represented a way to merge art and life: "After the long isolation of artists, we have loudly summoned life and life has invaded art, it is time for art to invade life. The painting of our faces is the beginning of the invasion."[38] While they acknowledged the beauty of aboriginal tattoos, they dismissed them as a one-time, permanent art form that did not conform to their dynamic vision of perpetual newness. After emigrating to Paris in 1915 to design sets and costumes for Diaghilev's *Ballets Russes*, Larionov and his wife Natalia Goncharova found a new realm in which to aestheticize the body: the costume ball. They participated most notably in the extraordinary Grand Bal Travesti Transmental on February 23, 1923. Organized for the financial benefit of the Union des Artistes Russes, the Grand Bal auctioned off masks designed by such prominent artists as Fernand Léger, Pablo Picasso, Juan Gris, and Albert Gleizes, as well as Goncharova, who also presided over her own boutique of masks (many of which betrayed an African influence) at the event.[39]

Mainstream "Futurist" Costume Parties

Perhaps not unexpectedly, given their public perambulations through the Moscow streets in outré attire starting in 1913, the avant-garde's revisionist attitude toward appearance began to influence costume designs at balls and parties. In some cases, the style of costumes joined in the playfully rebellious act of dislocating cultural expectations; in other cases, the avant-garde's sartorial and cosmetic rebellions were mocked and parodied. In his 1914 essay "Fashion" Lev Bakst addressed the public's consternation over the penetration of avant-garde aesthetics into the costumes and accessories favored by the beau monde: "I have been reading about the 'sad sensation'—the 'high-society ball' at which 'women appeared in blue, green, orange, and pink hair.' Even greater is our sorrow and surprise when we read that 'no one had anticipated such a spectacular victory of Futurism within a circle that claims to be an oasis of taste and good form.'"[40] Bakst mocked the laggards who lamented such innovation because the colored hair of which he wrote made its debut in Saint Petersburg's high society through his own creative initiative. In March 1914, Princess Elizaveta Shuvalova and Anastasia Leonard hosted concurrent Balls of Colored Wigs at which women sported bright blue, green, orange, and pink wigs that Bakst designed for the occasion.[41]

It has been suggested that Bakst's source of inspiration for the imaginative wigs was Aubrey Beardsley's *Venus and Tannhauser* (1896; 1907).[42] The wigs worn by Venus's entourage, however, were much more fanciful and made of exotic materials, including "wigs of black and scarlet

Балъ въ цвѣтныхъ парикахъ у А. С. Леонардъ (22 марта 1914 г.) въ ея роскошномъ особнякѣ въ Спб., бывшемъ князей Юрьевскихъ.

Слѣва направо: 1-й рядъ: княгиня Голицына-Муравлина, В. В. Дейтрихъ, А. С. Пестова, М. А. Шишкина, А. И. Колпашниковъ-Комакъ, Н. А. Шишкина, И. В. Игнатьева, В. В. Авиловъ. 2-й рядъ: А. В. Сулима-Самойло, Т. Е. Утина, П. В. Шиловскій, Е. Г. Земмеръ, бар. Вреде. 3-й рядъ: Е. В. Дельсаль, К. В. Сулима-Самойло, Е. В. фонъ-Розенбергъ, М. М. Бетулинская, М. С. Мамаевъ, В. П. Гаврилова, М. У. Защукъ, М. И. Поповичъ-Липовецъ, В. В. Длусская. 4-й рядъ: Е. П. Домерщикова, бар. В. Ф. Штакельбергъ, М. Г. Довичъ, А. А. Адлербергъ, М. А. Арапова, Э. Г. Гершельманъ, М. К. Каменевъ, А. А. Кузьмина-Караваева, А. Ф. Баумгартенъ, Р. С. Булацель, О. В. Верховская, бар. А. В. Аккурти, ген.-м. Максимовъ, бар. Арисгофенъ, Н. А. Лаппо-Данилевская, Т. М. Бельгардъ.

На стр. 15 по недосмотру поставлены ковычки около слова Ласло (худ. Laszlo).

Figure 23. Photo of Anastasia Leonard's Ball of Colored Wigs (March 22, 1914). (image courtesy of the Russian National Library)

wools, of peacocks' feathers, of gold and silver threads, of swansdown, of the tendrils of the vine, and of human hairs."[43] Among Venus's retinue, though, some women "had put on delightful little moustaches dyed in purples and bright greens, twisted and waxed with absolute skill."[44] While the unusual coloration of the moustaches accorded with Bakst's rainbow-hued wigs, Bakst himself pointed to Ida Rubinstein's blue wig worn in *Cléopâtre* in 1909, a performance for which he designed costumes.[45] Rubinstein donned a light-blue wig with golden braids on either side of her face; she was swathed in twelve veils, each of which was slowly unwound to reveal her nude body, painted a transfixing shade of turquoise.[46] Bakst commented that the brightly colored wigs represented a stage in the evolution of female appearance and a distinctively twentieth-century style. He believed that color was a powerful component of appearance, and that its importance in hair as well as dress was axiomatic. In "Fashion" he asserted, "naturally, with such a sumptuous array of pure and vivid colors, the woman of today is also obliged to apply color to her face and hair, enabling them to compete with the main colors of the dress."[47] Despite Bakst's view of colored wigs as a natural extension of fashion's reach, their formal deviation from the norm was a gesture of aesthetic estrangement. By substituting unnaturally colored synthetic strands for organic blond and brunette tresses, the artificially pigmented wigs transformed hair into something separate from the natural body and from cultural convention.

The colored wigs evoke Larionov's call to adorn the hair in addition to the body. He proposed painting the hair or donning a colored net atop one's head, and suggested that men could decorate their beards and moustaches by weaving colored threads into them.[48] However, whereas the wigs were worn within the private, contained sphere of the costume ball, Larionov envisioned the novel treatment of hair as an extension of the Rayonists' face-painting, which was a public demonstration of bold and rebellious noncompliance with status-quo appearance. Larionov's call to action was also transgressive because he advocated that men appropriate the pleasure and artistry of self-decoration, which had belonged almost exclusively to women and was part of the feminine toilette. No longer should women alone enjoy merging art and life by aestheticizing the body.

The Balls of Colored Wigs are an extreme example of how hair was an element of appearance that received particular stylizing at costume balls in the early twentieth century. Another instance can be found at the "powdered ball," or *bal poudré*, which was a type of historically themed costume ball at which women (and occasionally men) came with their hair powdered in the eighteenth-century style. In that historical period, aristocratic men and women in England and France dusted talc on their wigs and hairpieces for dress occasions. Women's powders were typically gray or bluish gray, but also included shades of violet, pink, and yellow; men, in contrast, favored staid and stately shades of white. On February 20, 1899, *The Petersburg Gazette* reported on a bal poudré organized by a certain Mrs. Ignatyeva, at which all the ladies were obliged to come either with powdered hair or wearing their hair in a historical style. The article noted that some attendees wore historical costumes, such as that of a French marquise, to go along with their coifs while others did not.[49] Another bal poudré, this time specifically in the style of Louis XV, took place in March 1908. While details of the ball are elusive, it is known that Michel Fokine and Alexander Benois participated in the event by producing for the guests a short harlequinade, *The Swindled Guest*.[50]

At such balls, the period dress and invocation of aristocratic refinement belied the events' playful temperament. One advertising poster for a bal poudré in 1903, drawn by Isaak Izrailevich Brodsky, a student of Ilyia Repin at the Saint Petersburg Academy of Arts, evokes eighteenth-century regality by featuring a grand dame wearing a conspicuous curled and powdered white wig, topped with a fascinator of arching feathers (figure 24). In keeping with contemporary aesthetic trends, the abstract pattern on her voluminous dress echoes the art-nouveau inspired wallpaper behind her, which together give an impression of her figure floating in a web of loosely and artistically entangled hairs. Art nouveau prominently featured women's curvaceous bodies and their long, sensuously flowing hair, both of which influenced the imagery on Brodsky's poster. While the buxom grande dame's own hair is firmly trapped beneath her wig, the curling, very thin script used in the announcement looks as if it were formed from a strand of hair and foregrounds the primacy of the event's trope of tresses. A ticket for yet another bal poudré (1903) has similarly fine, curling script resembling hair, and also features a stylized image of an aristocratic bewigged couple (figure 25). The anonymously drawn picture is framed on top and bottom with sinuous garlands, the cascading of which evokes tumbling hair. In a style that blends Konstantin Somov's rococo exuberance and the pen-and-ink pointillism of Nikolai Feofilaktov, this skillfully drawn image invites the viewer to enter its imaginary pastoral space. The vertical columns on either side and the horizontal garlands create a visual portal through which to enter the world of fantasy and escape that masquerade promises. A 1914 black-and-white photograph of guests in period costumes and wigs at the home of Wilhelm Wilhelmovich von Notbeck provides one documentary example of the painstaking attention dedicated to reproducing eighteenth-century fashions, including the powdered wig, at such early twentieth-century bals poudrés (figure 26).

Women's fashion magazines of the era also published suggestions for costume-ball hairstyles alongside costume recommendations. The

Figure 24. Advertising poster for a *bal poudré* by Isaak Brodsky (1903). (State Russian Museum, Saint Petersburg; reproduced from Iuliia Demidenko, ed., *Veseliashchiisia Peterburg*)

Figure 25. Honorary ticket to a *bal poudré* by an unknown artist (1903). (State Russian Museum, Saint Petersburg; reproduced from Iuliia Demidenko, ed., *Veseliashchiisia Peterburg*)

Figure 26. Photo of guests in period masquerade costumes and wigs at a ball in the home of Wilhelm von Notbeck (1914). (from the studio of Carl Bulla; image courtesy of TsGAKFFD, Saint Petersburg)

Figure 27. Photo of costume ball participants in period dress and wigs dancing a minuet at "The Aquarium" (1911). (from the studio of Carl Bulla; image courtesy of TsGAKFFD, Saint Petersburg)

Figure 28. Illustrations of women's "masquerade hairstyles." (from *Fashion World*, January 8, 1903; image Courtesy of the Russian National Library)

January 1, 1903, issue of *Fashion World*, for example, profiled two coifs, the "masquerade hairstyle with hanging ringlets" and the "masquerade hairstyle in the Empire [early nineteenth-century] style" (figure 28). Unlike the adventurous and whimsical wigs, nets, and colored hair accessories advocated by Larionov and Bakst, the coiffures featured in such mainstream publications adhered to established ideas of beauty and good taste. The journal's tastemakers sought neither to shock nor innovate, but rather to keep women's appearance within accepted standards. It was that kind of fashion status quo against which Bakst rebelled with his colored wigs.

While the Balls of Colored Wigs may not have been inspired directly by Beardsley's *Venus and Tannhauser*, the story's fanciful menagerie of costumes and masks offers a Decadent (Aestheticist) prelude to the Russian avant-garde's sartorial eccentricities and spirited experimentation with materials as such. Significantly, Blok alluded directly to Beardsley's story in *The Fairground Booth*'s stage directions, notably in the same passage that introduces the masquerade scene: "A Ball. The masks are spinning to the soft sounds of dancing. Among them wander yet more masks, knights, damsels, jesters. Sad Pierrot sits in the center of the stage on the bench where Venus and Tannhauser usually kiss."[51] This hint at the potential for riotous costumes in the scene has not, to my knowledge, been realized on stage in a manner consistent with Beardsley's spectacularly exotic decorations for the body, although Verigina remarks in her memoirs that the maskers were "in emphatically bold masquerade costumes."[52] In *Venus and Tannhauser*, some members of Venus's retinue had their faces and bodies painted with "extraordinary grotesques and vignettes," in addition to sporting whimsical wigs and moustaches: "Upon a cheek, an old man scratching his horned head; upon a forehead, an old woman teased by an impudent amor; upon a shoulder, an amorous singerie; round a breast, a circlet of satyrs; about a wrist, a wreath of pale, unconscious babes; upon an elbow, a bouquet of spring flowers; across a back, some surprising scenes of adventure; at the corners of the mouth, tiny red spots; and upon a neck, a flight of birds, a caged parrot, a branch of fruit, a butterfly, a spider, a drunken dwarf, or simply, some initials. But most wonderful of all were the black silhouettes painted upon the legs, and which showed through a white silk stocking like a sumptuous bruise."[53]

Other members of Venus's entourage wore masks made out of green velvet, colored glass, thin talc and India-rubber, as well as masks "... of the heads of birds, of apes, of serpents, of dolphins, ... of little embryons and of cats; masks like faces of gods."[54] Their costumes were as stunning as the body paintings and masks in their extravagance; some borrowed feathers and hides from exotic animals. There were "whole dresses of ostrich feathers curling inwards; tunics of panthers' skins that looked beautiful over pink tights; capotes of crimson satin trimmed with the wings of owls; sleeves cut into the shapes of apocryphal animals."[55] Beardsley's lavishly and sensuously detailed masks and costumes represent the same obsessive interest of the French Decadents in altering the natural world in the name of enhancing its beauty. Beardsley's resplendent images recall those in Joris-Karl Huysmans's novel *Against Nature*, the magnum opus of Decadent sensibilities, in which the central character Des Esseintes seeks to improve upon natural beauty. Des Esseintes's perverse insistence that human artifice is superior to nature's humble attempts at beauty (manifested in such acts as encrusting jewels in the shell of an exotic tortoise to make it more becoming) resonates with the avant-garde's efforts to expand the range of creative options for decorating the body. In both cases the aesthete wished to go beyond what is natural or conventional, and was motivated by a belief that the richness and variety of human imagination could improve upon nature.

The highly stylized, hyperbolic, and conspicuously artistic appearance of certain members of the avant-garde left them vulnerable to parody, despite their continuous efforts to reinvent and fashion themselves in such extravagant ways as to preempt ironic or sincere imitation. Virtually synonymous with rebel and/or madman, the label "futurist" was applied to any sort of misbehavior or public transgression of propriety or law. In 1914, one year after the face-painting manifestoes, several documented costume parties adopted the theme of "Futurism," the execution of which entailed exaggerated face-painting and flamboyant outfits in the "super-Futurist" (*sverkh-futuristskii*) style.[56] In keeping with the mumming tradition associated with Shrovetide in Russian culture, a group of students at the Saint Petersburg Academy of Arts organized a maslenitsa celebration in 1914 at which there were Futurist-style paintings hanging on the walls, Futurist-inspired toasts and speeches (presumably given in a zaum-like tongue), *bliny* cut in squares, rhomboids, and triangles and eaten off broken dishes, and, of course, students with painted faces. On March 9 of the same year the newspaper *Exchange Gazette* reported on a similar "Futurist masquerade" that took place at a Moscow student cafeteria: works of art in the

Futurist style decorating the walls, as well as Futurist costumes and face-painting, gave the event its parodic flavor.[57] At a traditional society masquerade held at the Moscow Hunters Club in the winter of 1914 one individual came dressed as a parody of Larionov in a costume called "Bird of Paradise." Poet Vsevolod Rozhdestvensky, whose own literary style inclined him more toward Acmeism, recalled a costume party in Koktebel', which was attended by various "Futurists," including one guest dressed as David Burliuk.[58] These costumes were, in a sense, parodies of parodies: the Futurists were parodying the dandy's effete concern with appearance, and the student-artists were parodying the Futurists' parody. The costume as an instrument of parody highlights an essential feature of masquerade: its tight connection to subversion and its openness to transgression. Masquerade costuming and travesties of appearance were powerful strategies for engaging polemically or playfully with an aesthetic standard.

The avant-garde's sartorial experiments challenged prevailing attitudes toward beauty by redefining ideas about what could be considered an aesthetic object and what constituted adornment. Their novel, frequently outlandish costumes also disrupted cultural paradigms that dictated how objects and materials ought to be used. Like the crepe-paper dresses at the Paper Ball and the cardboard costumes in *The Fairground Booth*, *Vladimir Mayakovsky: A Tragedy*, and *Victory over the Sun*, the vestimentary and cosmetic travesties enacted by members of the avant-garde exploited the artistic principles of displacement and material substitution, and demonstrated their estranging power. These cultural interventions were part of a project that sought to dismantle the barrier between life and art. By aestheticizing the body and transforming everyday objects like spoons and vegetables into fashion accessories, members of the avant-garde blurred the former distinctions between what is and is not art. The avant-garde's unbound relationship to the materials used for artistic self-expression (materials such as paper, cardboard, cloth, thread, and paint), which found expression in their experiments with their own physical appearance, represented creative revaluations of the subjective limitations imposed on those very materials. Their desire to shatter limitations that were based solely on convention resulted in sartorial deviations, which travestied the bourgeois notion of good taste and also reawakened the public to the playful potential of dress. While the Futurists have long been recognized as vestimentary iconoclasts, the challenges to dress conventions mounted by their contemporaries on Russia's dance stages are less well known. The following chapter shows how dancers' and other performers' bared bodies on public stages participated in the era's new view of costumes as occasions for individual expression and subjective interpretation.

7

> ─┼─◆➤─◯─◀➤┼─◄

Revealing Costumes
Bared Bodies on Stage

At modernist masquerades the body served as an exhibition space where a carefully curated set of garments and accessories constructed a temporary identity that had the potential to destabilize social paradigms. Just as certain modernist masquerade costumes challenged norms of artistic representation and cultural values at fin-de-siècle costume balls, the publicly bared bodies of dancers broke with conservative nineteenth-century conventions of stage performance and heralded a new era. In the years surrounding 1910, the subject of nudity (*nagota*) on stage gained public currency: opinions on its aesthetic value and moral propriety resounded in critical essays, newspaper articles, and interviews, as well as in letters to theater directors. Although this cultural obsession with nudity seemingly offered an antidote to Symbolism's penchant for obfuscation, masks, and veils, I wish to suggest that the nude body functioned for commentators as a blank page onto which they inscribed their own poetic interpretations in accord with the subjectivity of Symbolism and the individualism celebrated by the modern dance movement. In the critical descriptions that I examine, the dancing nude female body is a vehicle for spiritual transcendence, its physicality marginalized and subordinated to its ability to transport dancer and spectator into a realm of authentic, pure, metaphysical experience. I also apply these insights to nudity and nude dancing in Sologub's novel *Legend in the Making* (*Tvorimaia legenda*, also translated as *The Created Legend*), thereby further illuminating the relativism of nudity's cultural value and the subjectivity characteristic of its narrations.

Revolutions in Theater and Dance

At the end of the nineteenth century, theatrical costumes assumed a central role in stage productions, both in state-owned urban theaters and in private, provincial ones. The emergence of the ready-to-wear fashion industry in Russia and the translation of European fashion magazines into Russian created a sartorially savvy audience that rewarded stylish actresses with praise and popularity. Theater administration required actresses to purchase their own costumes, often in considerable quantity and at considerable expense. Catherine Schuler has noted that the public demand for plays and operas to double as fashion shows resulted in actresses changing their costumes multiple times during a performance.[1] In the late 1880s and 1890s, the frenzy for fashion among theatergoers precipitated what Schuler calls a "costume crisis," the crux of which was the heavy financial burden on actresses.[2]

The fervor for stylish apparel in theater was succeeded by an antithetical trend in ballet and modern dance: the popularity of bare legs and bare feet, which fell under the rubric of "nudity," as did various states of undress. In the first decade of the twentieth century Isadora Duncan, the subject of several Russian essays on nudity, was a prime force behind the trend of bodily liberation in modern dance, which also inspired modifications to the costumes of ballet dancers. Her theory of natural dance advocated simplicity and unfettered movement, and challenged classical ballet's rigid poses and constraining costumes. Duncan called for a return to the natural and free physical expression of ancient Greek dance, and accordingly she performed in a loose-fitting, translucent Grecian tunic without a corset (figure 29). In one of the earliest Russian responses to Duncan, a 1904 essay "Dance: Isadora Duncan," Symbolist poet Maksimilian Voloshin asserted that "nudity is a necessary condition of dance," and that "nudity and dance are inseparable and immortal."[3] Voloshin, himself a proponent of nude sunbathing and loose Grecian togas in Koktebel', used the term nudity to denote Duncan's freedom from a ballerina's traditional tutu and tights.[4]

Figure 29. Photo of Isadora Duncan in a loose Grecian tunic by Arnold Genthe (1916). (image courtesy of the New York Public Library)

Nudity, as used in Voloshin's essay and other theoretical and critical writings about stage performance in the nineteen naughts, designated various degrees of bodily exposure, but rarely did it mean complete bareness.

Nikolai Evreinov also used "nudity" broadly in juxtaposition to the restrictive costumes that hampered movement on stage. In a 1909 article "Language of the Body" (*Iazyk tela*), inspired by American dancer Maud Allan's stage performance as Salome, he wrote of the actress's "virginal nudity" (*devich'ia nagota*), although she wore a bikini-like garment. The semantic variability of the term nudity coincided with the Symbolist attenuation of signification more generally and conferred upon bodily exposure an artistic meaning that transcended physical appearance. Evreinov contrasted the aesthetic and spiritual glory of a body freed from vestimentary fetters to the vulgar state of maximal exposure, which he referred to as "nakedness" in the case of German-born Olga Desmond, whose "Evening of Beauty" was the impetus behind his 1908 essay "The Stage Value of Nudity" (*Stsenicheskaia tsennost' nagoty*). Desmond's performances consisted of her posing completely undressed as a classical Greek statue, creating a kind of tableau vivant. Evreinov advocated nudity for the functional purpose of liberating the active body: clothing hindered the performer's movement and thus interfered with her spirit's expression and compromised the aesthetic effect of her dance. Because Desmond's performances were static poses, Evreinov considered her bareness to be gratuitous and therefore differentiated her exposed body from that of active performers like Duncan. He chose to call Desmond naked (*golaia*) instead of nude, because nudity implied a level of artistry, which in his opinion she lacked no matter how perfect her bodily proportions. Desmond herself, however, engaged in no such semantic parsing and considered absolute exposure the defining essence of her artistry. So important was the state of complete bareness to her stage appearances that she filed a lawsuit against the editor of *The Petersburg Gazette* for 15,000 rubles because of a satirical picture of her fully clothed that appeared in the paper. Under the caption, "What the Public Awaited at Olga Desmond's 'Evening of Beauty' and What It Saw" were two drawings, one of her nude and the other clothed. Desmond feared that the libelous caricature would have a negative impact on attendance during her upcoming Russian tour.[5]

Duncan, Allan, and Desmond inspired much of the Russian intelligentsia's writing about nudity and nude performance. These American and German women represented the trend of exposing the female torso on stage, which captivated the Russian male theoreticians and critics but seemingly failed to inspire native imitators in modern dance. Even Ida Rubinstein, who famously stripped nude during Evreinov's 1908 private production of Oscar Wilde's play *Salome*, was Jewish, which gave her an outsider's status within Russian culture.[6]

This western proclivity toward bareness in modern dance did, however, influence Russian ballet. Dancer and choreographer Michel Fokine, for example, advocated for bare legs and feet. In addition to dispensing with the obligation of pointe shoes for ballet dancers, he challenged the convention of wearing tights and the Imperial theaters' prohibition against bare legs.[7] Pink tights (*triko*) were the norm among ballerinas at the turn of the last century, and their detractors argued that the unsuccessful attempt to simulate the look of flesh was more distracting on stage than bared legs. On at least one occasion Fokine painted "toes on the feet of the tights, even pink toe nails, and rouge on the knees, and heels," to give the illusion of bareness, so strong was his desire for mimetic realism.[8] For a 1908 performance of *Egyptian Nights*, Fokine did abandon tights for his dancers in favor of blackface. He

Figure 30. Photo by Foulsham & Banfield Photographers of Maud Allan in a revealing costume (1910). (image courtesy of the New York Public Library)

required the women to darken their skin with cosmetics, a move that proved unpopular among those who lacked ready access to baths for removing the color.[9] While the issue of wearing tights mainly concerned women, male dancers also experimented. Fyodor Shaliapin appeared on stage once in 1909 without tights in Paris. He flaunted bare legs for his role of Olofern in Alexander Serov's opera *Iudif'*, but "without producing a memorable effect." An article in *The Petersburg Gazette* drolly noted that Shaliapin always wore tights from then on.[10] The following year, also while in Paris, the opera singer and dancer Maria Kuznetsova refused to wear tights for her role in the opera *Thaïs* despite requests from the directors that she cover her legs. The audience sent in letters of complaint, but Kuznetsova held her ground and threatened to leave the show rather than wear tights.[11]

However, even wearing regular pink tights on stage was no certain protection against the ire of conservative state-owned theaters that feared charges of indecency. In February 1911 the Imperial ballet dismissed Vaslav Nijinsky for wearing a costume that was described as "way too bold" by the public seated in the front rows and by the Ballet's administration. Designed by Alexander Benois, Nijinksy's costume for *Giselle* comprised "an itty-bitty short bolero and tights, which revealed too much of the dancer's form," according to *The Petersburg Gazette*. Although days later the administration recanted its position, the offended Nijinsky reportedly refused the invitation to return.[12] As these examples show, tights were a highly contentious element of the stage performer's apparel, and their absence became a symbol of the new tendencies in modern dance. Later that same year *The Petersburg Gazette* bemoaned "the striving of actresses to bare themselves (*stremlenie artistok obnazhat'sia*)" on stage, and printed the names of these offenders and other "apologists of nudity."[13] Such conservatism was rooted in a misguided belief that the quality of a performance was directly correlated to the elaborateness of the costume.

Writing the Nude Body

While the new artistic agenda of modern dance and ballet may have guided the performers' self-exposure, the men who wrote about the female dancers focused on their own experience of spectatorship. For male discussants, the nude female body was an occasion for artistic reverie, not because of its sex appeal or the perfection of human form;

rather, the uncorseted and unconstrained body was a force of nature, an organic element, "a conduit to the soul," as Evreinov phrased it in "Language of the Body." The bared bodies of early twentieth-century performers in Russia were at risk of creative appropriation by the reviewers, critics, and theoreticians who wrote about their experience of spectating in subjective, metaphoric terms. However, such relativistic readings harmonized with the modernist spirit of individualism.

In his short study of striptease, Roland Barthes raised the question of nudity's relationship to performance: is nudity a condition inherent to an unclothed body, or is it the perception of that body by another? For Barthes, the performing body can never be authentic. In a striptease the body on stage is at first clothed or surrounded with props, which condition it to be a performance object even when the clothing and props are removed.[14] Once bared, the stripper is still not nude; she remains covered in the aura of her accessories. She is cloaked in the fiction of the narrative she and the spectator wove while she was undressing. The centrality of story in eroticizing the body, of enrobing the body in plot, is the essence of striptease, which relies on removing layers of clothing and accessories to create narrative suspense.

Evreinov and actor Fyodor Komissarzhevsky similarly commented on the role of clothing in creating intrigue and thereby inciting "animal feelings." In an essay called "Costume and Nudity," Komissarzhevsky wrote: "clothing is a mask, a mystifying cloak that makes the imagination work strenuously to finish drawing (*dorisovyvat'*) that at which it hints."[15] In his mind, fashion was the preserve of courtesans and flirts who had a romantic agenda. Komissarzhevsky further asserted that erotic feelings are aroused by the "plot of the dance" (*siuzhet tantsa*) and sensual movement of the body, suggesting that absent a storyline that motivates feeling and action, the body itself is neutral, blank, free from any signification other than that of naturalness.

For certain early twentieth-century Russian commentators, however, bodily authenticity was not as important as the emotional authenticity it promised to deliver. In "Language of the Body" Evreinov argued that the full expression of any emotion or condition of the soul can transpire only through the nude body, a position averred by Voloshin. Thus, for the sake of artistic achievement, in order to play a role convincingly, the dancer or actor must be free from inhibiting garments. The liberated performer could reach new heights of personal discovery and spiritual transcendence. As a consequence, the viewing public could enjoy a richer performance, which in turn elevated it to ecstatic experience.

Evreinov had a Symbolist's interest in what metaphysical meaning the nude body could communicate and the authenticity of this communicative act.

Voloshin, too, identified nudity as a precondition to the body's clear rhythmic expression of ineffable emotions (*dushevnye emotsii*). Alluding to the power of dance to communicate as a language, he observed that Isadora Duncan dances "everything that other people speak, drink, write, play and draw."[16] Voloshin conveyed the essence of her movement in poetic phrases that likened her dance to "the dance of a flower, that twirls in the wind's embrace," and compared the "measured swaying" of her arms above her head to that of "tree branches in the azure depths, bent by a summer breeze."[17] However, he refrained from detailing her actual movements. Instead, his impressionistic reading of her dance celebrates the power of motion to transform the nude body into a vision of beauty. Azure, a key color among Symbolists in France and Russia, represented the profound mysteries of life hidden in the limitless depths of the sky. By describing Duncan's arms as "tree branches in the azure depths, " Voloshin conferred upon her undulating body a privileged relationship to all that is transcendental.[18] As a series of movements unconstrained by clothing or convention, Duncan's dance was an act of revelation that bestowed an otherworldly beauty on an ordinary woman. Voloshin commented expressly on the transformative power of dance, noting in regard to Duncan that "The most unattractive body sparkles (*vspykhivaet*) with inspiration in the ecstasy of dance."[19]

The ability of dance to transform a physically flawed woman seems to have been one of its primary virtues for the period's male reviewers and theoreticians.[20] In "Language of the Body" Evreinov stated that "Maud Allen doesn't shine with beauty (*ne bleshchet krasotoi*)—her mouth is large, her nose is funny, she slouches, [and] her legs have veins."[21] Komissarzhevsky observed that "while dancing, Duncan who is very unattractive in life, is beautiful," a sentiment shared by Voloshin, Vasily Rozanov, artist Alexander Golovin, and other detractors who lamented everything from her uneven skin tone to her heavy legs. Sologub mocked this chorus of critics, bemoaning the fact that "[t]he shape of her chest isn't what one would like it to be, her foot is flat, her big toe is raised too much."[22] Andrei Bely was most diplomatic of all: he completely avoided any mention of Duncan's body and focused his attention on her radiant face. Commentary on the dancer's ungainly body highlights the magical transformation that occurs during the course of her performance. The dancer transcends her physical self, reaching a Dionysian height of spiritual rapture. In the words of Sologub, who references Cervantes's *Don Quixote*, "[the viewer] sees a true miracle, the transformation of normal flesh into an exceptional beauty in the making (*tvorimaia krasota*), he sees how a visible Aldonza is transformed into a true Dulcinea, a true beauty of that world—and the miracle of transformation he feels in himself."[23] The erasure of the dancing body's physical flaws through the transformative movement of dance elevates not only the dancer, but also the beholder who experiences this mysterious process. The female dancer's "beauty in the making," the movement from physical embodiment to spiritual transcendence, articulates a metaphysics of femininity based on carnal dynamism that differed from the Symbolist Eternal Feminine, a disembodied and unchanging ("eternal") ideal.

The Petersburg Gazette observed that nudity constituted a noteworthy trend in the artistic community not only on stage, but in paintings as well. In March 1911 a column complained that "There has never been so much female nudity at painting exhibitions as there has been this year."[24] Although the nude models ostensibly chose to pose for the artists, the journalist hinted at the women's financial need, thus highlighting the power imbalance between the nude body and the artist representing it. At early twentieth-century costume balls in Paris at L'École des Beaux-Arts, certain women "maskers" also ceded their power of bodily representation: these nude or seminude women were "dressed" as if for tableaux vivants, attired in the same "costumes" in which they had modeled for the artists' paintings. Like the nude model whose body was enrobed in someone else's narrative, the bared bodies of modern dancers performing on Russian stages were at risk of creative appropriation. Barthes argued that nudity is dependent on context and perception for its meaning: formed in the eyes of the beholder, nudity's value and significance is shaped by an individual's psychology and is open to interpretation. Evreinov, Komissarzhevsky, and Voloshin clothed nude dancers in their own subjective stories: they interpreted the dancing nude and translated its meaning into textual exposition. While the power they exerted over the historical documentation of the women's ephemeral appearances usurps narrative control over the women's bodies, the personal subjectivity they expressed harmonized with the individualism of modern dance as practiced by Duncan and her acolytes. In privileging the author's subjective interpretation of the bared body, the writings on stage nudity frame the performing woman as a bare interpretive field onto which the beholder inscribed his own aesthetic fantasies.

Nearly a decade after the furor over stage nudity roiled Russia, several individuals in Germany and Russia attempted to codify a language of the body. These endeavors transferred narrative control back to the dancers themselves by acknowledging the body's ability to communicate. Olga Desmond, whose immobile, statuesque poses earned her Evreinov's disapprobation, attempted to "transcribe the movements [of dance] one sees into a special grammar of symbols" in a 1919 pamphlet called "Rhythmografik." In the following years, also in Germany, Rudolf Laban constructed a vocabulary and grammar of movement, which he called Labanotation.[25] In Russia, Meierkhol'd elaborated his well-known system of biomechanics, which conceived of the performing body as a series of hieroglyphic poses that could be taught and perfected. Returning in a sense to the rigidity of classical ballet's limited repertoire of steps and its prioritizing of technical perfection, these lexicographers of the body ushered in an attitude toward its language that abandoned the metaphorical in favor of the denotative. Their technical codification of the body's movements prepared it for the Soviet-era idealization of the human body as a technological machine.[26]

Sologub's Legend in the Making

Sologub's association of the dancer with divinity, suggested in his image of Isadora Duncan as a "Dulcinea, a true beauty of that world," reappears in the first part of his trilogy Legend in the Making (published in 1907): the so-called quiet children and their governesses dance and bathe unclothed at the mysterious Edenic colony run by the writer and scientist Trirodov. The novel also voices a credo that Sologub expressed two years earlier in his essay "The Canvas and the Body": the joyfulness of nudity emanates from the body's direct connection to nature and organic vitality. Freed from societal restraints and bathed by the water, wind, and sun, the unclothed body regains its rightful place among the "native elements" (rodnye stikhii).[27] In Legend in the Making, the nudity of the young women and children symbolizes their liberation from animal passions and their elevation to a spiritual realm connected to creativity, art, and beauty. On one occasion, after having bathed nude in a lake, the children and governesses see their neighbors, the sisters Elena and Elizaveta Ramaev, approaching. They "formed a ring of beautiful wet bodies around them [the sisters], and twirled in a circle at a fast, furious pace. The discarded clothes that lay there close by seemed unnecessary to the sisters at that moment. What, after all, was more beautiful and lovely than the nude, eternal body?"[28] On the next page Sologub reinforced the pre-Lapsarian innocence of their activity: "So natural, indispensable, and inevitable seemed all the nakedness of these young, beautiful bodies that it appeared rather stupid to put on one's clothes afterwards. The sisters joined in with the naked dancers, and went into the water and lay on the grass under the trees. It was pleasant to feel the beauty, the grace, and the agility of their bodies among these other twirling, beautiful, strong bodies."[29] The simplicity of this narrative conveys a naïveté that accords with Sologub's belief in the naturalness and authenticity of the exposed and active bodies. The writer described them with generic adjectives such as "beautiful," "young," and "strong," and their dancing consists in nothing more than "twirling" at a "fast, furious pace" and with "agility." The generality and brevity of these descriptions results in a narrative chastity: Sologub refrained from burdening these innocents with the vestiture of elaborate language and thus allowed their nude bodies to remain veritable blank sheets of paper, reflective solely of purity.

Such portraits of nude dancing seem ekphrastically anemic when compared to the much more colorful, dynamic and verbally detailed depictions of bodies defiled by violence. During a Cossack raid upon a political meeting, a Decadent symphony for the senses resounds: "The knouts began to work rapidly. The thin textures upon the girls' shoulders were rent apart and delicate bodies were bared, and beautiful blue-and-red spots showed themselves on the white-pink skin like quickly ripened flowers. Drops of blood, large like bilberries, splattered into the air, which had already quenched its thirst on the evening coolness, on the odour of the foliage and the aroma of artificial scents. Delicately shrill, loud sobs were the accompaniment to the dull, flat lashings of whips across the bodies."[30] The graphic and sonic richness of this scene and the dynamism of the movement being portrayed quicken the reader's pulse and stand in complete opposition to the quiet and verbally spartan innocence of the previous descriptions. The incitement of the body to action and the tender vulnerability of the flesh in combat demonstrated for Sologub the aesthetic potential of the fighting human form. In "The Canvas and The Body" Sologub found a justification for the gloomy paintings of war by noting that the excessive violence of combat gives the painter a "panorama of fine movements, expressions and poses," which comprise a "celebration of the body" (*prazdnik tela*) and which connect war paintings with "representations of the body in general and the nude body in particular." He empha-sized, however, his preference for the joyful nude body, which for him is "a visual symbol of [. . .] human exaltation (*chelovecheskogo torzhestva*)."[31]

Sologub shared with fellow Decadent writers a fascination with the physical expressiveness and splendor of the besieged body that is capable of thrilling at intense sensation. In one of novel's tensest scenes, the near rape of Elizaveta, her body and those of her two male assailants are rendered as strong, agile, powerful, and aroused.[32] The stimulating narrative texture of this scene stems from its being fine-grained and protracted, as well as from the intense physicality of their struggle. The wrestling bodies gradually become bare as garments are ripped and torn, a narrative process that heightens desire as Barthes postulated in his essay on striptease. The handsome, swarthy young men become equally aroused by their own torn garments and soon-to-be-bare bodies as by Elizaveta's, and vice versa. She finds herself tempted to give in to the exposed, sweaty men, especially when they demand that she dance for them. By far the most sexually laden scene in the novel, it is also one of the lengthiest and most dynamic, making it an instructive example of how Sologub relied on narrative richness to stimulate and commu-nicate desire. In contrast to the ethereal nude dancing children and women at Trirodov's otherworldly colony whose innocence offers no narrative potential, the impassioned earthly bodies generate ample verbal exposition.

Sologub linked dynamism and sexuality, using the body's kinetic energy as expressed in its sinuousness and taught skin to index its de-sirousness and desirability. Although still a virgin, Elizaveta's budding womanhood rouses her at night and leads her to strip nude before a mirror, which reflects a tender yet seductive image: "Pearl-like were the moon's reflections on the lines of her graceful body. Palpitating were her white girlish breasts, crowned by two rubies. The living, passionate form stood flaming and throbbing, strangely white in the tranquil rays of the moon. The gradual curves of the body and legs were precise and delicate. The skin stretched across the knees hinted at the elastic energy that it covered. And equally elastic and energetic were the curves of the calves and the feet."[33] Her body's capacity for movement and its athleti-cism constitute a key component of its aesthetic appeal. Elizaveta's robust body reflects the period's gymnastic awakening and celebration of physical vitality as sports clubs and athletics (especially wrestling and bicycle riding) gained popularity among men and women. The naked body of Trirodov's lover Katya is likewise characterized as "graceful and flexible," and "the lines of [her] body are somewhat elongated but wholly elastic."[34] Sologub's extended narrative treatment of the sexualized body amplifies his reticence in regard to the innocents living in Trirodov's paradisiacal colony.

In contrast to the lithe, healthy, natural body is the grotesque body of the cabaret performer, whose cosmetics, costume, and unnatural acrobatic movement are depicted as artificial and alien: "An animated chansonnette-singer screeched and jerked her naked, excessively whitened shoulders, and winked with her exaggeratedly painted eyes; a woman acrobat, raising her legs, attired in pink tights, above her head, was dancing on her hands."[35] The pink tights are part of the cabaret performer's repellant artifice, recalling the criticisms of leg-wear among modern dance aficionados and ballet reformers. The chanteuse's crass, commercial use of her body on stage warrants narrative exposé, whereas the purity of the dancing children engenders silence.

Sologub acknowledged the relative value of nudity, locating salaciousness in the thoughts and prejudices of the beholder. In *Legend in the Making* Trirodov keeps nude pictures of his deceased wife in an album, and he even presents one such framed photo to Elizaveta after they proclaim their love for one another. Because she accepts the picture as pure and sacred art, the gift does not rouse her jealousy. Her rebuffed suitor Pyotr, however, worries "that making universal that which is intimate" and intended for a husband is indecent and pornographic.[36] The subjective value of nudity that Sologub highlighted accords with Barthes's theorization of the nude body as a screen onto which the beholder projects his own fantasies. By extension, Barthes's theory of the subjective meaning of nudity coincides more generally with the Symbolist attitude toward art: the object of the gaze is an occasion for the beholder to indulge his reveries, be they erotic or mystical.

The narrative reticence that Sologub exhibited in regard to the so-called quiet children who frolic in the buff preserves their innocence and purity, and implicitly equates the vestiture of language with corruption. Trirodov's edenic colony recalls the pre-Lapsarian innocence ascribed to Adam and Eve: in the Old Testament parable, covering the body with a fig leaf became symbolic of man's moral fall. The equivalence of nudity with authenticity and of clothing with dissimulation reverberates with Russian folk and Orthodox Church beliefs about the perils of dressing in costume: as we saw in chapter 1, the artifice of disguise imputes spiritual corruption. This valuation persisted in the officially atheist Soviet 1920s and 1930s: the state aligned seditious activity with figurative disguise and employed the rhetoric of unmasking (*razoblachenie*) to describe exposing the identities of enemies of the state. In the conclusion that follows, I elaborate on the cultural continuities from the late Imperial era to the early Soviet period in regard to the perception of social identity as a protean construct.

Conclusion
The Early Soviet Masquerade

The evolution of masquerade practices and imagery over the years that bridge the nineteenth and twentieth centuries illuminates the changing aesthetic priorities and the political tensions that defined late Imperial Russia. In particular, the masquerade motif in Russian modernism points out how the destabilization of essentialist paradigms of social identity and the consequent privileging of subjectivity ramified in the literary, visual, and performing arts, as well as in the emergent field of fashion design. It also foregrounds performative strategies for wielding political agency that the monarchy and its challengers used, such as wearing national costume and manipulating national identity. In the years after the Bolshevik Revolution of 1917, the leisure-time practice of attending masked and costume balls declined. However, modernist masquerades had left a legacy: lessons about the contingent nature of personal identity and the political power of self-fashioning undergirded early Soviet-era anxieties about betrayal at the hands of state enemies who were impersonating loyal citizens. In the years after the Civil War, when the state was eager to find and punish those who had fought against the Bolsheviks, the rhetoric of "unmasking" (*razoblachenie*) enemies became a pervasive metaphor for exposing purported traitors.

The early Soviets understood the contingency of social identity, which facilitated their re-conceptualization of society and the individual's relationship to it. Historian Sheila Fitzpatrick has explained that after the Bolshevik Revolution almost all Russians were forced to engage in some form of impersonation so that they could fit into the new order: "Post-revolutionary impersonation [. . .] included the universal task of learning to be a Soviet citizen (learning to 'speak Bolshevik,' in Kotkin's terms); the special role-learning tasks of the upwardly mobile (*vydvizhentsy*) and those who embraced new and specifically Soviet roles such as *aktivist, obshchestvennitsa* and *stakhanovets*; and the task of establishing an acceptable class identity, which bore most heavily on those of flawed (in Bolshevik terms) social background."[1] Fitzpatrick also observes that in the multiethnic Soviet Union, national identity played a less significant role in evaluating an individual's loyalty to the state than did his family background. In the 1920s and 1930s, she notes, the main axis of social identity was class, and it was therefore along this axis that most impersonations occurred. Individuals frequently revised their autobiographies to elide incriminating facts about their social origin, such as professional or familial connections to the bourgeoisie, the clergy, kulaks, and members of the tsarist regime.[2] Fitzpatrick points out that although the Soviets understood identity to be a social construct, there was one identity that no citizen could erase once it had been bestowed: enemy of the state.[3] Her study concluded that the destabilization of social roles in the wake of political revolution and the consequent mass revision of autobiographies led to the state's paranoia about enemy-impostors in the early postrevolutionary years. However, my study points to deeper cultural roots beneath the Soviet anxiety regarding the inconstancy of social identity and its potentially perilous consequences for the state.

The correlation between imposture and peril that informed the Bolshevik paranoia about ideological betrayal in the 1920s finds its earliest intimation in Russian folk and Orthodox Church beliefs about the link between disguise and demonism. Chapter 1 explained how religious dogma and popular superstitions about the violability of a masker's spirit colored literary representations of the masquerade as a site of transgression. The costume parties that Dostoevsky and Sologub portrayed in their novels *Demons* and *Petty Demon*, respectively, erupt into scandalous calamities that expose subversive social tendencies. Masks emblematize menace and confer upon the masquerade a Mephistophelian danger; incursions of the infernal at masked and costume balls also occurred in certain Romantic-era stories discussed in chapter 1, as well as in Andreev's play *Black Maskers* and Akhmatova's *Poem without a Hero*. The flip sides of disguise and demonism are authenticity and innocence, which exemplifies the binary thinking that governed early myth, as in the Old Testament parable of Adam and Eve. Chapter 7 examined modernist narratives of nudity, the presence of which on performance stages became a popular theme for cultural critics and theoreticians around the year 1910, and showed that nudity preserved its connotations of purity and enlightenment, at least in artistic circles. The Soviet-era metaphor of the politically dangerous traitor as a masked man thus perpetuated pre-revolutionary Russian cultural beliefs.

Historical experiences with political self-fashioning, starting in the years leading up to the inception of the Romanov dynasty and punctuating its duration, also influenced early Soviet-era anxieties about the expediency of impersonations undertaken for political gain. Chapter 2 detailed the story of the False Dmitry and other pretenders to the throne who attempted to gain power illicitly through social role-playing. It also examined instances of social role-playing undertaken by tsars in the name of affirming their political authority. Ivan IV and Peter the Great engaged in "games of tsar," a term Boris Uspensky used for their calculated and temporary renunciations of monarchial identity, as part of an act that demonstrated their absolute power. Empresses Elizabeth and Catherine the Great sported Russian men's military regalia at masquerade balls to legitimate their power as national leaders; this exercise was particularly important for the German-born Catherine. Such instances of rightful rulers and illicit upstarts using role-play and self-fashioning to assert or claim political power preceded the early Soviet-era masquerades of identity undertaken for the purposes of political expediency. Anxieties in the 1920s about the politically dangerous implications of manipulating public identity also grew out of Russia's experience with terrorists, such as Boris Savinkov and Yevno Azef, who actively manipulated their social and national identities as part of their combat operations in the years surrounding 1905. Prerevolutionary instances of Russians using disguise to confer and undermine political legitimacy thus played their part in catalyzing the vigilant campaign to unmask real and imagined traitors.

Public masquerades and stylizations of identity in the era of modernism sometimes carried polemical purposes or ideological implications that were less directly engaged with issues of influencing political power. The gender masquerades of male parodists and women writers, such as Zinaida Gippius and Elizaveta Dmitrieva, which were explored in chapter 3, were in dialog with conventions of femininity and female archetypes. Campy impersonations of the cosmetically enhanced modern woman on stage (such as that of female impersonator Alexander Galinsky) comically subverted cultural currents: hyperbolizing clichés carried polemical weight and thus enabled the self-stylizer to express opinion through his or her appearance. Costume designs that appeared at actual balls and parties around the turn of the last century also bespoke civic engagement, a phenomenon treated in chapters 2 and 4, as well as aesthetic engagement, which was addressed in chapter 6. The fundamentally social nature of masquerade facilitated the polemical and ideological aspects of costume design and self-styling: using the body as a public exhibition space for opinion and an instrument for social engagement conferred upon the individual a newfound political agency. Prerevolutionary ideas about the individual's empowerment as an agent of change threatened the postrevolutionary quest for political stability, and fueled fears about individuals being emboldened to act on their seditious thoughts.

Individuals who used their bodies as polemical billboards in the first two decades of the twentieth century operated on the premise that the body ought to be legible. Legibility imputed knowability and authenticity: a polemical costume was less a disguise and more an expression of personal belief. Certain costumes, however, resisted interpretation and refused to posit substitute identities for their wearers. In modernist literature, the anxiety of illegibility was emblematized by the enigmatic domino and half-mask. Such a costume revealed no identity or opinion; its communicative power lay in its intentional muteness, which signaled only danger. Akhmatova, Andreev, Blok, and Bely assigned allegorical meanings to the costumes represented in their literary portraits of masquerade, and chief among them was the masked domino who symbolized a menace so grave as to defy description. Chapter 4 investigated figurative costumes and the hermeneutic challenges they present. While nonrepresentational costumes at historical Artists' Balls in Saint Petersburg exemplified inventiveness and wit, examples of unintelligible costumes in literature often revealed epistemological or ontological crises, as for Lorenzo in *Black Maskers*. Chapter 7 also addressed the problematic legibility of the body, this time unclothed. Narrations of nudity from around 1910 proved to be highly subjective interpretations of the body and its movements; these interpretations reflected an awareness of their subject's fundamental ambiguity. In the Soviet 1920s and

1930s, the unreliability and potential illegibility of social identity generated a mood of fear similar to that represented in *Black Maskers*.

Chapters 5 and 6 of this book studied how conceptions of costume design at masquerades, on stage, and in life during the era of modernism reflected changing attitudes toward cultural patrimony. As we saw in chapter 5, Viacheslav Ivanov and Anna Akhmatova celebrated the past, whereas avant-garde artists scorned cultural tradition; the Bolsheviks continued this rejection of the past after the Revolution. Ivanov and Akhmatova embodied intertextual allusions in character costumes (which represented literary, mythological, or historical figures), with the effect of preserving the heritage of world culture, both at his Evenings of Hafiz and in her *Poem without a Hero*. The gathering of figures wearing costumes that evoke established cultural archetypes and historical heroes constituted what I call a philological masquerade, which has a syncretic chronotope that unites all epochs and nations. Ivanov and Akhmatova's respect for the past differs radically from the renunciation of cultural tradition enacted by the Russian Futurists and early Soviets.

David Burliuk, Vladimir Mayakovsky, and Mikhail Larionov, among others, brashly proclaimed their rejection of tradition and the social status quo, the visible manifestations of which were their outré attire and fanciful face-painting. They flamboyantly fashioned their appearance to disrupt customary aesthetic values and social principles, and they demonstrated their new vision of reality by theatricalizing life. Like the Futurists, the Bolsheviks envisioned a fresh reality. As part of their radical transformation of society they created new social roles, such as the political activist and hero of labor, and demanded new behaviors in accord with communist ideology. As Irina Gutkin has suggested, the legacy of the Futurists' aesthetic organization of behavior and appearance persisted into the Soviet era as a conspicuous theatricality.[4] The premium on transformative role-playing distinguished the visionary masquerades of the avant-garde and the Bolsheviks from earlier philological masquerades rooted in cultural history.

While one can discern certain through-lines connecting pre- and postrevolutionary attitudes toward masks, impersonation, and the theatricalization of life, the essential principles underlying the Soviet masquerades of identity diverged in key ways from the individualism and rich creativity that governed modernist leisure-time and metaphorical masquerades. Soviet charades of identity were utilitarian and geared toward navigating the exigencies of a new world order. After the Revolution, costume balls ceded their centrality in urban cultural life to ideologically didactic activities. With their bourgeois associations of elitism and the myths of socially transgressive behaviors, costume balls opposed the proletarian priorities of the young Bolshevik state and its preference for carefully scripted public festivals. The pleasures of masquerade such as temporary liberation from social strictures, intrigue, whimsical play, fantasy fulfillment, and creative self-expression did not accord with the goal-oriented program of socialist nation-building.

The artistic and diversionary richness of masquerade as a leisure-time activity at the fin de siècle locates it directly at the center of Russian Silver-Age cultural production. As totalizing aesthetic experiences, masquerades frequently incorporated sumptuous interior décor and stage sets, spectacular fireworks and fountains, inventive and extravagant costumes, exotic plants and flowers, orchestras and choruses, dancing, and culinary delights. By organizing my study of Russian modernism around these creative extravaganzas, I hope to have shown how costume balls participated in the formation and reproduction of the artistic values of the era's dominant aesthetic movements: Decadence, Symbolism, and Futurism. The masquerade's central position in urban cultural life gave it currency as a widespread literary motif that was intimately aligned with the period's literary sensibilities. Finally, the aptness of masquerade as a metaphor for experiments in constructing social identity opens up important insights into political agency and the exercise of power during the tumultuous years preceding and following the Bolshevik Revolution. It is my hope that this study of masked and costume balls has proved the fruitfulness of an interdisciplinary approach to studying neglected aspects of Russian cultural history, in addition to illuminating the ebullient creative spirit and social complexity that reigned at the turn of the last century.

Notes

Introduction

1. Pol' Assaturov. Poster for the "Monster Masquerade" ball (1901). In Eleanora Glinternik's *Reklama v Rossii XVIII–pervoi poloviny XX veka* (Saint Petersburg: Aurora, 2007), 99.

2. The contest for best costume at the "Monster Masquerade," held at the Saint Petersburg Noblemen's Assembly on January 24, 1901, included very specific categories for evaluation. Ladies could hope to win a prize for the costume judged most artistic (*khudozhestvennyi*), the most fashionable (*stil'nyi*), or the most original (*original'nyi*). Men's costumes, on the other hand, would be judged less on artistic qualities and more on social engagement: one prize each would be given to the best ideological (*ideinyi*) costume and the best topical (*zlobodnevnyi*) costume. Members and friends of members could enter for free, but the public had to purchase tickets, men at 3 rubles 10 kopecks and ladies at 2 rubles 10 kopecks. Ibid.

3. For an illuminating account of the fashion industry in Russia, see Christine Ruane, *The Empire's New Clothes: A History of the Russian Fashion Industry, 1700–1917* (New Haven and London: Yale University Press, 2009). For an account focused on fashion in modernism, see Elizabeth M. Durst, "A Cut Above: Fashion as Meta-Culture in Early-Twentieth-Century Russia" (PhD diss., University of Southern California, 2003).

4. Translations are mine unless otherwise noted. "Maslenitsa," *Severnaia pchela*, no. 17 (February 7, 1825): 4.

5. Another related early folk tradition in the Slavic lands was the *rusalii* or Rusalka week, which was a pagan celebration of fertility. The date of *rusalii* varied depending on geographic location, but it usually fell well after Easter in the month of June. Also, in Christian Russia urban fairs known as *gulian'ia* took place during Shrovetide and shared features with other folk festivals. For a discussion of annual urban folk festivities, see Nekrylova, *Russkie narodnye gorodskie prazdniki, uveseleniia i zrelishcha* (Leningrad: Iskusstvo, 1984).

6. Addressing Russia's emergent entertainment culture in the eighteenth century, N. V. Sipovskaia notes that the movement of holiday celebrations from the town square into private homes and country estates prompted entertainment to become an increasingly private, individual matter, which subsequently paved the way for the proliferation of amateur theaters. See Sipovskaia, "Prazdnik v russkoi kul'ture XVIII veka," in *Razvlekatel'naia kul'tura Rossii XVIII–XIX vv.*, ed. E. V. Dukov (Saint Petersburg: Rossiiskaia akademiia nauk, 2001), 36.

7. For an extended description of mumming, see I. I. Shangina and O. G. Baranova, *Russkii prazdnik: Prazdniki i obriady narodnogo zemledel'cheskogo kalendariia: Illiustrirovannaia entsiklopediia, Istoriia v zerkale byta* (Saint Petersburg: Iskusstvo-SPB, 2001), 493–501.

8. The binary structuring that often prevailed at carnival festivities, as in the example of the mummers' costumes, was a form of order that persisted, contrary to Bakhtin's assertion that carnival was characterized by a disruption of all existing order.

9. Iurii Lotman, *Besedy o russkoi kul'ture: byt i traditsii russkogo dvorianstva: XVIII–nachalo XIX veka* (Saint Petersburg: Iskusstvo-SPb, 1994), 100.

10. Iurii Alianskii, *Uveselitel'nye zavedeniia starogo Peterburga* (Saint Petersburg: Bank Petrovskii Publishing, 1996), 17.

11. A. E. Zarin, *Tsarskie razvlecheniia i zabavy za 300 let: Okhota, shuty i skomorokhi, teatry, baly i maskarady, uveselitel'nye progulki, karty, loto i drugie igry: Istoricheskie ocherki* (Leningrad: Mezhdunarodnaia fonda istorii nauki, 1991), 80.

12. Through the eighteenth century the court masquerades were highly structured and attentively planned, drawing on the creative expertise of theater directors and writers. Fyodor Volkov, founder of the first permanent theater in Russia, organized rehearsals for themed processions in the court of Elizabeth I, while Sumarokov (manager of the first permanent theater in Saint Petersburg until it was taken over by Volkov) composed songs for the events. See T. I. Pecherskaia, "Istoriko-kul'turnye istoki motiva maskarada," in *Siuzhet i motiv v kontekste traditsii*, ed. E. K. Romodanovskaia (Novosibirsk: Institut filologii SO RAN, 1998), 33.

13. Quoted in ibid., 33.

14. Richard Wortman, *Scenarios of Power: Myth and Ceremony in Russian Monarchy. Volume One: From Peter the Great to the Death of Nicholas I* (Princeton, NJ: Princeton University Press, 1995), 1:104.

15. According to Princess Ekaterina Romanovna Vorontsova-Dashkova, she and Catherine wore military garb during the coup of 1762 when she seized power. See *The Memoirs of Princess Dashkova*, ed. Kyril Fitzlyon (Durham and London: Duke University Press, 1995), 78.

16. Pecherskaia, "Istoriko-kul'turnye istoki motiva maskarada," 23.

17. *Severnaia pchela*, no. 17 (February 7, 1825): 4.

18. Quoted in Wortman, *Scenarios of Power*, 198.

19. Pecherskaia, "Istoriko-kul'turnye istoki motiva maskarada," 28–29. In addition to the politically expedient indoor masquerades and outdoor processions, the Imperial family hosted private masquerades for their own pleasure. In summertime the grounds at Peterhof were transformed into a sumptuously decorated backdrop for outdoor masquerades: fireworks and other light displays illuminated specially built outdoor structures, and gardens were elaborately decorated. Pecherskaia described one occasion when the grounds were transformed into a miniature map of the world, each garden styled to evoke the culture of a different country or epoch.

20. Ibid., 24.

21. As the reigning "manager of Diversions" in Moscow for the last third of the eighteenth century, Maddox also designed and managed the public gardens in southern Moscow, which came to be known in Russian as *voksal* (modeled on the public gardens in London, Waux Hall or Vauxhall). See Anthony Glenn Cross, *Anglo-Russica: Aspects of Cultural Relations between Great Britain and Russia in the Eighteenth and Early Nineteenth Centuries* (Providence: Berg, 1993), 37.

22. Quoted in Anna Kolesnikova, *Bal v Rossii XVIII–nachalo XX veka* (Saint Petersburg: Azbuka-klassika, 2005), 265–66.

23. Alianskii, *Uveselitel'nye zavedeniia starogo Peterburga*, 75.

24. In addition to the masquerade hall, Engel'gardt installed a restaurant and a costume rental shop. See N. I. Iakovkina, *Russkoe dvorianstvo pervoi poloviny XIX veka: byt i traditsii* (Saint Petersburg: Lan', 2002), 79.

25. Quoted in Pecherskaia, "Istoriko-kul'turnye istoki motiva maskarada," 34.

26. Quoted in Alla Marchenko, "Perechityvaia 'Maskarad'; k 170-letiiu so dnia rozhdeniia M. Iu. Lermontova," *Novyi mir* 10 (1984): 234.

27. Quoted in Pecherskaia, "Istoriko-kul'turnye istoki motiva maskarada," 32.

28. "Gorodskaia khronika," *Sibirskii listok* (January 19, 1909). "Gazetnye starosti." http://starosti.ru.

29. The same journal featured a couplet that likewise paired disguise at a masquerade with sexual frisson: "No one here will err: / Beneath the lace is hidden / A second face, but / All the rest is bared. . . ." The verse appeared beneath an illustration entitled "Maslenitsa masquerade." *Listok kopeiki*, no. 171 (February, 1913): 2.

30. *Listok kopeiki*, no. 4 (December, 1909): 2.

31. *Listok kopeiki*, no. 15 (1910): 7.

32. *Rul'* (January 10, 1911). "Gazetnye starosti." http://starosti.ru.

33. *Novoe vremia* (February 15, 1908). "Gazetnye starosti." http://starosti.ru.

34. Quoted in Kolesnikova, *Bal v Rossii XVIII–nachalo XX veka*, 270.

35. I. Porfirov "Bal-maskarad," in *Veseliashchiisia Peterburg: khudozhestvennaia khronika svetskoi zhizni*, ed. Iuliia Demidenko (Gosudarstvennyi Russkii muzei, 1994), 45.

36. O. Iu. Zakharova, *Russkie baly i konnye karuseli* (Moscow: Glasnost', 2000), 119.

37. The Russian Theatrical Society was particularly successful at raising money. The Society's records show that it took in 14,390 rubles from a masquerade on February 5, 1900, at the Mariinskii Theater. Compare that sum to the total amount taken in by the Society in 1901: 22,000 rubles. See Russkoe teatral'noe obshchestvo, "Otchet za 1900" (Saint Petersburg: Tip. Glavnago upravlenia udielov).

38. Alianskii, *Uveselitel'nye zavedeniia starogo Peterburga*, 166. Benefit masquerades and costume balls were popular well into the twentieth century. The Student Aid Office at the Saint Petersburg Academy of Arts had annual benefit costume balls up until 1908, as I discuss in chapter 4. In February 1907 another organization sponsored a costume ball at the Mikhailovskii Theater to benefit the Society for the Protection of the Mentally Ill. That event was made memorable by its beauty contest, which ranked the guests' overall allure instead of ranking only the costumes, as was customary. See Alianskii, *Uveselitel'nye zavedeniia starogo Peterburga*, 155.

39. In her memoirs about Tchaikovsky, A. I. Sokolova recalls a "very witty literary quadrille, all participants of which were supposed to paint their faces and dress with allusions to some tendency or other of extant Moscow and Petersburg newspapers." Quoted in S. Panov, "Literaturnaia kadril' v romane *Besy*," *Zven'ia* 4 (1936), 574. While Panov states that Dostoevsky would have read about it in *The Moscow Gazette* (*Moskovskie vedomosti*, no. 45), the editors of *Polnoe sobranie sochinenii* suggest that he would have encountered the description in the review "Moscow Life" (*Moskovskaia zhizn'*) that appeared in *The Voice* (*Golos*). The January 1, 1869 (no. 1) review describes a "scandalous ball" (*skandal'nyi bal*) to benefit invalids. *Polnoe sobranie sochinenii Dostoevskogo v 30-ti tomakh*, ed. V. G. Bazanov (Leningrad: Nauka, 1972), 12:314.

40. It was organized by a committee for aiding Saint Petersburg children's shelters. The committee was established by the Vedomstvo uchrezhdenii imperatritsy Marii, which was the governmental organ in Imperial Russia responsible for public welfare.

41. Alla Demidova, *Akhmatovskie zerkala* (Izdatel'stvo: Aleksandr Vainshtein, 2004), 150. Acmeist and Futurist poets as well as artists and actors regularly congregated at the Stray Dog in Saint Petersburg.

42. "Bal-maskarad na katke v Iusupovskom sadu 23-ogo fevralia,"*Ogonek*, no. 10 (March 19, 1910).

43. See Joan Delaney Grossman, *Valery Bryusov and the Riddle of Russian Decadence* (Berkeley: University of California Press, 1985), and Kirsten Lodge, ed., *The Dedalus Book of Russian Decadence: Perversity, Despair and Collapse* (Sawtry, UK: Dedalus, 2007).

44. For an extended discussion of life-creation, see Irina Paperno and Joan Delaney Grossman, eds., *Creating Life: The Aesthetic Utopia of Russian Modernism* (Stanford: Stanford University Press, 1994).

45. For more about the aesthetic theories of Symbolism, see Dee Reynolds, *Symbolist Aesthetics and Early Abstract Art* (Cambridge: Cambridge University Press, 2005).

46. Before Butler injected the metaphor into scholarly discourse in the field of gender studies, Joan Riviere examined the constructed nature of femininity,

which she termed a feminine masquerade, in her seminal 1929 essay "Womanliness as Masquerade." See Riviere, "Womanliness as a Masquerade," in *Formations of Fantasy*, ed. Victor Burgin, James Donald, and Cora Kaplan (London: Routledge, 1989).

47. See Olga Matich, *Erotic Utopia* (Madison: University of Wisconsin Press, 2005).

48. Bely articulated many of the group's fundamental premises in his writings between 1900 and 1904, most notably in his programmatic 1903 poem "The Golden Fleece" (*Zolotoe runo*).

49. Andrei Belyi, *Vospominaniia o Bloke: sobranie sochinenii* (Moscow: Respublika, 1995), 57.

50. Alexander Lavrov, "Andrei Bely and the Argonauts' Mythmaking," in *Creating Life: The Aesthetic Utopia of Russian Modernism*, ed. Irina Paperno and Joan Delaney Grossman (Stanford: Stanford University Press, 1994), 83–121.

51. For a discussion of the noumenal and phenomenal in Sologub's story "A Little Man," see Eric Laursen, "Transformation as Revelation: Sologub, Schopenhauer, and the Little Man" *Slavic and East European Journal* 39.4 (1995): 552–67. For a more general discussion of Sologub and Schopenhauer, see Edith Clowes, "Literary Decadence: Sologub, Schopenhauer, and the Anxiety of Individuation," in *American Contributions to the Tenth International Congress of Slavists*, ed. Jane Gary Harris (Columbus, OH: Slavica, 1988), 111–21.

52. Andrei Belyi, "Apokalipsis," in *Arabeski* (Moscow: Musaget, 1911), 228.

53. The action in Bely's novel *Masks* (also begun in 1928) takes place on the eve of the October Revolution. Intended as a sequel to *Moscow in Jeopardy*, the same characters appear, although, aptly, some appear in different guises. Kierko appears as Terentii Titych Titelev and Lizasha returns as his wife, Eleonora Leonova. Eduard Mandro comes back in anagrammatic form as Drua-Domarden (*Droit d'Homme Ardent*), a French journalist. While in *Moscow* the characters were "individuals," in *Masks* they undergo a transformation in concert with the political revolution, and their true selves are revealed. See J. D. Elsworth, *Andrey Bely, a Critical Study of the Novels* (New York: Cambridge University Press, 1983), 199.

54. Kornei Chukovskii followed suit in 1914 with *Faces and Masks* (*Litsa i maski*).

55. Maksimilian Voloshin, *Zapisnye knizhki* (Moscow: Vagrius, 2000), 124.

56. In 1904 Ivanov published the poem "Litso" (originally "Litso ili maska?") in *Novyi put'* in response to an article by D. Merezhkovskii, "Za i protiv," in which he ascribed to Ivanov the identification of Dionysus with Christ. Ivanov published a poem in 1914 entitled "Demony maskarada," in connection with his theory of man's multifacetedness. He dedicated the poem to Fyodor Stepun, philosopher and sociologist.

57. Mikhail Bakhtin, *Rabelais and His World* (Bloomington: Indiana University Press, 1984), 102.

58. Ibid., 103.

59. Mikhail Bakhtin, *Problems of Dostoevsky's Poetics* (Minneapolis: University of Minnesota Press, 1984), 159.

60. Ibid., 160.

61. Terry Castle, *Masquerade and Civilization: The Carnivalesque in Eighteenth-Century English Culture and Fiction* (Stanford: Stanford University Press), 1986.

62. Chapters 4 and 5, respectively, in Bakhtin, *Problems of Dostoevsky's Poetics.*

63. Bakhtin, *Problems of Dostoevsky's Poetics,* 194.

64. See Norma Claire Moruzzi, *Speaking through the Mask: Hannah Arendt and the Politics of Social Identity* (Ithaca, NY: Cornell University Press, 2000).

65. For more on female archetypes see Carl Jung, *The Archetypes and the Collective Unconscious,* trans. R. F. C. Hull (Princeton, NJ: Princeton University Press, 1968).

66. Barthes pays particular attention to the translation of clothing from its "technological" or physical incarnation (the garment itself), to its iconic representation in fashion photography, to (finally) the verbal description of the garment that accompanies the photograph. See *The Fashion System,* trans. Matthew Ward and Richard Howard (Berkeley: University of California Press, 1990).

Chapter 1. The Travestied Masquerade

1. A similar negative use of the mask as an emblem of the demonic can be found in non-Russian works of early nineteenth-century fantastic literature, such as Heinrich von Kleist's "Der Findling" (1811), E. T. A. Hoffmann's "Prinzessin Brambilla" (1821), Thomas De Quincey's *Klosterheim; or, The Masque* (1832), and Edgar Allan Poe's "The Masque of The Red Death" (1842).

2. I. I. Shangina and O. G. Baranova, *Russkii prazdnik: Prazdniki i obriady narodnogo zemledel'cheskogo kalendariia: Illiustrirovannaia entsiklopediia, Istoriia v zerkale byta* (Saint Petersburg: Iskusstvo-SPB, 2001), 501.

3. A. S. Famintsyn, *Skomorokhi na Rusi* (Saint Petersburg: Aleteiia, 1995), 152.

4. Quoted in Boris Uspenskii, "Tsar and Pretender: *Samozvanchestvo* or Royal Imposture in Russia as a Cultural-Historical Phenomenon," in *The Semiotics of Russian Culture,* ed. Ann Shukman (Ann Arbor: University of Michigan, 1984), 287.

5. In contrast, V. Dmitriev's "Masquerade" (1832) does not align the masquerade with holiday festivities or infernal powers: Dmitriev's story is a light romance with a happy ending.

6. Not all holiday tales that involved mummers or masquerades were sinister (S. A. Auslender's "Yuletide in Old Petersburg" [1912], for example, has a comic tenor). For a more comprehensive list and analysis of Yuletide masquerade stories, see E. V. Dushechkina, *Russkii sviatochnyi rasskaz: stanovlenie zhanra* (Saint Petersburg: SPbGU, 1995), 117–21.

7. Sigmund Freud, "The Uncanny," in *The Uncanny* (New York: Penguin Classics: 2003), 135.

8. V. N. Olin, "Strannyi bal," in *Russkaia romanticheskaia povest' pisatelei 20–40 godov XIX veka,* ed. V. I. Sakharov (Moscow: Pressa, 1992), 337.

9. Ibid.

10. M. N. Zagoskin, "Kontsert besov," in *Russkaia romanticheskaia povest' pisatelei 20–40 godov XIX veka,* ed. V. I. Sakharov (Moscow: Pressa, 1992), 315.

11. Olin, "Strannyi bal," 335.

12. Ibid., 335–36.

13. V. A. Sollogub, *Sochineniia* (Saint Petersburg: Izd. A. Smirdina, 1855).

14. See I. Chistova, "Belletristika i memuary Vladimira Solloguba," in *Povesti, vospominaniia V. A. Solloguba* (Leningrad: Khudozhestvennaia literatura, 1988). Available online at http://az.lib.ru/s/sollogub_w_a/text_0170html.

15. In France, the Goncourt Brothers and Victor Ponpin also took up the theme of the innocent woman who loses her virtue at the masquerade in *Henriette Maréchal* (1865) and *Le bal de l'Opéra* (1867), respectively.

16. In an early draft of the play, the masquerade ball venue was identified as being that of Engel'gardt. It has been suggested that one reason why censors were strict with Lermontov's play was because the tsar and grand duke attended Engel'gardt's masquerades and were protective of their reputation. See Alla Marchenko, "Perechityvaia Maskarad; k 170-letiiu so dnia rozhdeniia M. Iu. Lermontova," *Novyi mir* 10 (1984): 239.

17. Robert Louis Jackson, *Dostoevsky's Quest for Form* (New Haven. Yale University Press, 1966), 58.

18. Ibid.

19. Quoted in John Opie, "Ikonostas and Its Context," in *P. A. Florenskij i kul'tura ego vremeni. P. A. Florenskij e la cultura della sua epoca: Atti del Convegno Internazionale, Università degli Studi di Bergamo, 10–14 gennaio 1988*, ed. Michael Hagemeister and Nina Kauchtschischwili (Marburg: Blaue Hörner, 1995), 507, n4.

20. Pavel Florenskii, *Iconostasis*, trans. Donald Sheehan and Olga Andrejev (Crestwood, NY: St. Vladimir's Seminary Press, 1996), 55–56.

21. Upon returning home from Petersburg, Stavrogin commits three brazen affronts to the faces of others, thereby violating the sanctity of the countenance. He pulls Pavel Pavlovich Gaganov's nose, he kisses Madame Liputin thrice on the lips in public, and he bites Ivan Osipovich's ear.

22. Dostoevsky may have modeled the literary matinee (*literaturnoe utro*) on actual philanthropic readings in which he and Turgenev (along with Goncharov, Pisemsky, Ostrovsky, and Nekrasov) participated, and which had grown popular under the aegis of the Literary Fund in Saint Petersburg. As a member of the Fund, Dostoevsky participated in such public benefit readings, including one on March 2, 1862, to aid needy students, the atmosphere of which he may have used as a template for this scene. Dostoevsky, *Polnoe sobranie sochinenii v 30-ti tomakh*, ed. V. G. Bazanov (Leningrad: Nauka, 1972), 12:310.

23. Fyodor Dostoevsky, *Demons*, trans. Richard Pevear and Larissa Volokhonsky (New York: Vintage Books, 1995), 301.

24. Ibid., 464.

25. Ibid., 463.

26. Ibid., 469.

27. Ibid., 467.

28. Ibid., 461.

29. Ibid., 503.

30. The *Polnoe sobranie sochinenii* editors interpret the literary quadrille as a satirical portrayal of three periodicals from the years 1860–1870. The editors

suggest that the line "[. . .] it was this huskiness of his voice [*okhriplost' golosa*] that was meant to signify one of the well-known newspapers" alludes to the Petersburg newspaper *The Voice* (*Golos*, 1863–1883). They posit that the masker described as "one elderly gentleman, short, in a tailcoat—dressed like everyone else, in a word—with a venerable gray beard" is a reference to A. Kraevsky, publisher of *The Voice* (*Pss* 12:754). Kraevsky is also mentioned by name earlier in *Demons* (*Pss* 10:22; Pevear 23). Next is the monthly radical-democratic journal *The Deed* (*Delo*, 1866–1888), which Dostoevsky alludes to in the line "Under this [Honest Russian] thought's arm was a briefcase containing some 'dossier' [*portfel' s kakim-to'delom'*]." Finally, the "non-Petersburg but formidable publication" is *The Moscow Gazette*. Its two-time publisher M. N. Katkov wrote condemnatory articles about "progressive organs of the press" (12:315). *The Moscow Gazette* also printed the advertisement for a "buffoonish dance [*shutovskaia pliaska*]," which S. Panov proposes that Dostoevsky might have used as a model for the literary quadrille.

31. Dostoevsky, *Demons*, 508.

32. Ibid., 508.

33. *Pss* 12:315. S. Panov proposes that Dostoevsky might have used an advertisement for a "buffoonish dance [*shutovskaia pliaska*]" published in *The Moscow Gazette* as a model for the literary quadrille. Panov, "Literaturnaia kadril' v romane *Besy*," *Zven'ia* 4 (1936): 573–82.

34. Dostoevsky, *Demons*, 510.

35. Ibid., 511.

36. Fyodor Sologub, "Bessmertnaia plamen'," in *Teatr i iskusstvo* (1912), 51. In this essay Sologub echoed the words of a character in *Queen Ortruda*, the second part of his incomplete trilogy *Legend in the Making* (*Tvorimaia legenda*, 1907–14). The novel expressed his belief in the importance of the creative process as a soulful act of spiritual fulfillment. In response to a question posed by Ortruda's lady-in-waiting about whether aesthetics should be subordinate to ethics, the character Filippo Meccio (Mechchio) responds, "There's a great friendship between those two sisters. Whoever offends one makes the other one cry."

37. *Legend in the Making* does intertwine the theme of grassroots political activism with disguise in the figure of Elizaveta, who cross-dresses when attending political meetings.

38. The "Costume Party on Ice" was described as a "magical scene." "Kostiumirovannyi vecher na l'du," *Peterburgskaia gazeta*, no. 54 (February 24, 1899): 5.

39. "Izo dnia v den'," *Peterburgskaia gazeta*, no. 48 (February 18, 1899): 3.

40. "Izo dnia v den'," *Peterburgskaia gazeta*, no. 50 (February 20, 1899): 3.

41. "Kostiumirovannye, udalennye s bala." *Utro Rossii* (September 7, 1910). "Gazetnye starosti." http://starosti.ru.

42. "Nochnoi smotr Peterburgu," *Ogonek*, no. 2 (January 13/26, 1913).

43. *Teatr i iskusstvo*, January 7, 1907.

44. Elena Obatnina, *Tsar' Asyka i ego poddannie: Obez'ian'ia velikaia i volnaia palata A. M. Remizova v litsakh i dokumentakh* (Saint Petersburg: Izdatel'stvo Ivana Limbakha, 2001), 61.

45. Remizov wore the monkey-tail costume as a testament to his make-believe literary society, The Great Simian and Free Chamber (*Obez'an'ia velikaia i volnaia palata*, or *Obezvelvolpal*), which itself was not transgressive but did depart from standards of ordinary behavior.

46. The Sologubs hosted costume parties at their apartment in Saint Petersburg. One night several of the guests participated in the debut performance of Sologub's 1908 play *Night Dances*. Remizov compiled a list of guests at Sologub's masquerade under the title: "3 January 1909. The masks that came to F. K. Sologub." Next to each name is the sketch of a mask. Names include, in order of their appearance, V. E. Meierkhol'd, O. M. Meierkhol'd, A. M. Remizov, S. P. Remizova, M. A. Kuzmin, Sved Siunnerberg, V. M. Siunnerberg, V. K. Shvarsalon. A photo of the list is in Irina Miller's "From Home Masquerade to Public Performance: Nikolai Evreinov's Production of Fyodor Sologub's Play *Night Dances*," *Slavic and East European Performance* 19.1 (1999): 68–79.

47. Fyodor Sologub, *Petty Demon*, trans. Samuel Cioran (Ann Arbor: Ardis, 1983), 253.

48. Ibid., 250–51.

49. Ibid., 257.

50. Ibid., 261.

51. *Problems of Dostoevsky's Poetics*, 162.

52. Sologub, *Petty Demon*, 97.

53. Ibid., 209.

54. This thematic association of madness and masquerade in *Petty Demon* is also found in French Decadent writer Jean Lorrain's collection of stories, *Histoires de masques* (1900), in which the possibly insane figures commit crimes of perversion.

55. Sologub, *Petty Demon*, 210.

56. Boris Uspenskii, "Tsar and Pretender: *Samozvanchestvo* or Royal Imposture in Russia as a Cultural-Historical Phenomenon," in *The Semiotics of Russian Culture*, ed. Ann Shukman (Ann Arbor: University of Michigan, 1984), 264.

57. *Nedotyka* is listed in Vladimir Dahl's *Interpretive Russian Dictionary* under "nedotroga," which means someone or something that cannot be touched. Sologub coined the neologism *nedotykomka*. It is appropriate that the vaguely defined and referentially challenged *nedotykomka* makes its appearance at the masquerade, where signification is inherently problematized.

58. Sologub, *Petty Demon*, 264.

Chapter 2. The Political Masquerade

1. Azef also held meetings with Combat Organization members in other public places such as bars, bathhouses, theaters, and outdoor locations. Peri and Evans write, "The terrorists also implicated the city's [Saint Petersburg's] most popular promenades, including the Summer and Yusupov Gardens, Petrovsky Park, and the city zoo, in the assassinations, carrying out their meetings in these innocent, recreational surroundings in broad daylight." See Alexis Peri and Christine Evans, "How Terrorists Learned to Map: Plotting in *Petersburg* and Boris Savinkov's *Recollections of a Terrorist* and *The Pale Horse*," in

"Petersburg"/Petersburg: Novel and City, 1900–1921, ed. Olga Matich (Madison: University of Wisconsin, 2010), 164.

2. Norma Moruzzi, *Speaking through the Mask: Hannah Arendt and the Politics of Social Identity* (Ithaca, NY: Cornell University Press, 2000), 154.

3. Ibid., 36.

4. See Boris Uspenskii, "Tsar and Pretender: *Samozvanchestvo* or Royal Imposture in Russia as a Cultural-Historical Phenomenon," in *The Semiotics of Russian Culture*, ed. Ann Shukman (Ann Arbor: University of Michigan, 1984).

5. The recurrent problem of Pretenders throughout Russian history, impostors claiming their rights to the throne, can be attributed in part to the belief that bodily markings such as birth marks in the shape of a cross, an eagle, or the tsar's coat of arms signaled divine selection as monarch. This implies the possibility that the "rightful" tsar might be masquerading as a commoner and that any member of society might be the divinely selected monarch. See Marcia Morris, *The Literature of Roguery in Seventeenth- and Eighteenth-Century Russia* (Evanston, IL: Northwestern University Press, 2000), 20.

6. E. V. Dukov, "Bal v kul'ture Rossii XVIII–pervoi poloviny XIX veka," in *Razvlekatel'naia kul'tura Rossii XVIII–XIX vv.: ocherki istorii i teorii*, ed. E. V. Dukov (Saint Petersburg: "Dmitrii Bulanin," 2000), 173.

7. A. M. Iakovleva, "'Ustav o zhizni po pravde i s chistoi sovest'iu' i problema razvlechenii v Rossii XVI–XVII vv," in *Razvlekatel'naia kul'tura v Rossii*, ed. E. V. Dukov (Saint Petersburg: Rossiiskaia akademiia nauk, 2001), 23–24.

8. Uspenskii, "Tsar and Pretender," 270.

9. Ibid.

10. A. M. Panchenko has pointed to Ivan's separation of the *zemskie* and the *oprichniki* as an early example of the theme of doubles in Russia. He noted that the *zemskie* wore the old uniforms whereas the *oprichniki* were given new ones as an external symbol of their cleavage. See Panchenko, *Russkaia kul'tura v kanun petrovskikh reform* (Leningrad: Nauka Leningradskoe otd-nie, 1984), 189.

11. Uspenskii, "Tsar and Pretender," 273.

12. Zitser offers the colorful example of the Most Comical and All-Drunken Council (*vseshuteishii i vsep'ianeishii sobor*): with the members of this council, Peter engaged in outrageous indulgences and mocked all that was holy in Russian Orthodoxy in the name of affirming his power to enact such sweeping changes. See Ernest Zitser, *The Transfigured Kingdom: Sacred Parody and Charismatic Authority at the Court of Peter the Great* (Ithaca, NY: Cornell University Press, 2004), 6.

13. On the occasion of Catherine's coronation she organized the legendary allegorical masquerade "Triumphant Minerva" that had overtly instructive goals: the costumed characters represented virtues and vices and acted out small vignettes (in which virtue always defeated vice) as they paraded for three days through the streets of Saint Petersburg. A painting by Stefano Torelli at the Tretyakov entitled, "Ekaterina II v obraze Minervy, okruzhennaia muzami" (late 1760s) captured the event.

14. A. E. Zarin, *Tsarskie razvlecheniia i zabavy za 300 let: Okhota, shuty i skomorokhi, teatry, baly i maskarady, uveselitel'nye progulki, karty, loto i drugie igry: Istoricheskie ocherki* (Leningrad: Mezhdunarodnaia fonda istorii nauki, 1991), 82.

15. Boris Uspenskii notes in "Historia sub specie semioticae" that as late as 1652 foreigners living in Russia were not allowed to wear Russian clothing, per the order of Patriarch Nikon. See B. A. Uspenskii, "Historia sub specie semioticae," in *Izbrannye trudy*, vol. 1 (Moscow: Iazyki russkoi kul'tury, 1996), 78.

16. Richard Wortman, *Scenarios of Power: Myth and Ceremony in Russian Monarchy* (Princeton: Princeton University Press, 1995), 1:401.

17. Wortman, *Scenarios of Power*, 2:45.

18. From 1869 to his death in 1909, Vladimir Alexandrovich served as president of the Academy of Arts, which sponsored imaginative student-run costume balls, which I discuss in chapter 4.

19. Wortman, *Scenarios of Power*, 2:273–74.

20. The second ball took place on February 11 at the Concert Hall for the benefit of the dowager, who had missed the first ball.

21. In the same article Stasov also recalled in tremendous detail the originality and splendor of the 1867 All-Slavic Ethnographic Exhibition that took place in Moscow, noting that "the Russian initiative, always so weak and timid, showed itself on this occasion in its full strength and sparkle." Stasov, "Vystavki," *Novosti i birzhevye vedomosti*, no. 86 (April 1903).

22. Particularly abundant were the items borrowed from artist and professor K. E. Makovsky, which took up ten large display cases. Other donors Stasov named included A. A. Parland, Vs. Rost. Apukhtin, N. I. Rukavishnikov, F. P. Kruchinin, N. F. Romanchenko, and P. S. Kuznetsov. Stasov, "Vystavki," in *Novosti i birzhevye vedomosti*, no. 86 (April 1903).

23. *Novosti dnia* (May 26, 1903). "Gazetnye starosti." http://starosti.ru.

24. Moscow Kremlin website. http://www.kreml.ru/en/virtual/exposition /regalia/introduction/.

25. *Novosti dnia* (May 7, 1903). "Gazetnye starosti." http://starosti.ru.

26. *Moskovskii listok* (December 8, 1902). "Gazetnye starosti." http://starosti .ru.

27. *Gazeta-kopeika* (December 23, 1911). "Gazetnye starosti." http://starosti .ru.

28. *Fashion World*, no. 2 (January 8, 1904): 14–15. The journal began as a foreign edition of the German *Die Modenwelt* and was the most popular fashion magazine in the 1890s, with a circulation of 12,500. See Christine Ruane, *The Empire's New Clothes: A History of the Russian Fashion Industry, 1700–1917* (New Haven: Yale University Press, 2009), 99–100.

29. *Women's Affair* 1 (1911).

30. *Novosti dnia* (January 8, 1904). "Gazetnye starosti." http://starosti.ru.

31. "Telefon." *Russkoe slovo* (February 14, 1906). "Gazetnye starosti." http://starosti.ru.

32. "Arest v maskarade za kostium." *Russkoe slovo* (February 12/January 30, 1907). "Gazetnye starosti." http://starosti.ru.

33. Vadim Shkolnikov, "Terrorism and the Text: Dostoevsky, Savinkov, and the Representation of Terrorist Violence in Russia, 1872–1909." Lecture, University of Illinois at Chicago, February 21, 2012.

34. The discourse of theater that surrounds Verkhovensky and the Group of Five makes use of a longstanding "anti-theatrical prejudice": a distrust and

disparagement of actors based on their facility with dissimulating. The fear that the professionalization of disingenuousness could challenge the entrenched moral superiority of truthfulness and authenticity motivated this prejudice. Jonas Barish discusses the centuries of bias against thespians and the stage in Western culture in *Anti-Theatrical Prejudice* (Berkeley and Los Angeles: University of California Press, 1981).

35. *Demons*, 494.

36. Quoted in Claudia Verhoeven, *The Odd Man Karakozov: Imperial Russia, Modernity, and the Birth of Terrorism* (Ithaca, NY: Cornell University Press, 2009), 46.

37. Lynn Ellen Patyk, "'The double-edged sword of word and deed': Revolutionary Terrorism and Russian Literary Culture" (PhD diss., Stanford University, 2006), 155.

38. Peri and Evans, "How Terrorists Learned to Map," 162.

39. Peri and Evans argue eloquently that a large part of the terrorists' activity surrounded the tasks of mapping Saint Petersburg and mastering its topography.

40. Peri and Evans, "How Terrorists Learned to Map," 164.

41. Terrorist Dora Brilliant played McCullough's "wife," David Borishansky played their chauffeur, veteran terrorist Praskovyia Ivanovskaia performed the role of cook, and Egor Sazonov played the butler (Peri and Evans, "How Terrorists Learned to Map," 165).

42. Port Arthur was named for William C. Arthur, a Royal Navy Lieutenant. In October 1904, the Russian Navy confused some British fishing vessels for Japanese warships and attacked them. Aggravated by the careless mistake, Britain contemplated joining Japan's war against Russia.

43. *Russkoe slovo* (December 22 1904). "Gazetnye starosti." http://starosti .ru.

44. Sergei Nechaev, "The Revolutionary Catechism." Marxists Internet Archive. http://www.marxists.org/subject/anarchism/nechayev/catechism .htm.

45. V. Ropshin (B. Savinkov), *Kon' blednyi* (Saint Petersburg: Shipovnik, 1909).

46. Gippius even encouraged Savinkov to use her nom de plume Ropshin to publish *Pale Horse*. She had published the article "Toska po smerti" under the name Ropshin in *Poliarnaia zvezda*, no. 7 (1906). Savinkov had, in fact, already established the practice of writing under a nom de plume: his first story published in *Kur'er* in 1903 was under the name Kanin (Patyk, "'The double-edged sword of word and deed,'" 211–12).

47. Quoted in Patyk, "'The double-edged sword of word and deed,'" 220.

48. Savinkov, *Vospominaniia terrorista*, 143.

49. I develop this idea based on Terry Castle's observation that the domino (a cloak worn loosely over the entire body) has a "somewhat sinister power of effacement" and an "utter incommunicativeness." See Terry Castle, *Masquerade and Civilization: The Carnivalesque in Eighteenth-Century English Culture and Fiction* (Stanford: Stanford University Press, 1986), 59.

50. Andrei Bely, *Petersburg*, trans. and ed. Robert Maguire and John Malmstad (Bloomington: Indiana University Press, 1978), 19.

51. Andrei Belyi, *Mezhdu dvukh revoliutsii*, vol. 3 (Moscow, 1990), 65. Lynn Ellen Patyk has suggested that *Petersburg* might be read as a parody of *The Pale Horse* ("'The double-edged sword of word and deed,'" 277).

52. Azef Russified his name to Evgeny Filipovich in order to disguise his Belorussian-Jewish heritage.

53. Olga Matich, "Backs, Suddenlys, and Surveillance," in *"Petersburg"/Petersburg: Novel and City, 1900–1921*, ed. Olga Matich (Madison: University of Wisconsin Press, 2010), 35.

54. In response to a question from Valentinov, an active member of the Social-Democratic party in their correspondence from 1907–08 about why Bely chose to bring with him a copy of *Demons* on their trip together, Bely responded: "I wanted to check a few thoughts and feelings inside me. [. . .] For two years I've been contemplating a big novel about revolution. At its foundation is the Revolution of 1905." See A. V. Lavrov, "Dostoevskii v tvorcheskom soznanii Andreia Belogo (1900-e gody)," in *Andrei Bely: problemy tvorchestva* (Moscow: Sovetskii pisatel', 1988), 146.

55. Bely, *Petersburg*, 38.

56. Mark Steinberg, "'Chernye Maski'; Zrelishcha, obrazy i identichnost' na gorodskikh ulitsakh," in *Kul'tury gorodov rossiiskoi imperii na rubezhe XIX–XX vekov*, ed. Mark Steinberg and Boris Kolonitskii (Saint Petersburg: Evropeiskii dom, 2009), 102.

57. In *Recollections about Blok*, Bely avers that the black half-mask that appears on Nikolai Apollonovich was an actual mask, which he himself donned during a period of distress: "Indeed I was not normal in those days [of his romance with Liubov' Mendeleeva Blok]; I found a black masquerade mask among some old things." Belyi, *Vospominaniia o Bloke: sobranie sochinenii* (Moscow: Respublika, 1995), 243. Akhmatova's 1940 poem "My young hands" (*Moi molodye ruki*) describes the Russo-Japanese War as a masquerade, perhaps taking a page from Bely's *Petersburg*.

58. Bely, *Petersburg*, 123.

59. Ibid., 112.

60. Ibid., 115.

61. Opie, John. "Ikonostas and Its Context," in *P. A. Florenskij i kul'tura ego vremeni. P. A. Florenskij e la cultura della sua epoca: Atti del Convegno Internazionale, Università degli Studi di Bergamo, 10–14 gennaio 1988*, ed. Michael Hagemeister and Nina Kauchtschischwili (Marburg: Blaue Hörner, 1995. 431–42), 439.

62. Andrei Belyi, *Arabeski* (Moscow: Musaget, 1911), 131.

63. Ibid., 132. Two of Bely's poems from the same decade, "Bacchanalia" (*Vakhanaliia*, 1906) and "Masquerade" (*Maskarad*, 1908), associate the half-mask and domino with death. In "Bacchanalia" the half-mask is explicitly associated with death when the two Harlequins "with their hammer [pound] a half-mask to the cover of the coffin." In "Masquerade," from which Bely quotes in *Petersburg*, a red domino arrives at a masquerade and foretells of death.

64. Bely, *Petersburg*, 239.
65. Ibid., 27.
66. Ibid., 219.

Chapter 3. The Gender Masquerade

1. Miss Urania's name derives from "Uranian," originally used to signify an androgyne-like third sex. By the close of the nineteenth century the term had evolved to mean love between men. Neil McKenna, *The Secret Life of Oscar Wilde* (New York: Basic Books, 2006), 58.

2. Iuliia Demidenko, "Kostium i stil' zhizni," *Panorama iskusstv* 13 (1990): 75.

3. Demidenko also asserts that Nikolai Gumilev wore makeup but does not supply evidence. "Kostium i stil'," 78.

4. Leonard Koos, "Improper Names: Pseudonyms and Transvestites in Decadent Prose," in *Perennial Decay: On the Aesthetics and Politics of Decadence* (Philadelphia: University of Pennsylvania Press, 1998), 211 n.7.

5. Demidenko, "Kostium i stil'," 77.

6. "Besporiadki iz-za sharovar." *Rannee utro* (May 14, 1911). "Gazetnye starosti." http://www.starosti.ru.

7. Olga Matich, "The Symbolist Meaning of Love: Theory and Practice," in *Creating Life: The Aesthetic Utopia of Russian Modernism* (Stanford: Stanford University Press, 1994), 30.

8. For a discussion of Weininger's reception in Russia, see Evgenii Bershtein's "Tragediia pola: dve zametki o russkom veiningerianstve," *Novoe literaturnoe obozrenie* 65.1 (2004): 208–22.

9. The newspaper *Rannee utro* was labeled bourgeois by the Soviet-era handbook *Russkaia periodicheskaia pechat' (1895–1917)* (Moscow 1957), which also notes that the newspaper was closed down in July 1918 because it was ostensibly hostile to the Soviet regime. However, literati including V. Briusov, A. Bely, M. Voloshin, and N. Gumilev contributed to the newspaper's literary department.

10. *Fashion World* (January 22, 1903).

11. S. Knapp, "Herbert Spencer in Cexov's 'Skucnaja istorija' and 'Duel': The Love of Science and the Science of Love," *The Slavic and East European Journal* 29.3 (Autumn, 1985), 280.

12. Although there were some instances of women impersonating men on stage, it was men who dominated the gender-bending genre. Louise McReynolds, *Russia at Play: Leisure Activities at the End of the Tsarist Era* (Ithaca, NY: Cornell University Press, 2003), 152.

13. Mark Konecny, "In the Second Act, there are no Fig Leaves: Risque Russian Theater in the 1910s." Paper presented at the annual ASEEES (formerly AAASS) convention in Los Angeles, CA, November 2010.

14. McReynolds, *Russia at Play*, 152.

15. Mikhail Bakhtin, *Problems of Dostoevsky's Poetics* (Minneapolis: University of Minnesota Press, 1984), 189.

16. "Staraia pogudka na novyi lad." *Utro Rossii* (January 29, 1910). "Gazetnye starosti." http://www.starosti.ru.

17. A character from Samuel Richardson's eighteenth-century novel *Clarissa*, Lovelace is a cruel rake who forces Clarissa to elope with him and keeps her at a brothel where he disguises the prostitutes as high-society ladies.

18. Bakhtin, *Problems of Dostoevsky's Poetics*, 190.

19. Sergei Makovskii, *Na Parnase serebrianogo veka* (Moscow: Agraf, 2000), 94.

20. Quoted in Jenifer Presto, *Beyond the Flesh: Alexander Blok, Zinaida Gippius, and the Symbolist Sublimation of Sex* (Madison: University of Wisconsin Press, 2009), 145.

21. Irina Odoevtsova, "Kak laskovaia kobra ia...," in *Sobranie Sochinenii Z.N. Gippius*, vol. 9 (Moscow: Russkaia kniga, 2005), 348. Also online at http://gippius.com/about/odoyevtseva_kak-laskovaya-kobra-ya.html#1.

22. Quoted in Zinaida Gippius, *Literaturnyi dnevnik, 1899–1907* (Munich: W. Fink, 1970), 7.

23. Presto, *Beyond the Flesh*, 136.

24. Miss Fay's séances were rumored to be hoaxes, although she routinely attracted enormous crowds of people who willingly paid 50 cents to attend a performance. Spiritualist detractors attempted to discredit Miss Fay, subjecting her to various scientific tests, which were intended to reveal her charlatanry. A friend of famed magician Harry Houdini and considered by some to be nothing more than a vaudeville performer, Miss Fay became a symbol for the Positivists of the deceptiveness of religion in general and the Spiritualist "sham" in particular. See Jim and Lis Warwood, "Anna Eva Fay: The Modern Oracle of Delphi," *The Voice Box* (2007).

25. Gustave Moreau's 1876 painting, Oscar Wilde's play, and Aubrey Beardsley's drawing are but a few of the most prominent examples of the Salome story's recapitulation among Decadents. In the first decade of the twentieth century, the Salome story gained cultural currency in Russia. See Olga Matich, "Pokrovy Salomei: Eros, smert' i istoriia," in *Erotizm bez beregov*, ed. M. M. Pavlova (Moscow: Novoe literaturnoe obozrenie, 2004), 90–121.

26. Auguste Villiers de l'Isle-Adam, *Tomorrow's Eve*, trans. Robert Martin Adams (Urbana: University of Illinois Press, 2000), 115.

27. The narrator describes how "a flock of birds, balanced atop the flowering plants, parodied Life to the extent that some of them [...] replaced the warble of birds with the sound of laughter." Ibid., 93–94.

28. Ibid., 118.

29. Ibid.

30. Max Beerbohm, *The Works of Max Beerbohm*.

31. Lev Tolstoy, *Kreutzer Sonata*, trans. Isai Kamen (New York: Modern Library, 2003), 23.

32. Fyodor Sologub, "The Poisoned Garden," in *The Dedalus Book of Russian Decadence: Perversity, Despair, and Collapse*, ed. Kirsten Lodge (Sawtry, UK: Dedalus Limited, 2007), 120.

33. Ibid., 123–24.

34. Gippius's physical masquerade of femininity and her frequently flamboyant behavior in the semi-public realm of the salon vividly contrasted with the enduring concerns of the spirit, which she held higher. Starting in 1901 she organized, with her husband, Dmitry Merezhkovsky, the Religious-Philosophical Meetings as a venue in which to discuss with intellectuals and Church leaders scriptural and spiritual problems, and ways to transform Christianity. For more, see Olga Matich, *Paradox in the Religious Poetry of Zinaida Gippius* (Munich: W. Fink, 1972).

35. Presto also notes the female narrator's dandy-like posture in Gippius's so-called special diary, the *Contes d'amour* (1893–1904), which chronicles the writer's supposed romantic adventures. Writes Presto, "Much like the dandy she [Gippius] evinces views about women and more specifically the female body that are misogynistic" (*Beyond the Flesh*, 167).

36. Gippius, "Dekadentstvo i obshchestvo," in *Literaturnyi dnevnik, 1899–1907* (Munich: W. Fink, 1970), 222. The article originally appeared in "Vesy" (1906) and was signed D. Merezhkovsky.

37. Ibid., 225.

38. Ibid., 224.

39. Gippius, "*Posledniaia belletristika,*" in *Literaturnyi dnevnik, 1899–1907* (Munich: W. Fink, 1970), 83.

40. See Hélène Cixous, "The Laugh of Medusa," in *Feminist Theory: A Reader*, ed. Wendy K. Kolmar and Frances Bartkowski (Boston : McGraw-Hill Higher Education, 2010), 215–21.

41. Gippius's Russian contemporaries Anna Akhmatova, Andrei Bely, and Fyodor Sologub also stylized their literary selves by changing their last names from Gorenko, Bugaev, and Teternikov, respectively. Their permanent name changes differ from the practice of adopting a range of temporary pseudonyms, which mirrors the contingent nature of masquerade costuming. Among Gippius's contemporaries, Anton Chekhov played most vigorously with pseudonyms, publishing under no fewer than forty nominal masks (including descriptive phrases, such as "A Doctor With No Patients" and "A Man With No Spleen").

42. Rhonda Garelick, *Rising Star: Dandyism, Gender, and Performance in the Fin de Siècle* (Princeton, NJ: Princeton University Press, 1998), 61.

43. Ibid., 62–63.

44. Born Sidonie-Gabrielle Colette, the writer assumed one of her husband Henry Gauthier-Villars's noms de plume, Willy, as her surname while living in Paris.

45. The French-speaking writer was born Wilhelm Albert Włodzimierz Apolinary Kostrowicki to a Polish mother and he was, until emigration to France in his late teens, when he changed his name, a subject of the Russian empire.

46. Bakhtin, *Problems of Dostoevsky's Poetics*, 189.

47. When Dmitrieva married, she became Elizaveta Vasil'eva, the name under which her autobiography was published. Toward the end of her life Dmitrieva penned the cycle of poems "Little house under the pear tree" using the Chinese male alias of Li Syan Tszi.

48. Ellis Hanson, *Decadence and Catholicism* (Cambridge, MA: Harvard University Press, 1997), 1.

49. More widely read, however, was Anastasia Verbitskaia's wildly popular "novel-digest" *Keys to Happiness* (1909). The central character, Mania, was an uncommon heroine whose rapacious sexuality and unusually free lifestyle stood in contrast to typical female literary figures.

50. Tat'iana Aleksandrova, "Poeticheskie otgoloski: Cherubina de Gabriak." *Mirra Lokhvitskaia: poeziia serebrianogo veka* (2005), http://www.mirrelia.ru /echo/?l=cherub.

51. Lokhvitskaia's poem begins "Naprasno v bezumnoi gordyne / Moiu obviniaiut mechtu" and the first line of Cherubina's poem is "Mechtoiu blizka ia gordyni." See the poem's commentary by Nikolai Dolia, "Cherubina de Gabriak," *Zhivoe slovo: Serebrianyi vek* (1999-2002), http://brb.silverage.ru /zhslovo/sv/chg/?r=stihi&s=sc&id=41. Tat'iana Alexandrova has also likened Cherubina's "Zolushka" to Lokhvitskaia's "Skazki i zhizn'."

52. Quoted in Aleksandrova, "Poeticheskie otgoloski."

53. Valerii Briusov, "Mirra Lokhvitskaia, Nekrologiia," *Retsenzii*, literaturovedcheskie stat'i, *Mirra Lokhvitskaia: poeziia serebrianogo veka* (2005), http:// www.mirrelia.ru/review/?l=review-2.

54. Tat'iana Aleksandrova, "Biografiia," *Mirra Lokhvitskaia: poeziia serebrianogo veka* (2005), http://www.mirrelia.ru/bio/.

55. "Mirra Aleksandrovna Lokhvitskaia: Stikhotvoreniia," *Russkie poetessy XIX veka*, ed. N. V. Bannikov (Moscow: Sovetskaia Rossiia, 1979), http://az.lib.ru /l/lohwickaja_m_a/text_0050.shtml.

56. Ibid.

57. Sergei Makovskii, "O Cherubine," in *Portrety sovremennikov* (New York: Chekhov, 1955), http://brb.silverage.ru/zhslovo/sv/chg/?r=about&id=2.

58. Maksimilian Voloshin, "Rasskaz o Cherubine de Gabriak," *Zhivoe Slovo: Serebrianyi vek* (1999-2002), http://brb.silverage.ru/zhslovo/sv/chg/?r= about&id=4.

59. Dmitrieva also penned parodies of Decadent and Symbolist verse, such as "From Sologub," which starts, "Kiss the sweet virgins without their mama," "From Blok" ("I have planted my luminous paradise"), and a parody of Mikhail Kuzmin that begins, "The sisters rustled . . ." (1907). See V. P. Kupchenko, "Khronika zhizni i tvorchestva E. I. Vasil'evoi (Cherubiny de Gabriak)," in *Cherubina de Gabriak "Ispoved'"* (Moscow: Agraf, 1999), 318–35.

60. Joan Riviere, "Womanliness as a Masquerade," in *Formations of Fantasy*, ed. Victor Burgin, James Donald, and Cora Kaplan (London: Routledge, 1989), 43.

61. Marina Tsvetaeva, *Zhivoe o zhivom* (Saint Petersburg: Izd-tvo Serdtse, 1993), 22.

62. As Voloshin recalled in "History of Cherubina," her last name derived from "Gabriakh," the name of a mythical demon who guarded against evil spirits. He had earlier conferred the name upon an anthropomorphic piece of driftwood he found in Koktebel'.

63. Demidenko, "Kostium i stil'," 82.

64. Ibid.

65. Tsvetaeva, *Zhivoe o zhivom*, 28.

66. See Solomon Volkov, *St. Petersburg: A Cultural History*, trans. Antonina Bouis (New York: Free Press, 1995), 170.

Chapter 4. Figurative Costumes

1. A group of artists broke with the Academy of Arts in 1870, establishing themselves as the Society for Traveling Art Exhibitions (later shortened to the Wanderers), a moment I treat later in this chapter. This rupture represented an avant-garde mentality, if not aesthetic, as the artists responsible for it formed the first autonomous (non-governmental) artistic alliance. Theater in Russia remained under imperial control until 1882, when Alexander III abolished the state monopoly and opened the way to private (commercial) enterprises. While unofficial private theaters had existed prior to the decree, with the tsar's sanction their presence became more visible and their cultural influence more significant.

2. Iuliia Demidenko, "Peterburgskie baly khudozhnikov," *Nashe nasledie* 38 (1996): 37.

3. Ibid., 36.

4. *Peterburgskaia gazeta* (February 27, 1899): 2.

5. Lela Felter-Kerley, "The Art of Posing Nude: Models, Moralists, and the 1893 Bal des Quat'z-Arts," *French Historical Studies* 33.1 (2010), 87. The female models who posed nude for the artists frequently "dressed" for tableaux vivants—staged reproductions of paintings—just as they would "dress" for a painting on a canvas. The existence of paintings featuring nude or near-nude women thus enabled artists to defend themselves, when charged in 1893 with public indecency, on the grounds that the nudity was artistic rather than gratuitous.

6. Rossiiskii gosudarstvennyi istoricheskii arkhiv (RGIA), f. 789, op. 11, 1892, no. 47, l. 14–15.

7. Anna Ostroumova-Lebedeva, *Avtobiograficheskie zapiski* (Moscow: Izobrazitel'noe iskusstvo, 1974), 77.

8. Arkadii Aleksandrovich Rylov, *Vospominaniia* (Mosco : Iskusstvo, 1954), 65.

9. Ibid., 76.

10. RGIA, f. 789, op. 11, 1889, no. 26, l. 11. However, Rylov recalls in his memoirs (1954, 75) that students in possession of neither costume nor tuxedo resorted to the Academy's own supply of "rather worn-out and stained" costumes (Polish pan, hussar, Circassian with a dagger, etc.).

11. In January 1909, citing "the great loss of energy and precious time" spent organizing the balls, Academy of Arts provost Vladimir Beklemishev proposed holding a concert instead, a proposition adopted by the Academy's board of directors by unanimous vote (RGIA, f. 789, op. 13, 1909, no. 58, l. 7). For further discussion of the demise, see Colleen McQuillen, "Artists' Balls and Conceptual Costumes at the Saint Petersburg Academy of Arts, 1885–1909," *Fashion Theory* 16.1 (March 2012): 29–48.

12. Demidenko, "Peterburgskie baly khudozhnikov," 37.

13. Christine Poggi, *In Defiance of Painting: Cubism, Futurism, and the Invention of Collage* (New Haven: Yale University Press, 1992), 19, 17.

14. V. G. Lisovskii, *Akademiia khudozhestv: istoriko-iskusstvovedcheskii ocherk* (Leningrad: Lenizdat, 1982), 136.

15. V. Prokof'ev, "Malen'kaia khronika. Bal khudozhnikov," *Novoe vremia,* no. 8609 (February 14, 1900): 3.

16. *Peterburgskaia gazeta* (February 3, 1904).

17. Sergei Diaghilev, "Peredvizhnaia vystavka" (1897), in *Sergei Diaghilev i russkoe iskusstvo,* ed. V. A. Samkov (Moscow: Izobrazitel'noe iskusstvo, 1982), 67.

18. Poggi notes that while Picasso's 1912–1913 collages touch on the war in the Balkans, it was the Futurists who would raise the use of newspaper to "overt propaganda" (*In Defiance of Painting,* 25).

19. Leonid Andreev, *Black Maskers,* in *Plays,* trans. Clarence Meader and Fred Newton Scott (New York: Charles Scribner's Sons, 1918), 206.

20. The play makes clear that Lorenzo's body putrefies, underscoring his moral failings (saints' bodies do not putrefy).

21. In speaking of the play's audience I will refer to the reader instead of the viewer because I study the dramatic script rather than the stage performance. The play premiered at Komissarzhevsky's theater in 1908.

22. Elizabeth Durst, "A Cut Above: Fashion as Meta-Culture in Early-Twentieth-Century Russia" (PhD diss., University of Southern California, 2003), 143.

23. Ibid., 150, 153.

24. Todorov writes that when a reader encounters a fantastic event, he "hesitates between a natural and a supernatural explanation of the events described" and must "reject allegorical as well as 'poetic' interpretations" in order for him to conclude that it was a supernatural event. See Tzvetan Todorov, *The Fantastic: A Structural Approach to a Literary Genre* (Ithaca, NY: Cornell University Press, 1975), 33.

Chapter 5. Character Costumes

1. *Peterburgskaia gazeta* (December 28, 1910). "Gazetnye starosti." http:// starosti.ru.

2. The *Oxford English Dictionary* defines philology as "Love of learning and literature; the branch of knowledge that deals with the historical, linguistic, interpretative, and critical aspects of literature; literary or classical scholarship."

3. John Mersereau, "The Nineteenth Century: Romanticism 1820–1840," in *The Cambridge History of Russian Literature,* ed. Charles Moser (Cambridge University Press: 1992), 159.

4. A. A. Shakhovskoi, *Komedii; stikhotvoreniia,* ed. A. A. Gozenpud (Leningrad: Sovetskii pisatel', 1961).

5. "Literaturnyi maskarad," *Sovremennik* 31.1 (1852): 155.

6. Among others are Tamarin from M. V. Avdeev's eponymous novel, Diletaev from Aleksei Pisemsky's "Comic," and an allusion to "Dead Lake" written by Panaev's former wife, Avdotyia.

7. *Sovremennik* (1852): 157–58.

8. Quoted in Bograd, "Neizvestnyi fel'eton 1859 goda," 3.

9. The trope also appears in Osip Senkovsky's 1839 "The Transformation of Heads into Books and Books into Heads." The character Maladetti Morto wears a patchwork of texts as a costume: "I'm putting on pants, festive, stripped, multicolored . . . sewn, as you will see, from historical atlases and statistical tables [. . .] I'm sticking one foot into a boot cut out of novels, the other I'm putting into a dramatic buskin [a high laced boot]. My vest is the color of German philosophy with small, speculative buttons. On my neck I'm tying a big bow from industry and trade. I'm putting on an antique book robe. I'm greasing my hair with technology and styling it with fine arts [. . .] instead of a hat I'll put on my head a chemical treatise." In *Russkaia romanticheskaia povest' pisatelei 20–40 godov XIX veka*, ed. V. I. Sakharov (Moscow: Pressa, 1992), 194.

10. *Zhenskoe delo* 1 (1911) and *Modnyi svet* 2 (January 8, 1896).

11. "Izo dnia v den'," *Peterburgskaia gazeta* 47 (February 17, 1899): 3. Juliette Récamier (1777–1849) was a socialite who hosted an influential Parisian salon that attracted leading literary and political figures.

12. Valerie Steele, "*Femme Fatale*: Fashion and Visual Culture in *Fin-de-Siècle* Paris," *Fashion Theory* 8.3 (2004): 322. Andrei Bely draws on these associations in *Petersburg* when he dresses the shapely, satin-haired Sofia Likhutina as Pompadour. Like her historical namesake, Sofia—with whom Nikolai Apollonovich is enamored—sets in motion events that could change history. While dancing with Nikolai, famously dressed as the red domino, she hands him a letter that invites him to commit an act of terrorism and patricide.

13. The costumes "A Parisian Milliner from 1800" and "A Costume from the Era of Louis the XVI" appeared in *Women's Affair* 1 (1911).

14. Berdiaev's wife was also invited to the first meeting, but her tentativeness and inability to give over to full participation led to her being immediately voted out.

15. Quoted in Nikolai Bogomolov, "Peterburgskie gafizity," in *Mikhail Kuzmin: stat'i i materialy* (Moscow: Novoe literaturnoe obozrenie, 1995), 73.

16. Ibid., 70.

17. Ibid., 73.

18. Ibid., 70.

19. Quoted in Nikolai Bogomolov, "Pervyi god 'Bashni,'" *Toronto Slavic Quarterly: Academic Electronic Journal in Slavic Studies* 24 (2008). Bogomolov also quotes Kuzmin's observation from his diary: "Like clothing, an uncustomary name [and] 'ty' change relationships" ("Peterburgskie gafizity," 71).

20. Vyacheslav Ivanov, *Selected Essays of Vyacheslav Ivanov*, trans. Robert Bird, ed. Michael Wachtel (Evanston, IL: Northwestern University Press, 2001), 51.

21. Quoted in Bogomolov, "Peterburgskie gafizity," 346 n.21.

22. Bogomolov also notes that Vladimir Solovyov translated Hafiz, and he asserts that it would undoubtedly have attracted the attention of Ivanov. He does not, however, supply the date for this translation ("Peterburgskie gafizity," 78). Kuzmin, one of the active participants in the Evenings, also translated the work in the 1930s.

23. Ibid., 79.

24. Other attendees' aliases: Berdiaev was Solomon; Somov was Aladdin (from *1,001 Arabian Nights*); and Auslender was the Trojan hero Ganymede (ibid., 71).

25. Ivanov, *Selected Essays of Vyacheslav Ivanov*, 30.

26. Zain Al-Abidin Maragai (1838–1910) was an Iranian-born writer who moved to the Russian Empire (first to the Caucasus then the Crimea). He wrote a three-volume novel *Dnevnik puteshestviia Ibrakhim-beka, ili ego zlokliucheniia po prichine fantasticheskoi liubvi k rodine* (1888–1906).

27. Hölderlin called Susette Borkenstein Gontard, who inspired him to write *Hyperion*, by the name Diotima.

28. In the essay "On the Reasons for the Decline, and the New Currents, in Contemporary Russian Literature" (1892) Dmitry Merezhkovsky articulated a similar thought: "Characters can be symbols. Sancho Panza and Faust, Don Quixote and Hamlet, Don Juan and Falstaff are, according to Goethe's definition, *Schwankende Gestalten* [fluctuating figures]. . . . It is impossible to convey the idea of these *symbolic characters* with any words, for the words only define, delimit a thought, and symbols express the limitless side of thought." In *The Russian Symbolists: An Anthology of Critical and Theoretical Writings* (Ann Arbor: Ardis, 1986), 20.

29. Ivanov, *Selected Essays of Vyacheslav Ivanov*, 13.

30. Ibid.

31. Ibid., 30.

32. Renate Lachmann, *Memory and Literature: Intertextuality in Russian Modernism* (Minneapolis: University of Minnesota Press, 1997), 243.

33. Ibid., 251.

34. Akhmatova writes in the *Poem*, "Since I lack sufficient paper, I am writing on your first draft." Margo Rosen has convincingly argued that the "draft" that Akhmatova uses is Kniazev's "Sonnet," the lyrical "I" of which is Pierrot. See Margo Rosen, "The *Poem without Dante*: Akhmatova's History of Poetic Failure in Russia and the World," M.A. thesis, Columbia University, 2004.

35. Anna Akhmatova, *Sobranie sochinenii v shesti tomakh*, ed. S. A. Kovalenko (Moscow: Ellis Lak, 1998), 3:214.

36. Thomas Glahn was the hero of Knut Hamsun's *Pan* (1894) and Dorian Gray was the hero of Oscar Wilde's novel *The Picture of Dorian Gray* (1891).

37. Roland Barthes, "Literature and Signification," in *Critical Essays* (Evanston, IL: Northwestern University Press, 1972), 262.

38. Carl Proffer, *The Silver Age of Russian Culture* (Ann Arbor, MI: Ardis, 1975), 230.

39. The title of the journal *The Love for Three Oranges* referenced a play by the eighteenth-century Venetian playwright Carlo Gozzi, which drew on the commedia dell'arte tradition. The commedia tradition figures prominently in Akhmatova's poem (and in much Symbolist literature, especially drama), notably in the person of Colombina played by Olga Sudeikina, an actress, dancer, and close friend of Akhmatova. Her husband Sergei painted the walls of the Saint Petersburg cabaret *Prival komediantov* with frescoes of Italian masks, including one of Dapertutto-Meierkhol'd wearing a Venetian carnival mask. The painterly doubling of Meierkhol'd and his connection to the theater is

echoed in the stage designer Golovin's 1917 portrait of Meierkhol'd looking into a mirror. That same year, Golovin placed mirrors on the proscenium in Meierkhol'd's production of Lermontov's *Masquerade* to obscure the divide between actors and audience. Akhmatova asserted that the idea for the *Poem* was born after watching the dress rehearsal of *Masquerade* at the Aleksandriiskii Theater in February 1917. Staging his production on the eve of the 1917 Revolution, Meierkhol'd commented on how the dominos and half-masks of the Venetian carnival tradition, and eighteenth-century Venice itself, produced an atmosphere appropriate to the end of an Empire, bringing full circle the connection to Venetian dramatist Gozzi. See Anna Lisa Crone, "'Balaganchik,' 'Maskarad' and *Poema bez geroia*: Meierkhol'dian Expressions of the Artist's Crisis in Twentieth-Century Russia," *Canadian Slavonic Papers* 36.3–4 (1994): 330.

40. Roman Timenchik, "Rizhskii epizod v 'Poeme bez geroia,'" *Daugava: Literaturnyi zhurnal* 2.80 (February 1984): 113–21.

41. For more on the allusions to Mandel'shtam in the dedications, see Rory Childers and Anna Lisa Crone, "The Mandel'stam Presence in the Dedications of *Poèma bez geroja*," *Russian Literature* 15.1 (January 1984): 51–82.

42. The whispered words she hears are a near mirror inversion of Dragoon-Kniazev's words before his death in the fourth chapter. Compare "Farewell! It's time! / I leave you still breathing / But you will be my widow / You—my sweetheart, sun, sister!" to "You—my sweetheart, sun, sister! / I leave you still breathing / But you will be my widow / And now . . . / It's time to say farewell!" According to Nadezhda Mandel'shtam, "A few more months were to pass [in 1937], and [Osip Mandel'shtam] would say to Akhmatova: 'I am ready for death'" (Proffer, *The Silver Age of Russian Culture*, 202).

43. Wendy Rosslyn exhaustively treats the topic of performance as a theme and source of imagery in the *Poem*. Rosslyn has identified a broad spectrum of theatrical allusions, including the performers and performances that appeared in Petersburg between 1910, when Akhmatova arrived from Kiev, and the outbreak of the Revolution in 1917. Plays include: Maeterlinck's *L'Oiseau bleu*, Shakespeare's *Hamlet*, *Macbeth*, and *Romeo and Juliet*, Wilde's *Salome*, Beliaev's *Putanitsa, ili 1840 god*, and *Psisha*, the miracle play *Put' iz Damaska*, Molière's *Don Juan*, Lermontov's *Maskarad*, Mérimée's *Le Theatre de Clara Gazul*, and the plays of Sophocles. Operas and ballets include: Mozart's *Don Giovanni*, Tchaikovsky's *Pikovaia dama*, Rubinstein's *Demon*, Massenet's *Don Quichotte*, Dargomyzhsky's *Kamennyi gost'*, Gounod's *Faust*, Boito's *Mefistofele*, Fokine's *Tamara*, *Evnika*, *Karnaval*, *Zhar-ptitsa*, *Pavil'on Armidy*, and *Petrushka*, Petipa's *Don Kikhot*, Nijinsky's *Le Sacre du Printemps*, and Ilyia Satz's *Kozlonogie*. Performers mentioned or alluded to include: Karsavina, Nijinsky, Pavlova, Shaliapin, and Glebova-Sudeikina. She also discusses how sections of the *Poem* resemble stage directions or events that are described as if taking place on stage. See Wendy Rosslyn, "Theatre, Theatricality and Akhmatova's *Poema bez geroia*," in *Essays in Poetics: The Journal of the British Neo-Formalist School* 13.1 (1988): 94.

44. Iu. Lotman, "Ikonicheskaia ritorika," in *Semiosfera* (Saint Petersburg: Iskusstvo-SPB, 2000), 200.

45. As I discussed in chapter 1, masquerade ball guests (especially men) were not always obligated to dress in costume, which meant that a divide

between full and partial participants could exist. Masquerades held in theaters often had viewing galleries in certain loges for spectators. And through the eighteenth century, members of the royal family sometimes elected to observe court masquerades from a special room or balcony.

46. Examples of themes include Pushkin (1899), Fairy Tales (*Bal-skazka*, 1901), Ancient Egypt (1902), Spring (*Bal-vesna*, 1906), and Ancient Greece (1907). In 1896 there was a "Decadent" kiosk, erected atop supersized collections of the works, beloved by French and Russian Decadent writers, of Baudelaire and Edgar Allan Poe (Demidenko, "Peterburgskie baly khudozhnikov," 38).

47. V. Prokof'ev, "Malen'kaia khronika. Bal khudozhnikov," *Novoe vremia*, no. 8609 (February 14, 1900): 3.

Chapter 6. Avant-Garde Costumes

1. Guests included the playwright and his wife, Liubov', and the director Vsevolod Meierkhol'd. Writers Mikhail Kuzmin, Georgy Chulkov, and Sergei Gorodetsky also attended. Kuzmin's 1907 story "Cardboard House" ("Kartonnyi domik") was inspired by this evening.

2. Valentina Verigina, *Vospominaniia* (Leningrad, 1974), 107.

3. Quoted in Vladimir Novikov, *Aleksandr Blok* (Moscow, 2010), 142.

4. Verigina, *Vospominaniia*, 108. Liubov' Blok's costume differed, however, and positioned her as an outsider, according to Verigina. She wore a light-weight pink dress made from petals of thin paper.

5. For the costume instructions see *Modnyi svet*, no. 3 (January 15, 1895). Paper costumes also enjoyed popularity in France. "Zamechatel'nye baly i maskarady v Parizhe," *Zhenskoe delo*, no. 1 (1911): 45–47, identifies the costume balls given by the artist Madeleine Lemaire as the most spectacular, citing one in particular at which all costumes, in accordance with the hostess's wishes, were to be made of paper. Although no year is given, the article also notes that in 1900 the same actress gave another memorable costume ball called "Ball of Exhibits," which implies that her "paper ball" took place before 1900.

6. Viktor Shklovskii, "Stroenie rasskaza i romana," in his *O teorii prozy* (Moscow, 1929), 79–80.

7. Already in the 1880s, French Symbolist poet Stéphane Mallarmé articulated an idea later advanced by Viacheslav Ivanov: the unification of actors and spectators in a communal rite (or so they imagined the idealized mystery play). While the Catholic mass influenced Mallarmé's vision, the mystery play's similarities with Dionysian ritual inspired Ivanov. See Harold Segel, *Twentieth-Century Russian Drama: From Gorky to the Present* (Baltimore, 1993), 51.

8. Friedrich Nietzsche, *The Birth of Tragedy*, trans. Douglas Smith (Oxford: Oxford University Press, 2000), 54.

9. Michael Wachtel has explained that Ivanov appropriated the term from the Orthodox Church and applied it to his ideas on performance: "Sobornost' fits neatly with Ivanov's understanding of the ideal relationship of artist and audience, which is predicated on eradicating individualism and creating in its place a true community of believers." See Vyacheslav Ivanov, *Selected Essays of Vyacheslav Ivanov*, trans. Robert Bird, ed. Michael Wachtel (Evanston, 2001), xiv.

10. Ibid., 104.

11. Sologub also wrote a sketch in 1908 for another mystery play, *Torment in Other Lives: A Mystery.*

12. Fyodor Sologub, "Teatr odnoi voli," in his *Sobranie sochinenii,* ed. T. F. Prokopov (Moscow: NPK "Intelvak," 2001), 2:490.

13. A. F. Nekrylova, *Russkie narodnye gorodskie prazdniki, uveseleniia i zre-lishcha* (Leningrad: Iskusstvo, 1984), 155.

14. In the course of the show, the clown falls forward, intruding into the children's space and violating expectations about the divide between play and reality. The clown's physical transgression of the threshold between stage and audience momentarily connects the actor and spectator, only there is no mystical communion between clown and children. The folk nature of the balagan is inscribed into the poem formally through the use of the *raeshnyi stikh,* or *raeshnik* (a poetic form traditionally used in folk theater), in the last two lines. Characterized by imprecise rhymes and irregular meter, the balagan's oral, improvisational nature is at odds with the "high art" poetry penned by Blok and his circle.

15. The love triangle linking Pierrot, Colombina, and Harlequin resonated autobiographically for Blok. The characters' romantic imbroglio recalled that in which Blok, Liubov', and fellow Symbolist Andrei Bely had been embroiled. The play communicates Blok-Pierrot's rejection of sexual relations (part of his efforts to renounce or suppress his carnal self in pursuit of the spiritual) with his wife through the Colombina figure's cardboard body, devoid of warmth and sensuality. For more on Blok's renunciation of the carnal see Jenifer Presto, *Beyond the Flesh: Alexander Blok, Zinaida Gippius, and the Symbolist Sublimation of Sex* (Madison: University of Wisconsin Press, 2008).

16. Alexander Blok, "Balaganchik," in *Sobranie sochinenii v shesti tomakh,* ed. Mikhail Latyshev and S. A. Nebol'sin (Moscow: Terra knizhnyi klub, 2009), 4:13.

17. Verigina, *Vospominaniia,* 105.

18. Ibid., 107.

19. Along with Ivanov, Andrei Bely drew inspiration from medieval mystery plays, as is evident in his 1903 drama *He Who Has Come (Prishedshii).* Such prose writers as Dmitry Merezhkovsky and Valery Briusov also identified with the pre-Enlightenment privileging of the spiritual over the rational in such novels as *Leonardo da Vinci* and *The Fiery Angel,* respectively.

20. Verigina, *Vospominaniia,* 104.

21. Ibid., 102.

22. Vsevolod Meierkhol'd, *Stat'i, Pis'ma, Rechi, Besedy, 1891–1917* (Moscow: Iskusstvo, 1968), 1:218.

23. Ibid.

24. Ibid., 1:219.

25. The commedia dell'arte tradition enjoyed its height of popularity in eighteenth-century Venice. Venetian actors played "comedies of masks" in eighteenth-century Petersburg on the square known as Mars Field. Two hundred years later that same space was occupied by "The Comedians' Rest-Stop" ("Prival komediantov") (formerly the "Stray Dog" cabaret), which Sergei Sudeikin decorated with frescoes of, among other things, Italian masks (one of

which was Meierkhol'd dressed as Dr. Dapertutto wearing a Venetian "bautta," or half-mask). See V. N. Toporov, "Italiia v Peterburge," in *Italiia i slavianskii mir: Sovetsko-ital'ianskii simpozium in Honorem Professore Ettore Lo Gatto* (Moscow: Akademiia nauk SSSR, 1990), 69. The commedia's reemergence in fin-de-siècle Russian culture was fueled by its popularity with French Symbolists, most notably Paul Verlaine and his cycle *Fêtes Galantes*. Even though Verlaine's *Fêtes Galantes* was already in its third publication in Russia in the early 1890s, suggesting its wide popularity, Blok explicitly disavowed Verlaine's influence on him. For more on the extraordinary popularity of Italian commedia dell'arte at the fin de siècle and its influence on Silver Age Russian culture see Catriona Kelly, *Petrushka: The Russian Carnival Puppet Theatre* (New York: Cambridge University Press, 1990); J. Douglas Clayton, *Pierrot in Petrograd: The Commedia dell'arte/Balagan in Twentieth-Century Russian Theatre and Drama* (Montréal: McGill-Queen's University Press, 1993), and Andrew Wachtel, ed., *Petrushka: Sources and Contexts* (Evanston, IL: Northwestern University Press, 1998). Prior to *The Fairground Booth* the play, the Italian commedia dell'arte characters appeared in several of Blok's poems from 1902–4: "Light in the window wavered" ("Svet v okoshke shatalsia") (August 6, 1902), which speaks of a "farcical masquerade" (shutovskoi maskarad); "He appeared at a harmonious ball" ("Iavilsia on na stroinom bale") (October 7, 1902); "The Double" ("Dvoinik") (July 1903); and "At the hour when daffodils are tipsy" ("V chas, kogda p'ianeiut nartsissy") (May 26, 1904). See Blok, *Sobranie sochinenii v shesti tomakh*, vols. 1 and 2.

26. Katherine Lahti, "On Living Statues and Pandora, *Kamennye baby* and Futurist Aesthetics: The Female Body in *Vladimir Mayakovsky: A Tragedy*," *Russian Review* 58 (July 1999): 434.

27. Quoted in Robert Leach, "A Good Beginning: *Victory over the Sun* and *Vladimir Mayakovsky: A Tragedy* Reassessed," *Russian Literature* 13.1 (1983): 109.

28. Svetlana Boym, *Death in Quotation Marks: Cultural Myths of the Modern Poet* (Cambridge, MA: Harvard University Press,1991), 130.

29. Aleksei Kruchenykh, "Pervye v mire spektakli futuristov," in his *Nash vykhod: K istorii russkogo futurizma* (Moscow: RA, 1996), 71.

30. See *Kharmsizdat predstavliaet: Avangardnoe povedenie: Sbornik materialov*, ed. Valerii Sazhin (Saint Petersburg: M. K. & Kharmsizdat : In-t Otkrytoe obshchestvo, 1998), 40. The book incorrectly identifies the left figure as Kruchenykh instead of Matiushin. The photo, dated 1913, is a deformation of Carl Bulla's original photograph from the same year.

31. "A Slap in the Face of Public Taste" (1912), in *Manifesto: A Century of isms*, ed. Mary Ann Caws (Lincoln: University of Nebraska Press, 2000), 230.

32. Iuliia Demidenko, "Nadenu ia zheltuiu bluzu," in *Kharmsizdat predstavliaet*, 67.

33. Ibid., 73.

34. "Raskrashennyi Larionov," *Moskovskaia gazeta* (September 9, 1913). One of Larionov's most widely recognized canvases, "Rayonist Composition" (c. 1912–13), was also painted in blue, yellow, and green.

35. Quoted in Demidenko, "Nadenu ia zheltuiu bluzu," 68.

36. Ibid., 69.

37. Vladimir Novikov, *Aleksandr Blok* (Moscow: Molodaia gvardiia, 2010), 143.

38. Mikhail Larionov and Ilya Zdanevich, "Why We Paint Ourselves," in *Manifesto: A Century of isms*, 244.

39. Karen Elizabeth Gordon, *Paris Out of Hand: A Wayward Guide* (San Francisco: Byzantium Books, 1996), 62.

40. Lev Bakst, "Fashion," in *Theater of Reason, Theater of Desire: The Art of Alexandre Benois and Leon Bakst*, ed. John Bowlt (Lugano: Fondazione Thyssen-Bornemisza, 1998), 157.

41. Bakst was also responsible for designing the costumes for a maslenitsa ball hosted by Countess Kleinmikhel' in Saint Petersburg, January 1914. Many of the costumes were inspired by *A Thousand and One Nights* and had the same oriental exoticism and opulence that made Bakst's Ballets Russes costumes so remarkable (Bakst, "Fashion," 146).

42. Demidenko, "Nadenu ia zheltuiu bluzu," 74.

43. Aubrey Beardsley, *The Story of Venus and Tannhauser or Under the Hill* (London: Academy Editions, 1974), 36.

44. Ibid., 37.

45. Bakst, "Fashion," 146.

46. Vicki Woolf, *Dancing in the Vortex: The Story of Ida Rubinstein* (London: Routledge, 2001), 30.

47. Bakst, "Fashion," 157.

48. Demidenko, "Nadenu ia zheltuiu bluzu," 70.

49. *Peterburgskaia gazeta* 50 (February 20, 1899): 3.

50. Tim Scholl, *From Petipa to Balanchine: Classical Revival and the Modernization of Ballet* (London and New York: Routledge, 1994), 54.

51. Blok, *Sobranie sochinenii v shesti tomakh*, 4:13.

52. Veregina, *Vospominaniia*, 103.

53. Beardsley, *Story of Venus*, 37.

54. Ibid., 36.

55. Ibid., 36–37. The article "Zamechatel'nye baly i maskarady v Parizhe," in *Zhenskoe delo*, no. 1 (1911): 45–47, notes that in 1885 a certain Princess de Sagan gave a "Ball of Animals" for which she herself dressed as a peacock. Among her guests were a rooster, a giraffe, a monkey, a mouse, a lion, a pelican, a bat, a panther, and a swallow. While I did not discover records of any such balls in Russia, *Listok kopeiki*, no. 15 (1910), featured an anonymous cartoon-style illustration of a whimsical "zoological ball" in which animals are dressed in ball gowns and tuxedos, perhaps parodying the trope of humans dressing as animals for costume balls. French Decadent writer Jean Lorrain famously wore a pink swimming suit and panther-skin cloak to the Bal des Quat'z-Arts, a ball given annually by the students of the L'École des Beaux Arts in Paris. See Robert Ziegler, *Asymptote: An Approach to Decadent Fiction* (New York: Rodopi, 2009).

56. The first such parodic costume party took place in 1913. According to Andrei Kursanov and Boris Shifrin, a group of young actors organized a winter holiday party in the Futurist style (*elka futuristov*). They do not supply further details (Kursanov and Shifrin, "Zakliatie smekhom: futurizm v karikaturakh," in *Kharmsizdat predstavliaet*, 100).

57. Ibid.
58. Demidenko, "Nadenu ia zheltuiu bluzu," 71.

Chapter 7. Revealing Costumes

1. Catherine Schuler, "Actresses, Audience and Fashion in the Silver Age: A Crisis of Costume," in *Women and Russian Culture: Projections and Self-Perceptions*, ed. Rosalind Marsh (New York: Berghahn Books, 1998), 108.

2. In Act 3 of Chekhov's *Seagull*, Irina Arkadina famously laments that she has no money for her son to go abroad because she is an actress and the costumes alone have completely bankrupted her.

3. Maksimilian Voloshin, "Tanets: Aisadora Dunkan," in *Liki tvorchestva*, ed. V. A Manuilov, V. P. Kupchenko, and A. V. Lavrov (Leningrad: Nauka, 1988), 395.

4. Another essay by Voloshin from the same year entitled "Sizeranne on Contemporary Aesthetics: Contemporary Clothing" celebrates the superiority of togas and draped clothing over western styles that he viewed as deforming the body. See "Sizeran ob estetike sovremennosti: Sovremennaia odezhda," in *Liki tvorchestva*, ed. V. A Manuilov, V. P. Kupchenko, and A. V. Lavrov (Leningrad: Nauka, 1988), 183–87. The quest to reclaim mankind's intrinsic purity, which was to be found in his natural, unclothed state, motivated an interest in nude sunbathing among such members of the cultural elite as Voloshin in Koktebel' and Leonid Andreev on the Gulf of Finland.

5. *Rannee utro* (December 10, 1908). "Gazetnye starosti." http://starosti.ru.

6. According to Alexander Benois, Rubinstein would sometimes strip in public to create a "special artistic effect." See Olga Matich, "Gender Trouble in the Amazonian Kingdom: Turn-of-the-Century Representations of Women in Russia," in *Amazons of the Avant-Garde*, ed. John E. Bowlt and Matthew Drutt (New York: The Solomon R. Guggenheim Foundation, 1999), 85.

7. In a 1908 newspaper interview, however, Fokine opined that nudity (*nagota*) was not necessary for dance, the goal of which is unimpeded harmonic movement. Bare legs and bare feet, though, might be introduced into ballet for the sake of dispelling the monotony of classicism as well as freeing the dancer. See "Bosonogie tantsovshchitsy. Novaia era v balete (beseda s M. M. Fokinym)," in *Protiv techeniia: vospominaniia baletmeistera, stat'i, pis'ma*, ed. Iurii Slonimskii and Galina Dobrovol'skaia (Leningrad: Iskusstvo, 1981), 299.

8. Michel Fokine, *Fokine: Memoirs of a Ballet Master* (Boston: Little, Brown, 1961), 96.

9. "Zhaloby tantsovshchits," "Teatral'noe echo," *Peterburgskaia gazeta*, March 4, 1909. "Gazetnye starosti." http://starosti.ru.

10. *Peterburgskaia gazeta* (June 8, 1909). "Gazetnye starosti." http://starosti.ru.

11. *Novoe vremia* (May 27, 1910). "Gazetnye starosti." http://starosti.ru.

12. *Peterburgskaia gazeta* (February 8, 1911). "Gazetnye starosti." http://starosti.ru.

13. Those who dared to bare their legs included Gvozskaia, Verdinskaia, Kuznetsova, Shaliapin, Fokine, Mordkin, Valerskaia, Liubavina, Svobodina,

Barynskaia, Rigler, and Urvantsev. "Eskizy i kroki." *Peterburgskaia gazeta* (May 13, 1911). "Gazetnye starosti." http://starosti.ru.

14. Roland Barthes, "Striptease," in *Mythologies*, trans. Annette Lavers (New York: Hill and Wang, 1972), 85.

15. Fedor Komissarzhevskii, "Kostium i nagota," in *Maski* 2 (1912), 52.

16. Maksimilian Voloshin, "Tanets: Aisadora Dunkan," in *Liki tvorchestva*, ed. V. A Manuilov, V. P. Kupchenko, and A. V. Lavrov (Leningrad: Nauka, 1988), 392.

17. Ibid., 394.

18. Ibid., 395.

19. Ibid.

20. French writer Stéphane Mallarmé had an ecstatic response to the American performance artist Loie Fuller, whose dancing he described as "multiple emanations round a nakedness." An illusion artist, Fuller skillfully employed light and veils to create a new type of performance art. Mallarmé's enthusiasm is accompanied by that of artists and lithographers who depicted her as scantily clad and shapely, whereas photos and films reveal "a chunky body, thick around the belly and hips and quite well-draped." See Sally Banes, *Dancing Women: Female Bodies on Stage* (London and New York: Routledge, 1998), 71.

21. Nikolai Evreinov, "Iazyk tela," in *Nagota na stsene: illiustrirovannyi sbornik statei* (Saint Petersburg: Tip. Morskogo Ministerstva, 1911).

22. Fedor Sologub, "Mechta o Done Kikhote: Aisadora Dunkan," in *Sobranie sochinenii*, ed. T. F. Prokopov (Moscow: NPK "Intelvak," 2001), 2:511–12.

23. Ibid., 2:511.

24. *Peterburgskaia gazeta* (March 22, 1911). "Gazetnye starosti." http://starosti.ru.

25. Karl Toepfer, "Nudity and Modernity in German Dance, 1910–30," *Journal of the History of Sexuality* 3.1 (1992): 62, 89.

26. See Julia Vaingurt's *Wonderlands of the Avant-Garde: Technology and the Arts in Russia of the 1920s* (Evanston, IL: Northwestern University Press, 2013).

27. Fyodor Sologub, "Polotno i telo," in *Sobranie sochinenii*, ed. T. F. Prokopov (Moscow: NPK "Intelvak," 2001), 2:543.

28. Fyodor Sologub, trans. John Cournos, *The Created Legend* (Gloucester, UK: Dodo Press, 2008), 61.

29. Ibid., 62.

30. Ibid., 150.

31. Sologub, "Polotno i telo," 542–43.

32. Sologub, *The Created Legend*, 178–79.

33. Ibid., 41.

34. Ibid., 88.

35. Ibid., 150.

36. Ibid., 208.

Conclusion

1. Sheila Fitzpatrick, "Making a Self for the Times: Impersonation and Imposture in 20th-Century Russia," *Kritika* 2.3 (Summer 2001), 473.

2. Ibid., 477.

3. Ibid., 478.

4. See Irina Gutkin, "Legacy of the Symbolist Aesthetic Utopia: From Futurism to Socialist Realism," in *Creating Life: The Aesthetic Utopia of Russian Modernism*, ed. Joan Delaney Grossman and Irina Paperno (Stanford: Stanford University Press, 1994), 167–96.

Bibliography

"Arest v maskarade za kostium." *Russkoe slovo* (February 12/January 30, 1907). "Gazetnye starosti." http://starosti.ru.

"Bal-maskarad na katke v Iusupovskom sadu 23-ogo fevralia." *Ogonek*, no. 10 (March 19, 1910).

"Besporiadki iz-za sharovar." *Rannee utro* (May 14, 1911). "Gazetnye starosti." http://starosti.ru.

"Eskizy i kroki." *Peterburgskaia gazeta.* May 13, 1911. "Gazetnye starosti." http://starosti.ru.

Gazeta-kopeika (December 23, 1911). "Gazetnye starosti." http://starosti.ru.

"Gorodskaia khronika." *Sibirskii listok* (January 19, 1909). "Gazetnye starosti." http://starosti.ru.

"Izo dnia v den'." *Peterburgskaia gazeta*, no. 48 (February 18, 1899): 3.

"Izo dnia v den'." *Peterburgskaia gazeta*, no. 50 (February 20, 1899): 3.

"Kostiumirovannye, udalennye s bala." *Utro Rossii* (September 7, 1910). "Gazetnye starosti." http://starosti.ru.

"Kostiumirovannyi vecher na l'du." *Peterburgskaia gazeta*, no. 54 (February 24, 1899): 5.

"Literaturnyi maskarad." *Sovremennik* 31.1 (1852): 155.

"Maska." *Listok kopeiki*, no. 15 (1910): 7.

"Maslenitsa masquerade." *Listok kopeiki*, no. 171 (February, 1913): 2.

Moskovskii listok (December 8, 1902). "Gazetnye starosti." http://starosti.ru.

Moskovskie vedomosti (February 1869).

"'Nikolai Stavrogin' v Khudozhestvennom teatre." *Russkoe slovo*, October 24, 1913.

"Nochnoi smotr Peterburgu." *Ogonek*, no. 2 (January 13/26, 1913).

"Noveishie mody." *Modnyi svet* (January 22, 1903): 1.
Novoe vremia (May 27, 1910). "Gazetnye starosti." http://starosti.ru.
Novosti dnia (May 7, 1903). "Gazetnye starosti." http://starosti.ru.
Novosti dnia (May 26, 1903). "Gazetnye starosti." http://starosti.ru.
Novosti dnia (January 8, 1904). "Gazetnye starosti." http://starosti.ru.
"Opisanie maskaradnykh kostiumov." *Zhenskoe delo*, no. 1 (January 1, 1911): 40–41.
"Otchet za 1900." Russkoe teatral'noe obshchestvo. Saint Petersburg: Tip. Glavnago upravlenia udielov, 1901.
Peterburgskaia gazeta (June 8, 1909). "Gazetnye starosti." http://starosti.ru.
Peterburgskaia gazeta (December 28, 1910). "Gazetnye starosti." http://starosti.ru.
Peterburgskaia gazeta (February 8, 1911). "Gazetnye starosti." http://starosti.ru.
Peterburgskaia gazeta (March 22, 1911). "Gazetnye starosti." http://starosti.ru.
"Prisuzhdenie prizov na balu khudozhnikov." *Peterburgskii listok*, no. 42 (February 12, 1901): 3.
Rannee utro (December 10, 1908). "Gazetnye starosti." http://starosti.ru.
"Raskrashennyi Larionov." *Moskovskaia gazeta* (September 9, 1913).
Rul' (January 10, 1911). "Gazetnye starosti." http://starosti.ru.
"Staraia pogudka na novyi lad." *Utro Rossii* (January 29, 1910). "Gazetnye starosti." http://starosti.ru.
"Telefon." *Russkoe slovo* (February 14, 1906). "Gazetnye starosti." http://starosti.ru.
"V maskarade." *Listok kopeiki*, no. 4 (December, 1909): 2.
"V maskarade." *Novoe vremia* (February 15, 1908). "Gazetnye starosti." http://starosti.ru.
"Vcherashnie baly. V Tavricheskom dvortse." *Peterburgskii listok*, no. 42 (February 12, 1901): 3.
"Zamechatel'nye baly i maskarady v Parizhe." *Zhenskoe delo*, no. 1 (1911): 45–47.
"Zhaloby tantsovshchits." *Peterburgskaia gazeta* (March 4, 1909). "Gazetnye starosti." http://starosti.ru.

Akhmatova, Anna. *Sobranie sochinenii v shesti tomakh*. Ed. S. A. Kovalenko. Vol. 3. Moscow: Ellis Lak, 1998.
Aleksandrova, Tat'iana. "Poeticheskie otgoloski: Cherubina de Gabriak." *Mirra Lokhvitskaia: poeziia serebrianogo veka*, 2005.
Alianskii, Iurii. *Uveselitel'nye zavedeniia starogo Peterburga*. Saint Petersburg: Bank Petrovskii Publishing, 1996.
Allen, Elizabeth Cheresh. "Unmasking Lermontov's Masquerade: Romanticism as Ideology." *Slavic and East European Journal* 46.1 (2002): 75–97.
Andreev, Leonid. *Plays*. Trans. Clarence Meader and Fred Newton Scott. New York: Charles Scribner's Sons, 1918.
Arendt, Hannah. *On Revolution*. New York: Viking Press, 1965.
Aucouturier, Michel. "Theatricality as a Category of Early Twentieth-Century Russian Culture." In *Theater and Literature in Russia 1900–1930*. Eds. Lars

Kleberg and Nils Ake Nilsson. Stockholm: Almqvist & Wiksell International, 1984. 9–22.

Auslander, Philip. *Performance: Critical Concepts in Literary and Cultural Studies.* London and New York: Routledge, 2003.

Bakhtin, Mikhail. *Problems of Dostoevsky's Poetics.* Minneapolis: University of Minnesota Press, 1984.

———. *Rabelais and His World.* Bloomington: Indiana University Press, 1984.

Bakst, Lev. "Fashion." In *Theater of Reason, Theater of Desire: The Art of Alexandre Benois and Leon Bakst.* Ed. John Bowlt. Lugano: Fondazione Thyssen-Bornemisza, 1998.

Banes, Sally. *Dancing Women: Female Bodies on Stage.* London and New York: Routledge, 1998.

Banjanin, Milica. "From Fact to Fiction: The Role of the Red Domino in Bely's *Petersburg.*" *Russian Language Journal* 40.135 (1986): 63–79.

Bannikov, N. V., ed. "Mirra Aleksandrovna Lokhvitskaia: Stikhotvoreniia." In *Russkie poetessy XIX veka.* Moscow: Sov. Rossiia, 1979.

Barcan, Ruth. *Nudity: A Cultural Anatomy.* New York: Berg, 2004.

Barish, Jonas. *The Anti-theatrical Prejudice.* Berkeley and Los Angeles: University of California Press, 1981.

Barsht, Konstantin. "Defining the Face: Observations on Dostoevskii's Creative Process." In *Russian Literature, Modernism and the Visual Arts.* Eds. Catriona Kelly and Stephen Lovell. Cambridge: Cambridge University Press, 2000. 23–57.

Barthes, Roland. *Critical Essays.* Evanston, IL: Northwestern University Press, 1972.

———. *The Fashion System.* Trans. Matthew Ward and Richard Howard. Berkeley: University of California Press, 1990.

———. "Literature and Signification." In *Critical Essays.* Trans. Richard Howard. Evanston, IL: Northwestern University Press, 1972.

———. "Striptease." In *Mythologies.* Trans. Annette Lavers. New York: Hill and Wang, 1972.

Basker, Michael. "Symbolist Devils and Acmeist Transformation: Gumilev, Demonism, and the Absent Hero in Akhmatova's *Poem without a Hero.*" In *Russian Literature and Its Demons.* Ed. Pamela Davidson. New York: Berghahn Books, 2000. 401–39.

Baudelaire, Charles. "In Praise of Cosmetics." In *Painter of Modern Life and Other Essays.* Trans. and ed. Jonathan Mayne. London: Phaidon Press, 1995. 31–34.

Beardsley, Aubrey. *The Story of Venus and Tannhauser or Under the Hill.* London: Academy Editions, 1974.

Beerbohm, Max. *The Works of Max Beerbohm.* "Project Gutenberg."

Belyi, Andrei. *Arabeski.* Moscow: Musaget, 1911.

———. *Mezhdu dvukh revoliutsii.* Vol. 3. Moscow: Khudozhestvennaia literatura, 1990.

——— *Petersburg.* Trans and ed. Robert Maguire and John Malmstad. Bloomington: Indiana University Press, 1978.

———. *Vospominaniia o Bloke: sobranie sochinenii.* Moscow: Respublika, 1995.

Bershtein, Evgenii. "Tragediia pola: dve zametki o russkom veiningerianstve." *Novoe literaturnoe obozrenie* 65.1 (2004): 208–22.

Blessing, Jennifer. "The Art(ifice) of Striptease: Gypsy Rose Lee and the Masquerade of Nudity." In *Modernism, Gender, and Culture: A Cultural Studies Approach.* Ed. Lisa Rado. New York: Garland Publishing Inc., 1997. 47–63.

Blok, Aleksandr A. "Balaganchik." In *Sobranie sochinenii v shesti tomakh.* Eds. Mikhail Latyshev and S. A. Nebol'sin. Vol. 4 Moscow: Terra knizhnyi klub, 2009.

Bogomolov, Nikolai. "Pervyi god 'Bashni.'" *Toronto Slavic Quarterly: Academic Electronic Journal in Slavic Studies* 24 (2008).

———. "Peterburgskie gafizity." In *Mikhail Kuzmin: stat'i i materialy.* Moscow: Novoe literaturnoe obozrenie, 1995. 67–98.

Bograd, Ganna. n.d. "Neizvestnyi fel'eton 1859 goda." Unpublished manuscript.

———. *Proizvedeniia izobrazitel'nogo iskusstva v tvorchestve F. M. Dostoevskogo.* New York: Slovo-Word, 1998.

Borisova, L. M. *Na izlomakh traditsii: dramaturgiia russkogo simvolizma i simvolistskaia teoriia zhiznetvorchestva.* Simferopol: Tavricheskii natsional'nyi universitet im. V. I. Vernadskogo, 2000.

Bowlt, John. "Body Beautiful: The Artistic Search for the Perfect Physique." In *Laboratory of Dreams: The Russian Avant-Garde and Cultural Experiment.* Eds. John Bowlt and Olga Matich. Stanford: Stanford University Press, 1996.

———. *Theater of Reason, Theater of Desire: The Art of Alexandre Benois and Leon Bakst.* Lugano: Fondazione Thyssen-Bornemisza, 1998.

Boym, Svetlana. *Death in Quotation Marks: Cultural Myths of the Modern Poet.* Cambridge, MA: Harvard University Press, 1991.

Briusov, Valerii. "Mirra Lokhvitskaia, Nekrologiia." Retsenzii, literaturovedcheskie stat'i. *Mirra Lokhvitskaia: poeziia serebrianogo veka,* 2005.

Bugaeva, K. N. *Vospominaniia o Belom.* Ed. John E. Malmstad. Berkeley: Berkeley Slavic Specialties, 1981.

Bulgakov, S. N. "Russkaia tragediia." In *Besy: Antologiia russkoi kritiki.* Ed. L. I. Saraskina. Moscow: Soglasie, 1996. 489–507.

Burliuk, David, et al. "A Slap in the Face of Public Taste." In *Manifesto: A Century of isms.* Ed. Mary Ann Caws. Lincoln: University of Nebraska Press, 2000. 230.

Butler, Judith. *Gender Trouble.* New York: Routledge, 2007 (reprint).

Carlson, Maria. *No Religion Higher Than Truth.* Princeton, NJ: Princeton University Press, 1993.

Castle, Terry. *The Female Thermometer: Eighteenth-Century Culture and the Invention of the Uncanny.* New York: Oxford University Press, 1995.

———. *Masquerade and Civilization: The Carnivalesque in Eighteenth-Century English Culture and Fiction.* Stanford: Stanford University Press, 1986.

Chaianova, Ol'ga. *Teatr Maddoksa v Moskve, 1776–1805.* Moscow: Rabotnik prosveshcheniia, 1927.

Chebotarevskaia, Anastasiia. *O Fedore Sologube: kritika, stat'i i zametki.* Saint Petersburg: Navi Chary, 2002.

Childers, Rory, and Anna Lisa Crone, "The Mandel'stam Presence in the Dedications of *Poèma bez geroja.*" *Russian Literature* 15.1 (January 1984): 51–82.

Chistova, I. "Belletristika i memuary Vladimira Solloguba." In *Povesti, vospominaniia V. A. Solloguba.* Leningrad: Khudozhestvennaia literatura, 1988.
Chukovskaia, L. K. *Zapiski ob Anne Akhmatovoi.* Moscow: Soglasie, 1997.
Cixous, Hélène. "The Laugh of Medusa." In *Feminist Theory: A Reader.* Eds. Wendy K. Kolmar and Frances Bartkowski. Boston: McGraw-Hill Higher Education, 2010. 215–21.
Clark, Katerina. *Petersburg, Crucible of Cultural Revolution.* Cambridge, MA: Harvard University Press, 1995.
Clayton, J. Douglas. *Pierrot in Petrograd: The Commedia dell'arte/Balagan in Twentieth-Century Russian Theatre and Drama.* Montréal: McGill-Queen's University Press, 1993.
———. "The Play-within-a-Play as Metaphor and Metatheater in Modern Russian Drama." In *Theater and Literature in Russia 1900–1930.* Eds. Lars Kleberg and Nils Ake Nilsson. Stockholm: Almqvist & Wiksell International, 1984. 71–82.
Clowes, Edith. "Literary Decadence: Sologub, Schopenhauer, and the Anxiety of Individuation." In *American Contributions to the Tenth International Congress of Slavists.* Ed. Jane Gary Harris. Columbus, OH: Slavica, 1988. 111–21.
Cornwell, Neil. *The Society Tale in Russian Literature: From Odoevskii to Tolstoi.* Atlanta, GA: Rodopi, 1998.
Crone, Anna Lisa. "'Balaganchik,' 'Maskarad' and *Poema bez geroia*: Meierkhol'dian Expressions of the Artist's Crisis in Twentieth-Century Russia." *Canadian Slavonic Papers* 36, no. 3–4 (1994): 317–32.
———. "Genre Allusions in *Poema bez geroia*: Masking Tragedy and Satyric Drama." *Anna Akhmatova, 1889–1989: Papers from the Akhmatova Centennial Conference.* Ed. Sonia Ketchian. Oakland, CA: Berkeley Slavic Specialties, 1993. 43–59.
Cross, Anthony Glenn. *Anglo-Russica: Aspects of Cultural Relations between Great Britain and Russia in the Eighteenth and Early Nineteenth Centuries.* Providence: Berg, 1993.
Davidson, Pamela. *Russian Literature and Its Demons: Studies in Slavic Literature, Culture, and Society.* New York: Berghahn Books, 2000.
De Man, Paul. *Allegories of Reading: Figural Language in Rousseau, Nietzsche, Rilke, and Proust.* New Haven: Yale University Press, 1979.
De Marinis, Marco. *The Semiotics of Performance, Advances in Semiotics.* Bloomington: Indiana University Press, 1993.
Demidenko, Iuliia B., "Kostium i stil' zhizni." *Panorama iskusstv* 13 (1990): 71–83.
———. "Nadenu ia zheltuiu bluzu." In *Kharmsizdat predstavliaet: avangardnoe povedenie: sbornik materialov.* Ed. Valerii Sazhin. Saint Petersburg: M. K. & Kharmsizdat : In-t Otkrytoe obshchestvo, 1998. 65–76.
———. "Peterburgskie baly khudozhnikov." *Nashe nasledie* 38 (1996): 35–40.
———, ed. *Veseliashchiisia Peterburg.* Saint Petersburg: Gosudarstvennyi Russkii muzei, 1994.
Demidova, Alla. *Akhmatovskie zerkala. Akterskie zametki.* Izdatel'stvo: Aleksandr Vainshtein, 2004.
Derrida, Jacques. *Dissemination.* Trans. Barbara Johnson. Chicago, IL: University of Chicago Press, 1981.

Diaghilev, S. "Peredvizhnaia vystavka." In *Sergei Diaghilev i russkoe iskusstvo.* Ed. V. A. Samkov. Vol. 1. Moscow: Izobrazitel'noe iskusstvo, 1982. 67–71.

Dijkstra, Bram. *Idols of Perversity: Fantasies of Feminine Evil in Fin-de-Siècle Culture.* New York: Oxford University Press, 1986.

Dmitrenko, S. F. *Sviatochnye istorii: rasskazy i stikhotvoreniia russkikh pisatelei.* Moscow: Russkaia kniga, 1992.

Dmitriev, V. G. *Skryvshie svoe imia: iz istorii anonimov i psevdonimov.* Moscow: Nauka, 1977.

Dolia, Nikolai. "Cherubina de Gabriak." *Zhivoe Slovo: Serebrianyi vek.* 1999–2002.

Dostoevsky, Fyodor. *Demons.* Trans. Richard Pevear and Larissa Volokhonsky. New York: Vintage Books, 1995.

———. *Polnoe sobranie sochinenii v 30-ti tomakh.* Ed. V. G. Bazanov. Leningrad: Nauka, 1972.

Dukov, E. V. "Bal v kul'ture Rossii XVIII–pervoi poloviny XIX veka." In *Razvlekatel'naia kul'tura Rossii XVIII–XIX vv.: ocherki istorii i teorii.* Ed. E. V. Dukov. Saint Petersburg: "Dmitrii Bulanin," 2000. 173–95.

Durst, Elizabeth M. "A Cut Above: Fashion as Meta-Culture in Early-Twentieth-Century Russia." PhD diss., University of Southern California, 2003.

Dushechkina, E. V. *Russkii sviatochnyi rasskaz: stanovlenie zhanra.* Saint Petersburg: SPbGU, 1995.

Dushechkina, E. V., Henryk Baran, A. Shelaeva, and T. Shmakova, eds. *Chudo rozhdestvenskoi nochi: sviatochnye rasskazy.* Saint Petersburg: Khudozhestvennaia literatura, 1993.

Elsworth, J. D. *Andrey Bely, a Critical Study of the Novels.* New York: Cambridge University Press, 1983.

Engelstein, Laura. *The Keys to Happiness: Sex and the Search for Modernity in Fin-de-Siècle Russia.* Ithaca, NY: Cornell University Press, 1994.

Evreinov, Nikolai. "Iazyk tela." In *Nagota na stsene: illiustrirovannyi sbornik statei.* Saint Petersburg: Tip. Morskogo Ministerstva, 1911.

———. "Stsenicheskaia tsennost' nagoty." In *Nagota na stsene: illiustrirovannyi sbornik statei.* Saint Petersburg: Tip. Morskogo Ministerstva, 1911.

Famintsyn, A. S. *Skomorokhi na Rusi.* Saint Petersburg: Aleteiia, 1995.

Fedorov, A. V. *Teatr A. Bloka i dramaturgiia ego vremeni.* Leningrad: Leningradskii universitet, 1972.

Fedorov, V. V. *Repertuar Bol'shogo teatra SSSR, 1776–1955.* New York: Norman Ross, 2001.

Felter-Kerley, Lela. "The Art of Posing Nude: Models, Moralists, and the 1893 Bal des Quat'z-Arts." *French Historical Studies* 33.1 (2010): 69–97.

Fischer-Lichte, Erika. "The Avant-Garde and the Semiotics of the Antitextual Gesture." In *Contours of the Theatrical Avant-Garde: Performance and Textuality.* Ed. James Harding. Ann Arbor: University of Michigan Press, 2000. 79–95.

———. *The Semiotics of Theater.* Trans. Jeremy Gaines and Doris L. Jones. Bloomington: Indiana University Press, 1992.

———. *The Show and the Gaze of Theatre: A European Perspective.* Trans. Jo Riley. Iowa City: University of Iowa Press, 1997.

Fitzpatrick, Sheila. "Making a Self for the Times: Impersonation and Imposture in 20th-Century Russia." *Kritika* 2.3 (Summer 2001), 469–87.

Fletcher, Angus. *Allegory: The Theory of a Symbolic Mode*. Ithaca, NY: Cornell University Press, 1964.

Florenskii, P. A. *Iconostasis*. Trans. Donald Sheehan and Olga Andrejev. Crestwood, NY: St. Vladimir's Seminary Press, 1996.

———. *Pavel Florenskii i simvolisty: opyty literaturnye, stat'i, perepiska*. Ed. E. V. Ivanova. Moscow: Iazyki slavianskoi kul'tury, 2004.

Fokine, Michel. *Fokine: Memoirs of a Ballet Master*. Trans. Vitale Fokine, ed. Anatole Chujoy. Boston: Little, Brown, 1961.

———. *Protiv techeniia: vospominaniia baletmeistera, stat'i, pis'ma*. Eds. Iurii Slonimskii and Galina Dobrovol'skaia. Leningrad: Iskusstvo, 1981.

Frank, Joseph. "The Masks of Stavrogin." *Sewanee Review* 77 (1969): 660–91.

Freud, Sigmund. *The Uncanny*. New York: Penguin Classics, 2003.

Fried, Michael. *Absorption and Theatricality: Painting and Beholder in the Age of Diderot*. Berkeley: University of California Press, 1980.

Garber, Marjorie. *Vested Interests: Cross-Dressing & Cultural Anxiety*. New York: Routledge, 1992.

Garelick, Rhonda. *Rising Star: Dandyism, Gender, and Performance in the Fin de Siècle*. Princeton, NJ: Princeton University Press, 1998.

Gasperetti, David Wayne. *The Rise of the Russian Novel: Carnival, Stylization, and Mockery of the West*. DeKalb: Northern Illinois University Press, 1998.

Gattrall, Jefferson J. A. "Fictions of a Realist Christ: Jesus as a Literary Character in European and American Prose, 1830–1900." PhD diss., Columbia University, 2005.

Genette, Gerard. *Palimpsests: Literature in the Second Degree*. Trans. Channa Newman and Claude Doubinsky. Lincoln: University of Nebraska Press, 1997.

Gippius, Zinaida. *Literaturnyi dnevnik, 1899–1907*. Munich: W. Fink, 1970.

Glinternik, Eleanora. *Reklama v Rossii XVIII-pervoi poloviny XX veka*. Saint Petersburg: Aurora, 2007.

Goldberg, Stuart. "Blok's Living *Rampa*: On the Spatial and Conceptual Structuring of the Theater Poems." *Slavic and East European Journal* 49.3 (2005): 474–90.

Golub, Spencer. "The Silver Age, 1905–1917." In *A History of Russian Theatre*. Eds. Robert Leach and Victor Borovsky. Cambridge: Cambridge University Press, 1999. 278–301.

Gordon, Karen Elizabeth. *Paris Out of Hand: A Wayward Guide*. San Francisco: Byzantium Books, 1996.

Gray, Camilla. *The Russia Experiment in Art, 1863–1922*. New York: Thames & Hudson, 2002.

Green, Michael. *The Russian Symbolist Theatre: An Anthology of Plays and Critical Texts*. Ann Arbor: Ardis Publishers, 1986.

Greene, Diana. *Insidious Intent: An Interpretation of Fedor Sologub's "The Petty Demon."* Columbus, OH: Slavica Publishers, 1986.

Grinshtein, A. L. *Karnaval i maskarad v khudozhestvennoi literature*. Samara: Akademiia kul'tury i iskusstv, 1999.

Grossman, Joan Delaney. "Valery Briusov and Nina Petrovskaia: Clashing Models of Life in Art." In *Creating Life: The Aesthetic Utopia of Russian*

Modernism. Eds. Joan Delaney Grossman and Irina Paperno. Stanford: Stanford University Press, 1994. 122–50.

———. *Valery Bryusov and the Riddle of Russian Decadence.* Berkeley: University of California Press, 1985.

Gutkin, Irina. "Legacy of the Symbolist Aesthetic Utopia: From Futurism to Socialist Realism." In *Creating Life: The Aesthetic Utopia of Russian Modernism.* Eds. Joan Delaney Grossman and Irina Paperno. Stanford: Stanford University Press, 1994. 167–96.

Haber, Edythe C. "The Mythic Bulgakov: *The Master and Margarita* and Arthur Drews's *The Christ Myth.*" *Slavic and East European Journal* 43.2 (1999): 347–60.

Haight, Amanda. *Anna Akhmatova: A Poetic Pilgrimage.* Oxford: Oxford University Press, 1976.

Hanson, Ellis. *Decadence and Catholicism.* Cambridge, MA: Harvard University Press, 1997.

Harrington, Alexandra K. "Chaosmos: Observations on the Stanza Form of Anna Akhmatova's *Poem without a Hero.*" *Slavonica* 13.2 (2007): 99–112.

Hawthorne, Melanie. *Rachilde and French Women's Authorship: From Decadence to Modernism.* Lincoln: University of Nebraska Press, 2001.

Henry, Barbara. "Theatricality, Anti-Theatricality and Cabaret in Russian Modernism." In *Russian Literature, Modernism, and the Visual Arts.* Eds. Catriona Kelly and Stephen Lovell. Cambridge: Cambridge University Press, 2000. 149–71.

Hollander, Anne. *Seeing Through Clothes.* New York: The Viking Press, 1978.

Holmgren, Beth. "Stepping Out/Going Under: Women in Russia's Twentieth-Century Salons." In *Russia Women Culture.* Eds. Helena Goscilo and Beth Holmgren. Bloomington: Indiana University Press, 1996. 225–46.

Huysmans, Joris-Karl. *Against Nature: A rebours.* Trans. Margaret Mauldon. New York: Oxford University Press, 2009.

Iakovkina, N. I. *Russkoe dvorianstvo pervoi poloviny XIX veka: byt i traditsii.* Saint Petersburg: Lan', 2002.

Iakovleva, A. M. "'Ustav o zhizni po pravde i s chistoi sovest'iu' i problema razvlechenii v Rossii XVI–XVII vv." In *Razvlekatel'naia kul'tura v Rossii.* Ed. E. V. Dukov. Saint Petersburg: Rossiiskaia akademiia nauk, 2001. 7–27.

Iampol'skii, M. B. *Demon i labirint: diagrammy, deformatsii, mimesis.* Moscow: Novoe literaturnoe obozrenie, 1996.

Iezuitova, R. V. "Svetskaia povest'." In *Russkaia povest' XIX veka: istoriia i problematika zhanra.* Ed. B. S. Meilakh. Leningrad: Nauka, 1973.

Ivanov, Viacheslav. *Lik i lichiny Rossii: estetika i literaturnaia teoriia.* Moscow: Iskusstvo, 1995.

———. "Osnovnoi mif v romane *Besy.*" In *'Besy': Antologiia russkoi kritiki.* Ed. L. I. Saraskinaia. Moscow: Soglasie, 1996. 508–12.

———. *Selected Essays of Vyacheslav Ivanov.* Trans. Robert Bird, ed. Michael Wachtel. Evanston, IL: Northwestern University Press, 2001.

Jackson, Robert Louis. *Dostoevsky's Quest for Form.* New Haven: Yale University Press, 1966.

Johnson, Vida Taranovski. "The Thematic Function of Narrator in *The Master and Margarita.*" *Canadian-American Slavic Studies* 15.2–3 (1981): 271–86.

Jones, Malcolm V. *Dostoevsky and the Twentieth Century: The Ljubljana Papers.*
    Nottingham, England: Astra Press, 1993.
——. *Dostoyevsky: The Novel of Discord.* London: Elek, 1976.
Kalbouss, George. *The Plays of the Russian Symbolists.* East Lansing, MI: Russian
    Language Journal, 1982.
Kasatkina, T. S., ed. *Aisedora: Gastroli v Rossii.* Moscow: Izdatel'stvo "Artist.
    Rezhisser. Teatr," 1992.
Kelly, Catriona. *Petrushka: The Russian Carnival Puppet Theatre.* New York:
    Cambridge University Press, 1990.
Kelly, Catriona, and Stephen Lovell. *Russian Literature, Modernism and the Visual
    Arts.* New York: Cambridge University Press, 2000.
Khalizev, V. E. *Drama kak rod literatury: poetika, genezis, funktsionirovanie.*
    Moscow: MGU, 1986.
Kirpotin, V. Ia. *Dostoevskii i russkie pisateli: Traditsii. Novatorstvo. Masterstvo.
    Sbornik statei.* Moscow: Sovetskii pisatel', 1971.
Kirsanova, R. M. *Russkii kostium i byt XVIII-XIX vekov.* Moscow: Slovo, 2002.
Knapp, S. "Herbert Spencer in Cexov's 'Skucnaja istorija' and 'Duel': The Love
    of Science and the Science of Love." *The Slavic and East European Journal* 29.3
    (1985): 279–96.
Kolesnikova, Anna A. *Bal v Rossii XVIII–nachalo XX veka.* Saint Petersburg:
    Azbuka-klassika, 2005.
Komissarzhevskii, Fedor. "Kostium i nagota." *Maski* 2 (1912): 47–53.
Konechnyi, A. M., A. V. Leifert, and A. Ia. Alekseev. *Peterburgskie balagany.*
    Saint Petersburg: Giperion, 2000.
Konecny, Mark. "In the Second Act, There Are No Fig Leaves: Risque Russian
    Theater in the 1910s." Paper presented at the annual ASEEES (formerly
    AAASS) convention in Los Angeles, CA, November 2010.
Koos, Leonard R. "Fictitious History: From Decadence to Modernism." In *Turn
    of the Century: Modernism and Modernity in Literature and the Arts.* Eds.
    Chrisian Berg, Frank Durieux, and Geert Lernout. New York and Berlin:
    Walter de Gruyter, 1995. 119–31.
——. "Improper Names: Pseudonyms and Transvestites in Decadent Prose."
    In *Perennial Decay: On the Aesthetics and Politics of Decadence.* Philadelphia:
    University of Pennsylvania Press, 1998.
Korovin, V. I. *Russkaia svetskaia povest' pervoi poloviny XIX veka.* Moscow:
    Sovetskaia Rossiia, 1990.
Kozlovaia, M. G. "Menia udivliaet etot chelovek." In *Vstrechi s proshlym.* Ed. I. L.
    Andronikov. Moscow: Sovetskaia Rossiia, 1982. 224–43.
Kruchenykh, Aleksei. "Pervye v mire spektakli futuristov." In *Nash vykhod:
    K istorii russkogo futurizma.* Ed. R. V. Duganov. Moscow: RA, 1996.
Kumpan, K. A., and I. A. Paperno. "K deshifrovke pozitsii memuarista (Pavel
    I v zapiskakh N. A. Sablukova)." *Trudy po znakovym sistemam VII*, no. 365
    (1975): 112–18.
Kupchenko, V. P. "Khronika zhizni i tvorchestva E. I. Vasil'evoi (Cheruбiny de
    Gabriak)." In *Cherubina de Gabriak "Ispoved'."* Moscow: Agraf, 1999. 318–35.
Kursanov, Andrei, and Boris Shifrin. "Zakliatie smekhom: futurizm v karika-
    turakh." In *Kharmsizdat predstavliaet: avangardnoe povedenie: sbornik materialov.*

Saint Petersburg: M. K. & Kharmsizdat: In-t "Otkrytoe obshchestvo, 1998. 98–122.

Lachmann, Renate. *Memory and Literature: Intertextuality in Russian Modernism.* Trans. Roy Sellars and Anthony Wall. Minneapolis: University of Minnesota Press, 1997.

Lahti, Katherine. "On Living Statues and Pandora, *Kamennye baby* and Futurist Aesthetics: The Female Body in *Vladimir Mayakovsky: A Tragedy.*" *Russian Review* 58.3 (1999): 432–55.

Landa, M. S. "Simvolitskaia poetessa: opyt mifotvorchestva." *Russkaia literatura* 4 (1994): 120–33.

Larionov, Michel. "Icônes et loubki." In *Une Avant-garde explosive.* Eds. Michel Hoog and Solina de Vigneral. Lausanne: L'Age d'Homme, 1978. 115–20.

———. "Les Icônes." In *Une Avant-garde explosive.* Eds. Michel Hoog and Solina de Vigneral. Lausanne: L'Age d'Homme, 1978. 131–34.

Larionov, Mikhail, and Ilya Zdanevich. "Why We Paint Ourselves." In *Manifesto: A Century of isms.* Ed. Mary Ann Caws. Lincoln: University of Nebraska Press, 2000.

Laursen, Eric. "Transformation as Revelation: Sologub, Schopenhauer, and the Little Man." *Slavic and East European Journal* 39.4 (1995): 552–67.

Lavrov, A. V. "Andrei Bely and the Argonauts' Mythmaking." In *Creating Life: The Aesthetic Utopia of Russian Modernism.* Eds. Irina Paperno and Joan Delaney Grossman. Stanford: Stanford University Press, 1994. 83–121.

———. "Dostoevskii v tvorcheskom soznanii Andreia Belogo (1900-e gody)." In *Andrei Bely: problemy tvorchestva.* Moscow: Sovetskii pisatel', 1988.

Leach, Robert. "A Good Beginning: *Victory over the Sun* and *Vladimir Mayakovsky: A Tragedy* Reassessed." *Russian Literature* 13.1 (1983): 101–16.

———. *Makers of Modern Theatre: An Introduction.* New York: Routledge, 2004.

Leach, Robert, and Victor Borovsky. *A History of Russian Theatre.* New York: Cambridge University Press, 1999.

Leatherbarrow, W. J. "The Devils' Vaudeville: 'Decoding' the Demonic in Dostoevsky's *The Devils.*" In *Russian Literature and Its Demons.* Ed. Pamela Davidson. New York: Berghahn Books, 2000. 279–306.

Levitskaia, Liudmila. "Litso, maska, maskarad v russkoi khudozhestvennoi kul'ture nachala XX veka." *Iskusstvoznanie* 1 (2001): 414–36.

Lisovskii, V. G. *Akademiia khudozhestv: istoriko-iskusstvovedcheskii ocherk.* Leningrad: Lenizdat, 1982.

Lodge, Kirsten, ed., *The Dedalus Book of Russian Decadence: Perversity, Despair and Collapse.* Sawtry, UK: Dedalus, 2007.

Lokhvitskaia, Mirra Aleksandrovna. "Stikhotvoreniia." *Russkie poetessy XIX veka.* Ed. N. V. Bannikov. Moscow: Sov. Rossiia, 1979.

Lokotnikova, I. G. "Siurpriz dlia imperatritsy." *Pushkinskii muzeum* 2 (2000): 178–86.

Lotman, Iu. M. *Besedy o russkoi kul'ture: byt i traditsii russkogo dvorianstva: XVIII–nachalo XIX veka.* Saint Petersburg: Iskusstvo-SPb, 1994.

———. "Ikonicheskaia ritorika." In *Semiosfera.* Saint Petersburg: Iskusstvo-SPB, 2000. 194–202.

———. "Simvolika Peterburga i problemy semiotiki goroda." In *Istoriia i tipolo-giia russkoi kul'tury.* Saint Petersburg: Iskusstvo-SPb, 2002.

———. "Tema kart i kartochnoi igry v russkoi literature nachala XIX veka." *Trudy po znakovym sistemam* 7.394 (1975): 120–42.

———. "The Theater and Theatricality as Components of Early Nineteenth-Century Culture." In *The Semiotics of Russian Culture.* Ed. Ann Shukman. Ann Arbor: University of Michigan, 1984. 141–64.

Lotman, Iu. M., and B. A. Uspenskii. "Binary Models in the Dynamics of Russian Culture (to the End of the Eighteenth Century)." In *The Semiotics of Russian Cultural History.* Eds. Alexander D. Nakhimovsky and Alice Stone Nakhimovsky. Ithaca, NY: Cornell University Press, 1985. 30–66.

———. "The Poetics of Everyday Behavior in Russian Eighteenth-Century Culture." In *The Semiotics of Russian Culture.* Ed. Ann Shukman. Ann Arbor: University of Michigan, 1984. 231–56.

Makovskii, Sergei. *Na Parnase serebrianogo veka.* Moscow: Agraf, 2000.

———. "O Cherubine." In *Portrety sovremennikov.* New York: Chekhov, 1955

Mann, Iu. "Igrovye momenty v *Maskarade* Lermontova." *Izvestiia Akademii Nauk S. S. S. R., Seriia literatury i iazyka* 36 (1977): 27–38.

Marchenko, Alla. "Perechityvaia 'Maskarad'; k 170-letiiu so dnia rozhdeniia M. Iu. Lermontova." *Novyi mir* 10 (1984): 228–42.

Martinsen, Deborah. *Surprised by Shame: Dostoevsky's Liars and Narrative Exposure.* Columbus: Ohio State University Press, 2003.

Matich, Olga. "Backs, Suddenlys, and Surveillance." In *"Petersburg"/Petersburg: Novel and City, 1900–1921.* Ed. Olga Matich. Madison: University of Wisconsin Press, 2010. 31–54.

———. *Erotic Utopia.* Madison: University of Wisconsin Press, 2005.

———. "Gender Trouble in the Amazonian Kingdom: Turn-of-the-Century Representations of Women in Russia." In *Amazons of the Avant-Garde.* Eds. John E. Bowlt and Matthew Drutt. New York: The Solomon R. Guggenheim Foundation, 1999. 75–93.

———. *Paradox in the Religious Poetry of Zinaida Gippius.* Munich: W. Fink, 1972.

———. "Pokrovy Salomei: Eros, smert' i istoriia." In *Erotizm bez beregov.* Ed. M. M. Pavlova. Moscow: Novoe literaturnoe obozrenie, 2004. 90–121.

———. "The Symbolist Meaning of Love: Theory and Practice." In *Creating Life: The Aesthetic Utopia of Russian Modernism.* Stanford: Stanford University Press, 1994. 24–50.

McKenna, Neil. *The Secret Life of Oscar Wilde.* New York: Basic Books, 2006.

McQuillen, Colleen. "Artists' Balls and Conceptual Costumes at the Saint Petersburg Academy of Arts, 1885–1909." *Fashion Theory* 16.1 (March 2012): 29–48.

McReynolds, Louise. *Russia at Play: Leisure Activities at the End of the Tsarist Era.* Ithaca, NY: Cornell University Press, 2003.

Meierkhol'd, Vsevolod. *Stat'i, Pis'ma, Rechi, Besedy, 1891–1917.* 2 vols. Ed. Aleksandr V. Fevral'skii. Moscow: Iskusstvo, 1968.

Merezhkovsky, Dmitry. "On the Reasons for the Decline, and the New Currents, in Contemporary Russian Literature." In *The Russian Symbolists:*

An Anthology of Critical and Theoretical Writings. Trans. and ed. Ronald E. Peterson. Ann Arbor: Ardis, 1986. 17–21.

Mersereau, John. "The Nineteenth Century: Romanticism 1820–1840." In *The Cambridge History of Russian Literature.* Ed. Charles Moser. Cambridge, UK: Cambridge University Press, 1992. 136–88.

Mil'china, V. A. "Maskarad v russkoi kul'ture kontsa XVIII–nachala XIX veka." In *Kul'turologicheskie aspekty teorii i istorii russkoi literatury.* Ed. L. A. Kolobaeva. Moscow: MGU, 1978. 73–76.

Miller, Irina. "From Home Masquerades to Public Performance: Nikolai Evreinov's Production of Fyodor Sologub's Play *Night Dances.*" *Slavic and East European Performance* 19.1 (Spring 1999): 68–79.

Mondry, Henrietta. "Performing the Paradox: Rozanov and the Dancing Body of Isadora Duncan." *Essays in Poetics* 24 (1999): 91–116.

Morris, Marcia A. *The Literature of Roguery in Seventeenth- and Eighteenth-Century Russia, Studies in Russian Literature and Theory.* Evanston, IL: Northwestern University Press, 2000.

Moruzzi, Norma Claire. *Speaking through the Mask: Hannah Arendt and the Politics of Social Identity.* Ithaca, NY: Cornell University Press, 2000.

Murav, Harriet. *Holy Foolishness: Dostoevsky's Novels and the Poetics of Cultural Critique.* Stanford: Stanford University Press, 1992.

Murphy, Patrick D. *Staging the Impossible: The Fantastic Mode in Modern Drama.* Westport, CT: Greenwood Press, 1992.

Nechaev, Sergei. "The Revolutionary Catechism." Marxists Internet Archive. http://www.marxists.org/subject/anarchism/nechayev/catechism.htm.

Nekrylova, A. F. *Russkie narodnye gorodskie prazdniki, uveseleniia i zrelishcha.* Leningrad: Iskusstvo, 1984.

Nemirovich-Danchenko, V. I. *Tvorcheskoe nasledie v chetyrekh tomakh.* Ed. Inna Natanovna Solov'eva. Moscow: MXAT, 2003.

Nietzsche, Friedrich. *The Birth of Tragedy.* Oxford: Oxford University Press, 2000.

Nikol'skii, S. V. "Na grani metafor i alliuzii." *Izvestiia Akademii nauk. Seriia literatury i iazyka.* 58.1 (January–February 1999): 11–19.

Ninov, A. A., ed. *Dostoevskii i teatr: sbornik statei.* Leningrad: Iskusstvo, 1983.

———, ed. *M. A. Bulgakov-dramaturg i khudozhestvennaia kul'tura ego vremeni: sbornik statei.* Moscow: Soiuz teatral'nykh deiatelei RSFSR, 1988.

Novikov, Vladimir. *Aleksandr Blok.* Moscow: Molodaia gvardiia, 2010.

Obatnina, Elena. *Tsar' Asyka i ego poddannie: obez'ian'ia velikaia i volnaia palata A. M. Remizova v litsakh i dokumentakh.* Saint Petersburg: Izdatel'stvo Ivana Limbakha, 2001.

Odoevtsova, Irina. "Kak laskovaia kobra ia . . ." In *Sobranie Sochinenii Z.N. Gippius.* Eds. B. S. Bugrov and T. F. Prokopov. Vol. 9. Moscow: Russkaia kniga, 2005. 345–75.

Olin, V. N. "Strannyi bal." In *Russkaia romanticheskaia povest' pisatelei 20–40 godov XIX veka.* Ed. V. I. Sakharov. Moscow: Pressa, 1992. 329–42.

Opie, John. "Ikonostas and Its Context." In *P. A. Florenskij i kul'tura ego vremeni. P. A. Florenskij e la cultura della sua epoca: Atti del Convegno Internazionale, Università degli Studi di Bergamo, 10–14 gennaio 1988.* Eds. Michael Hagemeister and Nina Kauchtschischwili. Marburg: Blaue Hörner, 1995. 431–42.

Ostroumova-Lebedeva, Anna. *Avtobiograficheskie zapiski*. Moscow: Izobrazitel'noe iskusstvo, 1974.

Panchenko, A. M. *O russkoi istorii i kul'ture*. Saint Petersburg: Izdatel'stvo Azbuka, 2000.

———. *Russkaia kul'tura v kanun petrovskikh reform*. Leningrad: Nauka Leningradskoe otd-nie, 1984.

Panov, S. "Literaturnaia kadril' v romane *Besy*." *Zven'ia* 4 (1936): 573–82.

Paperno, Irina, and Joan Delaney Grossman, eds. *Creating Life: The Aesthetic Utopia of Russian Modernism*. Stanford: Stanford University Press, 1994.

Patyk, Lynn Ellen. "'The double-edged sword of word and deed': Revolutionary Terrorism and Russian Literary Culture." PhD diss., Stanford University, 2006.

Pavis, Patrice. *Theatre at the Crossroads of Culture*. London and New York: Routledge, 1992.

Pavlova, M. M. "Iz tvorcheskoi istorii romana F. Sologuba *Melkii Bes*." *Russkaia literatura* 2 (1997): 138–54.

Pecherskaia, T. I. "Istoriko-kul'turnye istoki motiva maskarada." In *Siuzhet i motiv v kontekste traditsii*. Ed. E. K. Romodanovskaia. 2nd ed. Novosibirsk: Institut filologii SO RAN, 1998.

Peri, Alexis, and Christine Evans. "How Terrorists Learned to Map: Plotting in *Petersburg* and Boris Savinkov's *Recollections of a Terrorist* and *The Pale Horse*." In *"Petersburg"/Petersburg: Novel and City, 1900–1921*. Ed. Olga Matich. Madison: University of Wisconsin, 2010. 149–73.

Picon-Vallin, Beatrice. "Les Années 10 à Petersbourg: Meyerhold, la commedia dell'arte et Le Bal masqué." In *Le masque. Du rite au théâtre*. Eds. Odette Aslan and Denis Bablet. Paris: Editions du Centre nationale de la recherche scientifique, 1985. 147–58.

Pisarenko, K. A. *Povsednevnaia zhizn' russkogo dvora v tsarstvovanie Elizavety Petrovny, Zhivaia istoriia — povsednevnaia zhizn' chelovechestva*. Moscow: Molodaia gvardiia, 2003.

Poggi, Christine. *In Defiance of Painting: Cubism, Futurism, and the Invention of Collage*. New Haven: Yale University Press, 1992.

Polosin, I. "Igra v tsaria (otgoloski smuty v Moskovskom bytu XVII veka)." *Izvestiia Tverskogo pedagogicheskogo instituta* 1 (1926): 59–63.

Pozniak, Telesfor. *Dostojewski w kregu symbolistów Rosyjskich*. Wrocław: Prace Wrocławskiego Towarzystwa Naukowego, 1969.

Presto, Jenifer. *Beyond the Flesh: Alexander Blok, Zinaida Gippius, and the Symbolist Sublimation of Sex*. Madison: University of Wisconsin Press, 2008.

———. "Women in Russian Symbolism: Beyond the Algebra of Love." In *The History of Women's Writing in Russia*. Ed. Adele Marie Barker and Jehanne M. Gheith. Cambridge University Press, 2002. 134–52.

Preston, Carrie. "The Motor in the Soul: Isadora Duncan and Modernist Performance." *Modernism/Modernity* 12.2 (2005): 273–89.

Proffer, Carl. *The Silver Age of Russian Culture*. Ann Arbor, MI: Ardis, 1975.

Prokof'ev, V. "Malen'kaia khronika. Bal khudozhnikov." *Novoe vremia*, no. 8609 (February 14, 1900): 3.

Pudelek, Janina. "Fokine in Warsaw, 1908–1914." In *Dance Chronicle* 15.1 (1992): 59–71.

Pyliaev, M. I. "Epokhi rytsarskikh karuselei i allegoricheskikh maskaradov." *Istoricheskii vestnik: istoriko-literaturnyi zhurnal* (August 1885): 309–39.

Rabinowitz, Stanley. "Fedor Sologub and His Nineteenth-Century Antecedents." *Slavic and East European Journal* 22.3 (1978): 324–35.

Reyfman, Irina. *Ritualized Violence Russian Style: The Duel in Russian Culture and Literature.* Stanford: Stanford University Press, 1999.

Reynolds, Dee A. "Dancing Free: Women's Movements in Early Modern Dance." In *Modernism, Gender, and Culture: A Cultural Studies Approach.* Ed. Lisa Rado. New York: Garland Publishing Inc., 1997. 247–79.

Reynolds, Dee. *Symbolist Aesthetics and Early Abstract Art.* Cambridge: Cambridge University Press, 2005.

Riviere, Joan. "Womanliness as a Masquerade." In *Formations of Fantasy.* Eds. Victor Burgin, James Donald, and Cora Kaplan. London: Routledge, 1989.

Rodina, T. *Aleksandr Blok i russkii teatr nachala XX veka.* Moscow: Nauka, 1972.

Ropshin, V. *Kon' blednyi.* Saint Petersburg: Shipovnik, 1909.

Rosen, Margo. "The *Poem without Dante*: Akhmatova's History of Poetic Failure in Russia and the World." M.A. Thesis, Columbia University, 2004.

Rosenthal, Bernice Glatzer. *Nietzsche in Russia.* Princeton, NJ: Princeton University Press, 1986.

Rosslyn, Wendy. "Painters and Painting in the Poetry of Anna Akhmatova: The Relation between the Poetry and Painting." In *Anna Akhmatova: 1889–1989.* Ed. Sonia Ketchian. Berkeley: Berkeley Slavic Specialties, 1993. 170–85.

———. "Theatre, Theatricality and Akhmatova's *Poema bez geroia.*" *Essays in Poetics: The Journal of the British Neo-Formalist School* 13.1 (1988): 89–108.

Ruane, Christine. *The Empire's New Clothes: A History of the Russian Fashion Industry, 1700–1917.* New Haven: Yale University Press, 2009.

Rylov, Arkadii Aleksandrovich. *Vospominaniia.* Moscow: Iskusstvo, 1954.

Sakharov, V. I., ed. *Russkaia romanticheskaia povest' pisatelei 20–40 godov XIX veka.* Moscow: Pressa, 1992.

Sandler, Stephanie. "Pleasure, Danger, and the Dance: Nineteenth-Century Russian Variations." In *Russia, Women, Culture.* Eds. Helena Goscilo and Beth Holmgren. Bloomington: Indiana University Press, 1996. 247–72.

———. "The Stone Ghost: Akhmatova, Pushkin, and Don Juan." In *Literature, Culture and Society in the Modern Age: In Honor of Joseph Frank.* Vol. 2. Stanford: Department of Slavic Languages at Stanford University, 1992. 35–49.

Savinkov, Boris. *Vospominaniia terrorista.* Moscow: Mysl', 1991.

Sazhin, Valerii, ed. *Kharmsizdat predstavliaet: Avangardnoe povedenie: Sbornik materialov.* Saint Petersburg: M. K. & Kharmsizdat : In-t Otkrytoe obshchestvo, 1998.

Scholl, Tim. *From Petipa to Balanchine: Classical Revival and the Modernization of Ballet.* London and New York: Routledge, 1994.

Schorman, Rob. *Selling Style.* Philadelphia: University of Pennsylvania Press, 2003.

Schuler, Catherine. "Actresses, Audience and Fashion in the Silver Age: A Crisis of Costume." In *Women and Russian Culture: Projections and Self-Perceptions.* Ed. Rosalind Marsh. New York: Berghahn Books, 1998. 107–22.

Segel, Harold B. *Twentieth-Century Russian Drama: From Gorky to the Present.* Baltimore: Johns Hopkins University Press, 1993.

Senkovskii, Osip. "Prevrashchenie golov v knigi i knigi v golovy." In *Russkaia romanticheskaia povest' pisatelei 20–40 godov XIX veka.* Ed. V. I. Sakharov. Moscow: Pressa, 1992.

Serova, S. A. *Teatral'naia kul'tura serebrianogo veka v Rossii i khudozhestvennye traditsii Vostoka (Kitai, Iaponiia, Indiia).* Moscow: IV RAN, 1999.

Shakhovskoi, A. A. *Komedii; stikhotvoreniia.* Ed. A. A. Gozenpud. Leningrad: Sovetskii pisatel', 1961.

Shangina, I. I., and O. G. Baranova. *Russkii prazdnik: Prazdniki i obriady narodnogo zemledel'cheskogo kalendariia: Illiustrirovannaia entsiklopediia. Istoriia v zerkale byta.* Saint Petersburg: Iskusstvo-SPB, 2001.

Shklovskii, V. B. *O teorii prozy.* Ann Arbor, Michigan: Ardis, 1985.

Shkolnikov, Vadim. "Terrorism and the Text: Dostoevsky, Savinkov, and the Representation of Terrorist Violence in Russia, 1872–1909." Lecture, University of Illinois at Chicago, February 21, 2012.

Shubinskii, S. N. *Istoricheskie ocherki i rasskazy.* Moscow: Moskovskii rabochii, 1995.

Shugart, Helene. "Parody as Subversive Performance: Denaturalizing Gender and Reconstituting Desire in *Ellen*." *Text and Performance Quarterly* 21.4 (2001): 95–113.

Sipovskaia, N. V. "Prazdnik v russkoi kul'ture XVIII veka." In *Razvlekatel'naia kul'tura Rossii XVIII–XIX vv.* Ed. E. V. Dukov. Saint Petersburg: Rossiiskaia akademiia nauk, 2001. 28–42.

Smith, Susan Harris. *Masks in Modern Drama.* Berkeley: University of California Press, 1984.

Smoliarova, Tatiana. "Distortion and Theatricality: Estrangement in Diderot and Shklovsky." *Poetics Today* 27.1 (2006): 3–33.

Sobol, Valeria. "'Shumom bala utomlennyj': The Physiological Aspect of the Society Ball and the Subversion of Romantic Rhetoric." *Russian Literature* 49.3 (2001): 293–314.

Sofronova, L. A. *Maska i maskarad v russkoi kul'ture XVIII–XX vekov.* Moscow: Gosudarstvenniy institut iskusstvoznaniia, 2000.

Sollogub, V. A. *Sochineniia.* Saint Petersburg: Izdatel'stvo A. Smirdina, 1855.

Sologub, Fedor. "Bessmertnaia plamen'." *Teatr i iskusstvo* (1912): 51.

———. *The Created Legend.* Trans. John Cournos. Gloucester, UK: Dodo Press, 2008.

———. *Petty Demon.* Trans. Samuel Cioran. Ann Arbor: Ardis, 1983.

———. "Mechta o Done Kikhote: Aisadora Dunkan." In *Sobranie sochinenii.* Ed. T. F. Prokopov. Vol. 2. Moscow: NPK "Intelvak," 2001. 511–13.

———. "*Polotno i telo*." In *Sobranie sochinenii.* Ed. T. F. Prokopov. Vol. 2. Moscow: NPK "Intelvak," 2001. 541–44.

———. "The Poisoned Garden." In *The Dedalus Book of Russian Decadence: Perversity, Despair, and Collapse.* Ed. Kirsten Lodge. Sawtry, UK: Dedalus Limited, 2007.

———. "Teatr odnoi voli." In *Sobranie sochinenii.* Ed. T. F. Prokopov. Vol. 2. Moscow: NPK "Intelvak," 2001. 490–509.

Solov'eva, I. N. "Variatsii i temy Venetsii v russkom stsenicheskom iskusstve

1910-kh godov." *Vipperovskie chteniia*. Moscow: Sovetskii khudozhnik, 1988. 296–314.

Stasov, Vladimir. "Vystavki." *Novosti i birzhevye vedomosti* 86 (April 1903).

Steele, Valerie. "*Femme Fatale*: Fashion and Visual Culture in Fin-de-Siècle Paris." *Fashion Theory* 8.3 (2004): 315–28.

Steinberg, Mark. "'Chernye maski'; Zrelishcha, obrazy i identichnost' na gorodskikh ulitsakh." In *Kul'tury gorodov rossiiskoi imperii na rubezhe XIX–XX vekov*. Eds. Mark Steinberg and Boris Kolonitskii. Saint Petersburg: Evropeiskii dom, 2009. 97–111.

Szilard, Lena. "M. Bulgakov i nasledie simvolizma: Magiia kriptoanagram-mirovaniia." *Russian Literature* 56 (2004): 283–96.

———. "Ot *Besov* k *Peterburgu*: Mezhdu poliusami iurodstva i shutovstva." In *Studies in Twentieth-Century Russian Prose*. Ed. Nils Nilsson. Stockholm: Almquist & Wiksell, 1982. 80–107.

Thomas, D. M. *Anna Akhmatova: Requiem and Poem without a Hero*. Athens: Ohio University Press: 1976.

Timenchik, Roman. "Chuzhoe slovo u Akhmatovoi." *Russkaia Rech'* 3 (May–June 1989): 33–36.

———. "Rizhskii epizod v 'Poeme bez geroia.'" *Daugava: Literaturnyi zhurnal* 2.80 (February 1984): 113–21.

Todd, William Mills. "Periodicals in Literary Life of the Early Nineteenth Century." In *Literary Journals in Imperial Russia*. Ed. Deborah Martinsen. New York: Cambridge University Press, 1997.

Todd, William Mills, and Robert L. Belknap, eds. *Literature and Society in Imperial Russia, 1800–1914*. Stanford: Stanford University Press, 1978.

Todorov, Tzvetan. *The Fantastic: A Structural Approach to a Literary Genre*. Ithaca, NY: Cornell University Press, 1975.

Toepfer, Karl. *Empire of Ecstasy: Nudity and Modernity in German Body Culture, 1910–1935*. Berkeley and Los Angeles: University of California Press, 1997.

———. "Nudity and Modernity in German Dance, 1910–30." *Journal of the History of Sexuality* 3.1 (1992): 58–108.

———. "Nudity and Textuality in Postmodern Performance." *Performing Arts Journal* 18.3 (1996): 76–91.

———. "One Hundred Years of Nakedness in German Performance." *TDR* 47.4 (2003): 144–88.

Tolstoy, Lev. *Kreutzer Sonata*. Trans. Isai Kamen. New York: Modern Library, 2003.

Toporov, V. N. "Italiia v Peterburge." In *Italiia i slavianskii mir: Sovetsko-ital'ianskii simpozium in Honorem Professore Ettore Lo Gatto*. Moscow: Akademiia nauk SSSR, 1990. 68–70.

Tseelon, Efrat, ed. *Masquerade and Identities*. New York: Routledge, 2001.

Tsiv'ian, Tat'iana. "Akhmatova i muzyka." *Russian Literature* 10–11 (1975): 173–212.

Tsvetaeva, Marina. *Zhivoe o zhivom*. Saint Petersburg: Izdatel'stvo Serdtse, 1993.

Turovskaia, M. "Sblizhenie." *Teatr* 6 (1979): 35–37.

Tynianov, Iurii. "Dostoevskii i Gogol' (k teorii parodii)." In *Poetika. Istoriia litera-tury. Kino*. Moscow: Nauka, 1977. 198–226.

Ulanovskaia, B. Iu. "O prototipakh romana F. Sologuba *Melkii Bes.*" *Russkaia literatura* 3 (1969): 181–84.

Uspenskii, B. A. "Historia sub specie semioticae." In *Izbrannye trudy.* Vol. 1. Moscow: Iazyki russkoi kul'tury, 1996. 71–82.

———. "Tsar and Pretender: *Samozvanchestvo* or Royal Imposture in Russia as a Cultural-Historical Phenomenon." In *The Semiotics of Russian Culture.* Ed. Ann Shukman. Ann Arbor: University of Michigan, 1984. 259–91.

Vaingurt, Julia. *Wonderlands of the Avant-Garde: Technology and the Arts in Russia of the 1920s.* Evanston, IL: Northwestern University Press, 2013.

Vengerov, S. A., S. B. Dzhimbinov, and A. G. Fomin. *Russkaia literatura XX veka, 1890–1910. Dva veka russkoi filologii.* Moscow: XXI vek-Soglasie, 2000.

Verhoeven, Claudia. *The Odd Man Karakozov: Imperial Russia, Modernity, and the Birth of Terrorism.* Ithaca, NY: Cornell University Press, 2009.

Verigina, Valentina P. "Vospominaniia ob Aleksandre Bloke." In *Aleksandr Blok v vospominaniiakh sovremennikov.* Ed. V. N. Orlov. Moscow: Khudozhestvennaia literatura, 1980. 410–88.

———. *Vospominaniia.* Leningrad: Iskusstvo, 1974.

Vilenkin, V. *Vospominaniia s kommentariiami.* Moscow: Iskusstvo, 1982.

Villiers de l'Isle-Adam, Auguste. *Tomorrow's Eve.* Trans. Robert Martin Adams. Urbana: University of Illinois Press, 2000.

Volkov, Solomon. *St. Petersburg: A Cultural History.* Trans. Antonina Bouis. New York: Free Press, 1995.

Voloshin, Maksimilian. "Istoriia Cherubiny." In *Izbrannoe: stikhotvoreniia, vospominaniia, perepiska.* Minsk: Mastatskaia literatura, 1993.

———. "Rasskaz o Cherubine de Gabriak." *Zhivoe slovo: Serebrianyi vek.* 1999–2002.

———. "Sizeran ob estetike sovremennosti: Sovremennaia odezhda." In *Liki tvorchestva.* Eds. V. A. Manuilov, V. P Kupchenko, and A. V. Lavrov. Leningrad: Nauka, 1988. 183–87.

———. "Tanets: Aisadora Dunkan." In *Liki tvorchestva.* Eds. V. A. Manuilov, V. P. Kupchenko, and A. V. Lavrov. Leningrad: Nauka, 1988. 392–99.

———. *Zapisnye knizhki.* Ed. Vladimir Kupchenko. Moscow: Vagrius, 2000.

Vorontsova-Dashkova, Ekaterina. *The Memoirs of Princess Dashkova.* Ed. Kyril Fitzlyon. Durham and London: Duke University Press, 1995.

Wachtel, Andrew, ed. *Petrushka: Sources and Contexts.* Evanston, IL: Northwestern University Press, 1998.

Warwood, Jim and Lis. "Anna Eva Fay: The Modern Oracle of Delphi." *The Voice Box.* 2007.

Weiner, Adam. *By Authors Possessed: The Demonic Novel in Russia.* Evanston, IL: Northwestern University Press, 1998.

Weir, Justin. *The Author as Hero: Self and Tradition in Bulgakov, Pasternak, and Nabokov.* Evanston, IL: Northwestern University Press, 2002.

Wilshire, Bruce W. *Role Playing and Identity: The Limits of Theatre as Metaphor.* Bloomington: Indiana University Press, 1982.

Woolf, Vicki. *Dancing in the Vortex: The Story of Ida Rubinstein.* London: Routledge, 2001.

Worthen, W. B. "Drama, Performativity, and Performance." In *Performance:*

Critical Concepts in Literary and Cultural Studies. Ed. Philip Auslander. New
    York: Routledge, 2003. 86–108.
Wortman, Richard. *Scenarios of Power: Myth and Ceremony in Russian Monarchy.*
    Princeton, NJ: Princeton University Press, 1995.
Zagoskin, M. N. "Kontsert besov." In *Russkaia romanticheskaia povest' pisatelei
    20–40 godov XIX veka.* Ed. V. I. Sakharov. Moscow: Pressa, 1992. 315–28.
Zakharova, O. Iu. *Russkie baly i konnye karuseli.* Moscow: Glasnost', 2000.
Zarin, A. E. *Tsarskie razvlecheniia i zabavy za 300 let: Okhota, shuty i skomorokhi,
    teatry, baly i maskarady, uveselitel'nye progulki, karty, loto i drugie igry: Istori-
    cheskie ocherki.* Leningrad: Mezhdunarodnaia fonda istorii nauki, 1991.
Ziegler, Robert. *Asymptote: An Approach to Decadent Fiction.* New York: Rodopi,
    2009.
Ziskin, Grigorii. "K istorii postanovki maskarada na stsene Aleksandrinskogo
    teatra." *Zapiski russkoi akademicheskoi gruppy V USA.* Ed. Nadja Jernakoff.
    New York: Association of Russian-American Scholars in the USA, 1990.
    63–73.
Zitser, Ernest A. *The Transfigured Kingdom: Sacred Parody and Charismatic Authority
    at the Court of Peter the Great.* Ithaca, NY: Cornell University Press, 2004.
Zody, Patricia. "A Creative Passion: Revolutionary Terrorism in Dostoevsky's
    Demons and Beyond, 1871–1916." PhD diss., Northwestern University, 2002.

Index

Page references in italic refer to illustrations.